KIBBUTZ
Volunteer

956
.94

calum

Victoria Pybus

Published by Vacation Work, 9 Park End Street, Oxford
www.vacationwork.co.uk

KIBBUTZ VOLUNTEER
First edition 1978
Seventh Edition 2000

Copyright © Vacation Work 2000

ISBN 1-85458-228-3

ISSN 0143-3881

Cover design by Miller, Craig and Cocking Design Partnership

Typeset by Worldview Publishing Services (01865-201562)

Printed by William Clowes Ltd., Beccles, Suffolk, England

Contents

PART I – VISITORS' GUIDE TO ISRAEL

PART II – THE KIBBUTZ

PART III – MOSHAVIM & OTHER WORK

PART IV – KIBBUTZIM GUIDE

Maps

Acknowledgments

The author and publishers would like to thank all the people and organisations which have helped with or contributed to this new edition and in particular Louise Whetter (research on voluntary work organisations), Leoni at Aliya in London and Kathryn at Kibbutz Representatives.

Preface

In 1967 large numbers of non-Jewish volunteers went to Israel to help keep the kibbutzim running while every able-bodied Israeli was doing their military duty defending the country against simultaneous attacks from Egypt and Syria. Since then, hundreds of thousands of volunteers have visited and worked in Israel. The 1970's were the heyday for foreign volunteers; more than 50,000 of them visited Israel every year during that decade. Most of the volunteers came from Europe and North America to labour, mainly outdoors, under the burning sun. They were enjoying the liberated mood of the times and sharing the kibbutz ideal. By 1987 when the Palestinian Intifida (resistance) started, the total had fallen to 20,000 which included those working on moshavim (collective farms) as well as kibbutzim. The Gulf War also took its toll, not literally, but by adding to Israel's seemingly perilous involvment in the conflict. Two years later, by 1993 volunteer numbers were down to fewer than 10,000 a year. In the second millennium, there are signs that Israel is winning back its popularity amongst backpackers, following the Israeli-Arab peace accords and the on-going 'peace process'.

Three decades and a few years on from the arrival of the first volunteers, it is inevitable that the relationship between kibbutz members and volunteers has undergone a transformation, notably an increase of cynicism on both sides and a tendency to bemoan the falling standards of volunteers or the kibbutzim's exploitation of volunteer labour. The kibbutzim themselves are beleaguered by problems financial, ideological and social, that have brought many of them to a crisis and a turning point in their aims. Collectively they are massively in debt to the tune of four billion US dollars, while their very future in their present form looks to be in jeopardy as half the kibbutz youth leave their home settlements to pursue individual goals in the outside world, and the kibbutzim themselves may be privatised.

However, there are still as many as 80 to 100 of the 270-odd kibbutzim that continue to welcome volunteers, and some of these visitors will return to the same kibbutz several times, a few may even settle in Israel (more difficult now with the influx of nearly a million immigrants from Eastern Europe), and it is still possible for the system to work remarkably well on individual kibbutzim.

Whichever kibbutz you go to, it will almost certainly not be what you anticipated, and will require considerable adjustment on your part. One of the aims of *Kibbutz Volunteer* is to try to give you some idea of of what to expect. For instance few kibbutz members live very austere lives these days, but volunteers still arrive expecting a strong element of ideology and a pioneering mentality to exist on the kibbutz. There have been many changes, not all of them the same in every kibbutz. They include the provision of personal budgets for members and kibbutz families dining at home and not in the communal dining room. Volunteer accommodation is basic, but the beauty and opulence of some kibbutzim, as well as their size, (some are like small towns), and their degree of industrialisation, will probably come as a surprise to those expecting a collection of wooden houses in an agricultural setting. The 'industrial revolution' of the kibbutzim dates from the 1950's when the Israeli government provided loans to set up factories to provide jobs for the waves of new immigrants. Now most kibbutzim are at least 70% industrial. Areas such as the disputed Golan heights, where there are many younger kibbutzim may well be very isolated and spartan and not much fun for the volunteer. Some prospective volunteers allocated to prosperous kibbutzim may also like to question how those kibbutzniks who do enjoy a very high standard of living can justify not paying realistic wages to 'volunteers.'

Since the last edition of this book, more kibbutzim have reduced their volunteer intake, some have stopped taking volunteers altogether, yet others will only accept them from certain organisations and some have even blacklisted certain nationalities. Working hours for volunteers on most kibbutzim are eight hours a day, six days a week and excursions and free basic items such as toiletries etc. (once standard compensations) have been curtailed or reduced. Their provision is nowadays dependent on the policy (or cashflow) of individual kibbutzim.

It is some years since readers of this book pointed out that it is a myth that working on a kibbutz is one of the best ways to see Israel. One three-day trip only if the volunteer stays three months, and only arranged by some kibbutzim, and negligible pocket money, do not constitute much sightseeing or travelling expenses in a country where prices are comparable to those of Germany or Switzerland. However, travel by bus remains good value and there is a first class national network. The other travellers' support is the prolific supply of cheap sleeping places aimed at budget travellers. Israel is however concentrating more on mainstream non-budget tourism for obvious reasons. Palestine is also channelling its efforts into smarter tourism now that it has regained control of some of its territory and some key historic towns and sites.

Since there are several ways to finance travelling in Israel we have included a section on moshavim and other paid work in Israel, and as there is so much to see and do in this troubled, small, beautiful and endlessly fascinating land, we have also expanded the Visitors' Guide section to include more travel information. There is also a lengthier section on voluntary work, especially in Palestinian territories, where unfortunately, many basic human needs are still lacking.

This new edition is therefore better designed than ever to help you make the most of your time in Israel.

The peace process still has a long way to go and there are problems with Israeli religious fanatics who don't want any concessions to the Arabs, and Palestinians whose aim is to see the end of Israel and a Palestinian state in its place. However, progress has been made in handing over some territory in the West Bank to Palestinian government, and there is dialogue between the sides and signs that the majority hope that with perseverance, tolerance and concessions on both sides, a peaceful co-existence will be possible.

Victoria Pybus
January 2000

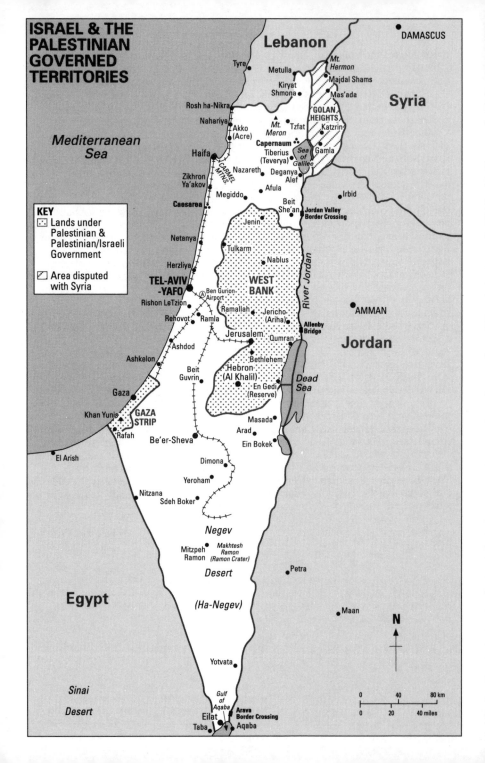

Visitors'Guide to Israel

Practical Information

Background, Troubles and Peace

Smaller than Belgium and about the same size as Wales, or New Jersey, Israel occupies 21,946 sq km including Arab East Jerusalem. However, its significance in world politics is out of proportion to its size. When the last edition of this book was published early in 1996, Israel was in the aftershock of Prime Minister Yitzak's Rabin's assassination. At the time of the assassination in November 1995, Israel had just begun the process of rethinking its borders, in recognition of the fact that peace with its remaining hostile neighbours would inescapably involve the handing back of territory seized from them in war. Territory, including the West Bank, Golan Heights and East Jerusalem has never been an internationally recognised part of Israel. At the time of press, Israel's new premier, Ehud Barak has promised to speed up the painfully slow progress towards 'permanent' settlement with the Palestinians. Failure to make headway in the peace settlement cost his predecessor, Benjamin Netanyahu, the premiership by a landslide in the May 1999 elections. *Barak* apparently means lightning in Hebrew and it remains to be seen if he lives up to his name.

Throughout its turbulent existence, Israel, before and after independence has never been ignorable. It is a focus of Jewish, Christian and Muslim religions, and the refuge of one of the most persecuted races in history. It is the dispossesor of the Palestinian nation and also an American-backed stronghold in the Middle East; it is the owner of an army which, in 1967 and 1973, was more than capable of taking on all its hostile Arab neighbours simultaneously, and winning (this would possibly not be the case now).

While its religious, historical and political turmoils have kept Israel in the spotlight of world attention, its licence to exist at all, probably arose from the horrors of Nazi Germany. However, at the beginning of a new century, the living memories of the Jewish holocaust have all but faded into the history books and neglected claims for justice, particularly relating to the territory of Palestinians have turned Israel into the oppressor.

Supporting the peace process, means Israel making concessions to the Palestinians, Syria and the Lebanon. These last two neighbouring countries are claiming back territory which was taken from them by Israel. Of the three outstanding territorial claims, the Palestinian one is the strongest.

The origins of Israel's dispute, with the Palestinians is not hard to find. By the time the state of Israel was founded in 1948, over a million Palestinians from that region had become dispossessed and stateless persons and 400 Palestinian villages had been destroyed. Since then, they have been consistently treated as second-class citizens and subjected to living in near apartheid conditions, in a land which was formerly theirs. It is this conflict of interests that has kept, and is still keeping, Israel at the forefront of today's news bulletins.

Despite having enormous public relations and political problems there is no denying, that Israel is a surpassingly beautiful and fascinating land. It is never difficult to forget the ever present tensions when travelling there. But even some of the dramatic landscapes are changing beyond all recognition, as the nearly six million strong population of Israel expands at a startling rate. This is happening from within the country, and also from continued immigration, most recently from the former Soviet Union, which has provided upwards of 700,000 new immigrants to Israel in the last decade, and from elsewhere in eastern Europe. The average population density is now 204 per sq mile. The most densely populated area is central Israel where it is estimated that in a few years there will be no agricultural land left as it will have been swallowed up by the growing towns and cities.

Jerusalem is one of the fastest growing cities in the world. The Jewish population of East Jerusalem more than tripled from 50,000 in 1979 to 168,000 by 1993.

History

There have been many eras to Israel: Jewish, Arab, Roman, Greek, Christian, Muslim to name but a few. As The Holy Land, its many sites provide the backdrop of Christianity, and biblical tourism is one of Israel's biggest money earners. The bible relates events (with some question as to their literal accuracy), that happened in Israel in the time of Moses (about 1300 BC) when the Israelite tribes escaped from slavery in Egypt, and crossed the Red Sea into Sinai. From thence they went to Palestine where they continued their existence largely as masters of that land, repelling from time to time the neighbouring Philistines and Assyrians when they ventured to become acquisitive.

The armies of Alexander the Great however, proved unstoppable even for the plucky tribes of Israel, who were no match for his steamroller passage through Palestine, which as a consequence was largely Greek by the 4th century AD. But in a reversal of fortune to which all empires are liable, the Greek one gave way to the Roman one, and by AD100 Palestine was part of the Roman Empire. As the rule of Rome disintegrated in its turn, the Arabs stepped into the vacuum only to fall foul of the Christian fanatics of Europe during the crusades. Amongst the many eminent crusaders was England's own Richard I (The Lionheart). Even today you meet fair-haired, blue-eyed Arabs in Israel, who claim to be the descendants of crusader by-blows, though they are more likely to be from the time of the British mandate (see below).

The Christians established several states (including Jerusalem), before they were well and truly routed by Salah ad-Din (Saladin) at Karnei Hittim (Horns of Hittim) near Tiberias in 1187. After this the Mamelukes and Ottomans poured in to Palestine to stake their various claims, and the Jews were forced out and dispersed all over Europe. Palestine remained part of the Ottoman (Turkish) Empire until the time of the First World War in Europe, when in 'a sideshow' of that war, the British, at a cost of more than 10,000 soldiers' lives, drove the Ottomans from Palestine and established a mandate there.

During the 19th century, when the Zionist movement emerged in Europe and the claim for a permanent Jewish homeland began to gather momentum. Palestine became the destination of the Zionists who began to reclaim what they regarded as the historical Jewish homeland, towards the end of the nineteenth century and at the beginning of the 20th. This was when the first communal settlements were founded in Palestine by Zionist idealists. This further increased tension between the Jews and the Arabs. The latter had been in Palestine for generations and regarded the land, not unreasonably, as theirs.

The Palestinian campaign of the First World War may have been derogated by Western powers to the status of a minor event, but Israel's troubled history for most of the 20th century was a direct legacy of British policy there. Palestine became a British Protectorate in 1920, and the worsening of the Arab-Jewish conflict can be traced to the Balfour Declaration of that time which gave *carte blanche* to Jews to continue settling in Palestine, much to the outrage of the Palestinians already there, who were being driven off their land by the Zionist settlers. There were several major violent interludes between the Jews and Palestinians during the British mandate; the worst was from 1936 to 1939 when there was virtually a civil war.

After the Second World War, in response to the genocide attempted on the Jews of the Nazi era, the United Nations favoured carving a separate Jewish state out of Palestinian territory. It was supposed to be a humanitarian response to compensate the Jews for their unimaginable suffering. As you would expect, the Arabs resisted the carving up of their land, but before the solution could be hammered out, the British Mandate expired. The British withdrew, harried by terrorists from the nascent Jewish state, and thus effectively abandoned the Palestinians. This was their second betrayal by the British; the first being the secret Franco-British pact (cf.The Sykes-Picot Agreement) which deceived them about the intended fate of arab lands after the First World War.

The Jews seized the whole of Palestine, except the area known today as the West Bank, and East Jerusalem. Both of these areas were occupied by Jordan. They declared the independence of the state of Israel in 1948, and the new Jewish nation was born. It was a highly emotional moment for Jews around the world, but for the Palestinians it was a well of bitterness for the years to come.

In 1967, nearly twenty years after the creation of the Israeli state, Israel struck out at its arab neighbours in an unwarranted pursuit of expansion (masquerading as self defence) by seizing not only the West Bank and East Jerusalem from Jordan, but also Sinai from Egypt, and the Golan Heights from Syria in the war with all its arab neighbours. As the Israelis will have it, it was 'a modern David and Goliath story' except that David had vastly superior weaponry and technology compared to Goliath.

Although it was not without great heroics, the '67 war was to produce a state of extraordinary tension in the region as subsequent attempts by its neighbours, trying to regain their territories, has shown.

The first peace between Israel and an Arab neighbour was the Camp David Accord of 1978, which was masterminded by the Americans. More recently, the Norwegians fostered the second phase in 1993 when secret talks in Oslo led to the at first incongrous meeting and handshake on the lawn of the White House in Washington of Yasser Arafat, the Palestinian representative and the late Israeli Prime Minister, Yitzhak Rabin. Mr Arafat was officially recognised as the Palestinian leader, and the Palestinians in Israel were immediately granted a modicum of autonomy in Jericho and Gaza, and autonomy in stages for the arab towns of the West Bank. In return Mr Arafat, renounced all violence against Israel. Mr Arafat may have hung up his battledress, but the hard line Palestinian agitators have not relinquished theirs, nor their aspirations to take all of Israel for the Arabs. They promptly disavowed Mr Arafat as their leader. As a result Mr Arafat has been weakened rather than strengthened by being officially recognised as the leader of the Palestinians, many of whom feel he has sold them short to the enemy. The strength of feeling of the Palestinian extremists has been shown in their suicide bomb attacks on Israelis, the most recent at the time of press were in Haifa and elswhere in the north. As recently as November 1999, there was a triple pipe bomb attack which injured over 30 Israelis in Netanya, the coastal resort just north of Tel-Aviv. It is in this inauspicious climate of extremes that a permanent settlement is intended, somewhat ambitiously, to be concluded by September 2000.

The symbolic agreement on the White House lawn was followed in 1994 by a peace treaty with Jordan, which subsequently has full diplomatic relations with Israel. The next phase, in progress at the time of writing, involves the Syrians who are likely to play ball, only if the Golan Heights, presently occupied by Israel, are returned to them. This leaves only a resolution of the volatile Lebanese border zone, which is a major security problem for Israel, not least because Hizbollah are bent on violating it from their strongholds in northern Lebanon. Also to be resolved is probably the most emotive problem of all – Jerusalem, which both Israel and Palestine claim as their capital. At the time of press it looks as though Mr Arafat will be forced into compromise by accepting Jewish rule over Jerusalem and a squeezing out of the Palestinians to the edge of the city, where they will be allowed to establish some kind of capital.

The West Bank negotiations seem to be the only part of the Israeli-Palestinian peace process in which visible progress has been made, but even here latent danger lurks. The problem of the 144,000 Israeli settlers still living in the Palestinian West Bank is feared by many to be a recipe for future confrontation. All through the peace discussions of the last seven years, the building of over 30 Israeli settlements in the West Bank has been continuing, against the wishes of the USA and others involved in brokering a peace. The right wing continues to be a hinderance to peaceful progress. There was the Goldstein massacre of 1994 when a fanatical Israeli settler in Hebron gunned down 30 Palestinians at prayer. The assassination of 'peacemaker' Yitzhak Rabin in November 1995 by a an Israeli student with links to the Israeli secret service, was a manifestation of the same kind of no compromise extremism. The West Bank Israeli settlers vowed to form their own private army for defending themselves and Israel.

The terms of the peace as regards the West Bank settlers are liberal, to say the least. The stand-alone settlements will be abandoned. Sixty other, large ones will be segregated off from arab territory and expanded into settlement blocks comprising up to 30% of the West Bank. These blocks will be linked to Israel via roads carved out of yet more Palestinian territory. Even when (or if?) the Wye accords are fully implemented, the Palestinians will only have full or partial control of 40% of the West Bank territory, plus most of the Gaza Strip. There is still much unresolved: the status of East Jerusalem, which the Israelis have claimed unilaterally as theirs, and the freedom or otherwise of Palestinian refugees to return to the fledgling Palestine from refugee camps outside Israel, and the size of the compensation settlement for the current figure of 3.5 million refugees created by the wars with Israel in 1948 and 1967.

For other details see the section *The Palestinians and the Palestinian Governed Areas.*

ENTRY AND VISA REGULATIONS

At one time, getting into Israel, extending your stay and even settling there was remarkably easy. However, regulations have tightened up dramatically in recent years for working travellers. On entry, new arrivals are issued with a visitor's visa, usually valid for three months and renewable (with the Ministry of the Interior) for a maximum of six months, though some people have found a way to stay longer. If you subsequently find work on a kibbutz, archaeological dig etc.

you are obliged to convert your visitor visa to a volunteer (B4) visa at a cost of about £15. If you go through an official organisation or are placed by the Volunteers' Office in Tel Aviv the process is relatively easy. If you fix up something direct with an employer it might not be so straightforward.

After three months, it is important to renew your B4 permit. The penalty for non-renewal is likely to be deportation from Israel. Currently, the total duration for B4s appears to be a six months maximum stay in Israel, but regulations are always changing, and certainly if you want to stay on and your employers are keen, they will probably find a way to get an additional extension. For other kinds of casual work favoured by working travellers, work permits are virtually impossible to get and many people find they have no choice but to work illegally with the threat of deportation and exploitative conditions blighting their stay. If you only have a tourist visa and are prepared to take chances, it is essential to renew the visa every three months. The usual way is to take a trip away from Israel and then re-enter it.

One last obvious, but easy to overlook point is that you should not enter Israel with a passport with less than six months to run before the expiry date.

Ministry of the Interior offices where application for visa extension can be made:

Eilat: Ha Temarim Boulevard; tel 07-6376332.
Jerusalem: General Building, 1 Shomzion Hamalka Street; tel 02-6228211.
Tel Aviv: Shalom Tower, 9 Ahad Haam Street; tel 03-5193222.
Haifa: Il Hassan Shukri Street; tel 04-9667781.

Or at District Commissions Offices in: Afula, Akko, Ashkelon, Beer'sheva, Hadera, Herzliya, Holon, Nazareth, Netanya, Ramle, Ramat Gan, Rehovot, Safed and Tiberias.

Egyptian, Jordanian & Syrian Visas

Egyptian Visa Application in the UK
To visit Egypt you will need a visa, which is obtainable in Israel, at Cairo International Airport, or from an Egyptian consulate or embassy before you leave home: In the UK, the Egyptian Consulate (Visa Section, 2 Lowndes Street, London SW1X 9ET) is open for personal applications from Monday to Friday 9.30am to 12.30pm. Visas can be processed in a day and can be collected from 2.30pm to 4pm. The cost is £15 (50% more than at Cairo airport). You can also apply by post having obtained an application form (tel 0891-887777, 60p per minute or fax 0891-669902 to have one sent to you). The consulate advises sending your application form, passport, £15 postal order, and passport-size photo by registered post with an S.A.E. for (non-registered) return of your passport. Note that it is necessary that your passport should not have an expiry date of less than six months away at the time of application.

Egyptian Visa Application in Other Countries:
In the USA: (3521 International Court NW, Washington, DC 20008 (tel 202-966-6342; fax 202-244 4319); In Canada: 454 Laurier Avenue, E Ottawa, Ontario K1N 6R3; tel 613-234 4931; fax 613-234 9347).

You can also get Egyptian visas from the Egyptian Embassy in Tel Aviv (54 Basel Street, off Ibn Givrol St; tel 03-546 4151; fax 03-544 1615) or the Egyptian Consulate in Eilat (68 Ha'Efroni St; tel 07-6376 882). The cost is NIS50-70 (free, if you are South African). The visa service is from 9am to 11am Sunday to Friday (closed Saturdays).

Visas are normally valid for travel within six months of the issue date. You can request a multiple entry visa for Egypt allowing you to make several trips back and forth across the border within the period of the visa.

If you are going to visit only the Sinai, Sinai-only visas are available at border crossings and are valid for two weeks.

Egyptian Embassies/Consulates

Australia: Egyptian Consulate, 112 Glen More, Paddington, Sydney, NSW 2028; tel 02-93624383; 02-9332-3288; also in Melbourne (tel 03-9654-8634.

Canada: Egyptian Embassy, 454 Laurier Ave, E Ottawa, Ontario K1N 6R3; tel 613-234 4931; fax 613-2349347; also Consulate in Montreal (tel 514-866-8455).

United Kingdom: Egyptian Embassy, 12 Curzon Street, London W1Y 6DD; tel 020-7499 2401; fax 020-7355 3568; also Consulate 2 Lowndes Street, London SW1 tel 020-7235 9777.

United States of America: Egyptian Embassy, 3521 International Court NW, Washington DC 20008; tel 202-966 6342; fax 244-4319; also a Consulate in New York (tel 212-759 7120).

Jordanian Visas

Since the Jordanian-Israel peace, crossing between Israel and Jordan has become more streamlined. The Allenby Bridge (called King Hussein Bridge by the Jordanians) has been supplemented by two other crossings between the two countries. For the Allenby Bridge near Jericho you must obtain a visa *in advance*.

If you turn up at the Allenby Bridge without a visa you will not be allowed to cross into Jordan. By the same token, you must retain the entrance slip given you by the Jordanian border police if you want to re-enter Israel by the same route. The distance from the Allenby Bridge to Amman, Jordan's capital is about 40km.

The two new border crossings used by Israelis and foreigners were opened in 1994. One is the Arava crossing 4km north of Eilat at Wadi Araba, the other, Peace Bridge or Jordan River crossing to the Israelis (*Jisr Sheik Hussein*, Sheik Hussein Bridge to the Jordanians), is near North Shona and east of Bet She'an in the north of Israel. Visas can be obtained at these border crossings but to avoid delays it is still advisable to get a visa in advance, either in Israel from the Jordanian Consulate in the Ramat Gan district of Tel Aviv (14 Aba Hillel Street; tel 03-7517722). The consulate opening times are Sunday to Thursday 9.30am-12.30pm, or from the Jordanian Embassy in your own country. On the whole, Israelis do not use the Allenby Bridge crossing. It is likely that you can also get a visa arranged through one or two travel agents when booking tours to Jordan. For additional information you can contact the Jordanian Tourism Board, P.O.Box 224, Amman, Jordan; tel. +962 06-4642311 or +962 06 4642312; fax 64648465.

Jordanian Embassies/Consulates

Australia: Jordanian Embassy, 20 Roebuck Street, Red Hill ACT 2603, Canberra; tel 02-6295 9951; fax 02-6239 7236.

Canada: Jordanian Embassy, 100 Bronson Avenue, 701, Ottawa, Ontario K1R 6G8; 613-238-8090; fax 613-232 3341.

6G8; 613-238-8090; fax 613-232 3341.

United Kingdom: Jordanian Embassy, 6 Upper Philimore Gardens, London W8 7HB (tel 020-7937 3685; fax 020-7937 8795.

United States: Jordanian Embassy, 3504 International Drive NW, Washington DC 20008; tel 202-966 2664; fax 202-966 3110; also Consulate in New York (tel 212-355 9342).

Syrian Visas

At the time of going to press, relations between Syria and Israel had not progressed to a peace accord. While the present state of affairs (i.e. no diplomatic relations) lasts, you cannot enter Syria from Israel, or if you have an Israeli stamp in your passport. If you wish to go to Syria you will have to obtain a visa in advance from any Syrian Embassy including those in Amman (Jordan) and Cairo (Egypt).

Syrian Embassies/Consulates

United Kingdom: Syrian Embassy, 8 Belgrave Square, London SW1; tel 020-7245 9012.

United States: Syrian Embassy, 2215 Wyoming Avenue, NW Washington DC 20008; tel 202-232 6613; Consulate in New York (tel 212-661-1553).

Passports

It is important to be aware that there is a lucrative black market in stolen passports. Your passport should be kept with you at all times or deposited in a safe place. Kibbutzim and moshavim will normally lock up your valuables in a safe place on request.

If you intend to visit Syria, or any other Middle-Eastern country (except Jordan and Egypt) after Israel, ask for a separate, detachable visa. If your passport is stamped by the Israelis it will close many Arab nation doors. If you are likely to have an extended stay in Israel, you may well get your passport stamped after applying for renewal which will have the same effect of excluding you from entering many Arab countries. Even Israeli-Egyptian border crossing stamps may bar you from entry to Syria. To be really sure, consider having two passports which the British Home Office will grant for a valid reason such as wanting to travel both to Israel and certain arab countries.

There is no problem entering Israel with a passport containing stamps from any arab country.

Customs

Luggage in Israel is subject to the most exacting scrutiny (see *Security* below). You can bring in certain items for personal use provided that they are re-exported and if they are portable and in use. These include cameras, binoculars, sound recorder, typewriter/word processor/computer etc., sports equipment, jewellery, musical instruments, bicycle and films/tapes/CDs if you have the appropriate equipment.

Security

Because of Israel's particular place in the world of politics, it is necessary to remember that for your own safety and for Israel's security, you will be subjected to the most thorough and extensive search of both your person and your baggage. This can take place both at your point of departure and on arrival in Israel. However, it is usually far worse at departure. For example, visitors leaving Ben Gurion Airport are routinely interrogated sometimes by three security personnel in rotation, as well as having their luggage searched. Nobody is exempt, and you must be prepared for quite long delays which these procedures can cause.

As the experience of being handled by Israeli security is never a relaxing one, keep reminding yourself that these searches are conducted for your own safety as well as Israel's and that getting up-tight will not benefit anyone. Besides, such searches are usually conducted with courteous efficency. If you can bring yourself to compliment the security personnel for their efficiency and thoroughness, you may even raise a smile.

Everything in your luggage can be examined, even your soap, tooth-paste or shoe heels. Electrical equipment, transistor radios and recorders may be dismantled and it is wise not to have film in your camera as it could be opened. Camping knives will be taken and returned later on arrival.

MONEY AND TOURISM

The Israeli currency seems to have suffered as many adversities as the country itself. In 1980 the Israeli pound was replaced by the shekel and greeted with much fanfare. It was hoped that returning to the old biblical currency would help revive the ailing economy: however, five years later inflation was raging at 400%. The problems caused by inflation were practical as well as financial. Cardboard, bearing the extra zeros had to be stuck on the petrol pumps and there was not enough room on a cheque to complete the payment details. The solution was to replace the shekel with the New Shekel which was worth 1,000 old shekels.

Nowadays the Israeli economy is described as 'booming' with an annual growth rate of about 6%, attributed among other things to Israel's nascent high tech industries, which have benefited enormously from an input of top grade talent from many Russian professionals, who are amongst the tide of new immigrants from the former Soviet-Union. High inflation is a thing of the past, and a tourism boom resulting from a permanent settlement with the Arabs would complete the picture of the present prosperity and outlook of the economy. Exchange rates are relatively stable and changing money on the black market is only slightly advantageous financially and not as safe as changing it in a bank.

Rates of exchange are posted daily in the banks and the *Jerusalem Post*.

Money

Currency & Exchange
New Israeli Shekels (NIS) come in notes of: NIS200, NIS100, NIS50, NIS20, NIS10 and coins of: NIS10, NIS5, NIS1, NIS0.50 , 0.10 and 0.05 agorot. 100 argorot 1 shekel.
UK£1=NIS6.6, US$1=NIS4.2, A$1=NIS2.8.

Money and travellers cheques can be exchanged at banks, some hotels, the airport etc. You will need to produce your passport for identification when cashing travellers cheques. If you wish to try the black market money changers, there are booths in Salah-el-Din Street, in the Old City of Jerusalem. It is advisable to record the exact amount of money you are changing and to memorise the colour and corresponding value of notes to avoid being short-changed.

You may bring into Israel an unlimited and undeclared amount of foreign currency in cash, travellers' cheques, letters of credit or State of Israel Bonds.

There are some advantages to paying in foreign currency (including travellers cheques, Eurocheques written in shekels but counted as foreign currency and credit cards) for services and purchases, as you will not have to pay domestic VAT (currently 17%). However, you will receive your change in shekels. Many shops have to be persuaded to deduct the VAT at the point of sale as it is more advantageous for them to have you pay them the VAT and then you claim it back from the bank when you leave Israel. To do this you will have to keep all receipts of purchase made with foreign currency for presentation at the airport bank.

There are a range of restrictions on VAT refunds including a minimum purchase value. Details can be found in the *Customs Guide for the Reimbursement of VAT* which you can pick up at the airport or port of your arrival. All in all, it is much less trouble if you can persuade the shopkeeper/service provider to deduct the VAT at the point of sale.

When you leave Israel you may change up to $5,000 worth of shekels back into foreign currency if you can show proof of the original conversion. Unless you want to keep them as a souvenir don't leave Israel with any shekels as they are completely ignored by banks outside Israel.

Bank Opening Hours
Sun. Mon. Tues. Thurs.:	8.30am to 12.30pm and 4pm to 5.30pm
Wednesday:	8.30am to 12.30pm
Friday & eves of holidays:	8.30am to midday

If you are stuck for a bank outside these hours you can try the branches of banks situated in major hotels which are open for additional hours.

Tipping
It will not be expected, except in western-type hotels and restaurants, that you tip and even then you should not feel it is obligatory. Taxi-drivers, bartenders etc. will accept tips but it always depends on whether you can afford it and whether you feel it is justified.

Student Discounts
The discounts offered to students in Israel are numerous. Buses, trains, youth hostels, hotels and restaurants, some entertainments, museums, parks and tourist facilities are among some of the providers of student discounts. To get an International Student Identity Card (ISIC) which is valid for 15 months from September, you will need an ISIC application form, proof of student status, two passport-type photos and a £6 (£6.50 if obtaining by ISIC mail order) fee is payable. The card is available from student travel offices and ISIC Mail Order (P.O. Box 36, Glossop, Derbyshire SK13 8HT; e-mail enquiries@nussl.co.uk). The card comes with a booklet *ISIC World Travel Handbook* giving a country-by-country guide to discounts. The card is valid for 15 months from September.

Americans can get ISEIC (International Exchange Identity Card) from ISE Cards, 5010 East Shea Blvd, A-104, Scottsdale, AZ 85254 (www.isecard.com) for $20.

An International Youth Hostel card, available from your own country's Youth Hostel Association will also entitle you to some discounts as will the Federation of Youth Travel Organisations (FIYTO) which issues a card, often through the same outlets as for ISICs.

You can also obtain from the main bus and train depots in Tel Aviv, Haifa and Jerusalem a card entitling you to discounts on all train and bus routes in Israel, but you must present one of the above-mentioned cards.

Israel Student Tourist Association (ISSTA)

ISSTA is a non-profit organisation whose aim is to cater for the needs of the student and youth traveller.

You should visit any of their offices (or write) to find out about the many services they are able to offer. There are always additions and changes being made, but some services they regularly offer are: discount charter flights, reservations in inexpensive hotels, and vacation centres, special tours, kibbutz volunteer groups and archaeological digs.

Tel Aviv: The Dizengof Centre, 3rd Floor; tel 03-5250037; fax 03-5251617. Open from 10am to 8pm.

Jerusalem: 31 Ha-Nevi'im Street, 95103; tel 02-6252799; fax 02-6240462; also at 5 Joel Solomon Street.

Haifa: 2 Balfour Street, 33121 (tel 04-8669139 and 04-8670222; fax 04-8676697). Other branches in the student building at Technion (tel 04-8326739), and in Haifa University (04-8253951).

Opening hours usually: 9am to 1pm and 3pm to 6pm unless otherwise stated.
Closed: Wednesday and Friday afternoons and all day Saturday.

ISSTA Poste Restante
Mail can be sent to you c/o ISSTA offices, to be collected during office hours. Passports must be shown at the time of collection. 'Poste Restante' (*doar shamur*) must be added to the address.

Israel Government Tourist Offices (IGTO)

There are IGTO offices in major Israeli towns and cities. They can offer a lot of help and carry a vast range of information on accommodation, bus and train times, recommended firms and stores, current events of interest and deal with complaints or any problems you may have. Unfortunately, their standard of service is very hit and miss and some offices make out they are doing you an enormous favour rather than their job when you ask for their assistance; yet others can be extremely helpful.

They also offer a range of other services, for instance arranging room rentals in private Israeli homes as an alternative to staying in hostels, and for a similar cost. They are also able to give discounts on some tourist attractions and stores. Also available are free maps of Israel and plans of large towns.

I.G.T.O.s:
Acre (Akko): Eljazar St, opp. Mosque (tel 04-9991764).
Allenby Bridge: Allenby Bridge (tel 02-9942626).
Arad: Visitors' Centre, 28 Eliezer Ben-Yair St. (opp. Community Centre); tel 07-99544; 07-9955866.
Arava: border crossing with Jordan; tel 07-6336811.
Ashdod: 4 Haim Moshe Shapira St. Rova Daled (tel 08-8640485; fax 08-8640090).
Ashqelon: 2 Hanassi, Afridar Commercial Centre (tel 07-6710312; fax 07-6732412).

Beer'Sheva: 6A Ben Zvi Street (tel 07-236001/3).
Ben Gurion International Airport: (tel 03-9711485).
Eilat: Arava Highway Corner, Yotam Road; tel 07-6372111; 07-6374233; fax 07-6376763.
Ein Hamifratz: Kibbutz Ein Hamifratz, 25210; tel 04-9852377.
Haifa: 18 Herzl St.; (tel 04-8666521; 04-8643616; fax 04-8622075) and 106 Sderot Hanassi; tel 04-8374010 and in the Central Bus Station tel 04-8512208.
Haifa Port: (tel 04-8663988).
Jerusalem: Jaffa Gate (tel 02-6280382, 02-6280457 and 17 Jaffa Road; (tel 04-6258844).
Jordan River Crossing (Sheik Hussein Bridge); tel 06-6586410; tel 06-6586392; fax 06-6586421.
Mahanayim: Zomet Mahanayim; tel 06-6935016.
Nahariya: Municipal Square, 19 Ga'aton Blvd. (tel 04-9879800' 04-9879811; fax 04-9922303).
Nazareth: Casanova St. (tel 06-6573003; fax 06-6573078).
Netanya: Kikar HaAtzmaut (tel 09-8827286).
Rafiah: border crossing with Egypt; tel 07-6734080.
Ramat Hanegev: Zomet Mashabay Sadeh; tel 07-6557314.
Safed: 50 Jerusalem Street (tel 06-6920961; 06-6920633.
Taba: border crossing into Sinai (Egypt); tel 07-6372104; tel 07-6373110.
Tel Aviv: Suite 6108, 6th Floor, New Central Bus Station; tel 03-6395660; fax 03-6395659 and 69 Ibn Givrol Street; tel 03-5218500.
Tiberias: HaBanim Street, The Archaeological Park (tel 06-6725666).

Egypt:
c/o The Embassy of Israel, 6 Ibn el Maleck, Giza, Cairo; tel 729734.

Green Card for National Parks

The Green Card is a special offer: for NIS50 you can visit any 6 (out of 54) National Parks and Reserves. The card is valid for two weeks only, and is issued by the Israel Nature and National Parks Protection Authority (3 Am ve Olamo Street, Jerusalem; tel 02-5006244; fax 02 5005444; and 35 Jabotinsky Street Ramat-Gan 52511 Tel Aviv; tel 03-5766888; fax 03-7511858). The Card can be obtained at any National Park and Reserve (e.g. Masada, Caesarea, Jerusalem Walls, Ein Gedi, Coral Beach etc.).

Useful Free Publications

The Israeli Ministry of Tourism publishes a booklet *Israel – A Visitor's Companion* available from Government Tourist Offices outside Israel. Unfortunately, it is not updated every year. The most recent available at time of press was from June 1998. A better bet might be *Israel Tourism Guide* of which there is one for every region published by Index Pirsumim Ltd (5 Petah Tikva Road, Tel Aviv; tel 03-5600281; fax 03-5662828; e-mail index@index.co.il www.index co il) or leaflets and maps published by the Ministry of Tourism and available from Israeli Government Tourist Offices.

Israeli Government Tourist Offices Abroad

Australia: Australia-Israel Chamber of Commerce, Tourism Department, 395 new south Head Road, Double Bay, Sydney, NSW 2028; tel 29326-1700; fax 29326-1676; e-mail alcc@mpx.com.au

North America: Tourism Commisioner for North America, 800 Second Avenue, New York, NY 10017; tel 212-499-5640; fax 212-499 5645; Information Centre e-mail info@goisrael.com Website www. goisrael.com

United Kingdom: Israel Government Tourist Office, UK House, 180 Oxford Street, London W1N 9DJ; tel 0207-299 1113; fax 020-7299 1112.

GETTING AROUND

The possibilities include buses, trains, taxis, sheruts and hitch-hiking (called tramping in Israel).

Bus

Although the Israelis constantly complain about the bus companies, they are by western standards cheap, reliable and the best and most convenient form of transport in Israel. The biggest company is Egged (tel 03-537 5555/03-694 8888), which serves most towns and cities and provides intercity services throughout the country. Students get 10% discount on production of an ISIC. The Dan company (tel 03-6394444) operates in Tel-Aviv while in the West Bank, (including East Jerusalem), Gaza and Galilee there are arab buses.

Buses are air-conditioned and their speakers relay Israeli radio broadcasts including news and music to the back of the bus. There are *yashir* (direct), express and *me-asef* (local) services. Express buses leave from marked platforms and you can pay on board. However, for long distance journeys, for instance Jerusalem to Eilat, advance reservations should be made.

Services start at about 5am. There are frequent buses throughout the day to all parts of the country, but late night services are scarce. Except for the routes between Tel-Aviv and Jerusalem and Tel-Aviv-Haifa where the last bus is about 11.30pm, most routes have finished by 10pm. Most buses stop running about 6pm on Friday, at the start of the Sabbath, and do not start running again until after sunset on Saturday, when they are liable to be very crowded. No buses run on Jewish holidays.

Egged also run excursion tours to all parts of the country and to Egypt and Sinai. For further information write to their head office at 15 Frishmann Street, Tel Aviv (tel 03-527 1222).

Bus Passes: Egged city bus passes for Jerusalem and Haifa offer unlimited travel for a calendar month for about NIS120. In Tel-Aviv the Dan pass costs about the same. The Israbus pass from Egged offers unlimited travel countrywide for 7/14/21/30 days from about NIS190 for seven days and is available at any Egged Tours office in Israel. There is a toll-free number for information concerning Egged Routes, timetables and fares – 177-022-5555.

Train

There is a limited single track network. Fares are slightly lower than the buses and trains run daily to the major cities except on the Sabbath and all religious occasions. The line from Haifa to Jerusalem is well worth taking as it passes through the Judean wilderness and is particularly scenic. Note that at the time of press, it was closed for an unspecified period for repairs to the line. The most used and useful line is the coastal route from Tel Aviv which goes as far north as Nahariya. These are regular services used by commuters as well as travellers.

The lines are:

Tel Aviv Central up the northern coast to Herzliya, Netanya, Hadera, Haifa, Akko (Acre) and Nahariya.

Tel Aviv South to Jerusalem (see note above), Ramla, Lod, Beer'sheva and Dimona.

For details telephone: Tel Aviv (03-5421515; Haifa (04-564564); Jerusalem (02-717764) or any Government Tourist Office. Ask about extra-generous student card discount – at present 50%.

Taxis

Sherut

These are large cars which take up to seven passengers. They are shared taxis which run a definite route at a fixed price per passenger only slightly higher than bus fares. They usually follow bus routes and will drop you and pick you up at bus stops, but you must hail them. There are city sheruts which cruise the streets looking for passengers and and inter-city sheruts for longer distances.

On the Sabbath, in many parts of the country, they are the only form of transport available so it is wise to agree a price before you get in. Prices are usually higher at night so if you are not sure whether you are being ripped off or not, check the price with the locals. Arabs call sheruts 'service taxis'.

Private taxis

Private taxis are known in Israel as 'Special' taxis. Legally they must have meters though you may have to insist that it be switched on or agree the fare in advance and haggle if it seems extortionate. You can summon taxis by phone or hail them in the street. The meter indicates three fare schedules, (0) telephone surcharge (to passenger pick up); (1) regular fare and (2) fare plus 25% surcharge for night (9.00pm to 5.30am) and Sabbath and holiday service. There is an official standard price list for urban fares which the driver should produce on request. Owing to the reputation special taxi drivers have for ripping off tourists and locals alike, make certain you know what the going rate is before you take a ride. Tourist offices and reception desks in hotel lobbies will be able to advise you of the standard fares if the drivers cannot.

Air

There is an inland air service run by Arkia that operates between the following cities:

Jerusalem to Tel Aviv, Haifa, Rosh Pina and Eilat.

Tel-Aviv to Jerusalem, Rosh Pina, Eilat and Masada.

Haifa to Jerusalem, Tel Aviv, Eilat.

Eilat to Jerusalem, Tel Aviv, Haifa.

Massada to Tel Aviv.

Schedules, fares and reservations for Arkia can be obtained by calling 03-5240220 in Tel Aviv or Arkia offices in main towns and cities or on the website: www.arkia.co.il

Hitch Hiking

On main roads and close to bus-stops there are clearly marked hitching points. They are mainly used for military personnel, who always take precedence, but young tourists will find it easy to get lifts, both locally and long distance. If you do not feel confident hitch-hiking then don't and even those who are confident should exercise caution and common sense. For instance no hitching alone, or at night etc..

It is important not to stick your thumb out when hitching a lift, as this is considered offensive in Israel. Instead, use your index finger to point to the side of the road.

Most drivers you meet will be friendly, hospitable and helpful but there are potential hazards to be aware of.

In recent years, incidents of sexual harassment and assault, have greatly increased and women contemplating hitching on their own should take warning from the fact that Israeli women soldiers are now prohibited from hitching on their own. As in many countries a boy-girl team is considered the safest way to travel, but even then, the girl should sit away from the driver.

The other potential hazard is hitching in a less populated area when the driver is not going all the way to your destination. You may run the risk of being stranded so always ascertain where exactly the driver is going to leave you, before you get in the car.

On long journeys you will probably travel through wild and remote areas, so before accepting a lift, you should have some confidence in the intentions of the driver and the condition of the car.

Girls should not reveal their exact name and address to drivers they do not feel at ease with. If you do, you could be pestered for weeks by follow-up visits and phone calls, not only from the driver, but his brothers, uncles, cousins and friends! If in doubt, invent details likely to deter them.

For boys travelling without girls, the most obvious way to improve your chances of getting a lift is to dress as conventionally as possible, and avoid a hippy-type appearance.

Car Hire and Driving

There are probably about 20 or so hire companies operating in Israel including international ones like Hertz, Eldan and Budget, not to mention The Youth Hostel Association which offers hostel accommodation/car rental packages. Car rental offices are located in main Israeli cities and at Ben Gurion Airport. In general, locally based companies are likely to have much better deals than the big international ones.

When driving in the West Bank or other Palestinian areas, reactions are less likely to be hostile if you avoid hiring an Israeli car (i.e. with yellow plates). There are several Palestinian hire companies; Orabi has branches near Jerusalem (02-995 3521, fax 02-995 3521) and in Bethlehem, Jericho and Nablus.

You can drive in Israel if you have a valid national or international driving licence and, depending on the company there is a minimum age requirement of 21. Drivers aged 21-23 pay higher insurance rates. You cannot take an Israeli hired car into Sinai or elsewhere in Egypt, or Jordan.

If you intend to bring your own car or motorbike into the country, the registration and insurance must be valid. Drivers' habits are aggressive but with that certain Israeli flair. However, the high accident rate is out of all proportion to the number of cars on the roads.

Petrol prices are comparable with the UK, but higher than in North America. Petrol stations close at night and on the Sabbath and Jewish holidays.

With such an extensive and reasonably priced transport system in Israel, hiring a car may only be necessary to reach out-of-the-way places. The cheapest rental will be approximately $50 a day with unlimited mileage. The Rent-a-Car deal offered by the Youth Travel Bureau (part of the Israeli Youth Hostel Association), offer an all-in package (car hire, unlimited mileage and seven nights' hostel accommodation with breakfast from $240 (four persons sharing) to $310 (2 persons sharing) for the smallest model car (Fiat Punto, Peugeot 205). In peak periods (last two weeks in April, the months of July and August and late December/January) there is a daily supplement of $15 per day. Drivers aged 18-21 pay extra cost for insurance. For further details contact the Youth Travel Bureau (1 Shezer Street, P.O. Box 2001, Jerusalem 91060; tel 02-6558400; fax 02-6558432).

For further information about driving regulations and car hire in Israel, contact the Israel Automobile Club (P.O. Box 36144 Tel Aviv).

Useful Contacts
Avis : 02-6249001 and 03-5271752.
Budget (Jerusalem): 02-6248991
Eldan (Jerusalem): 02-6252151
Hertz (Jerusalem): 02-6231351

Getting to Egypt

There are two main border crossings between Israel and Egypt: at Rafah in the Gaza Strip, or Taba, just south of Eilat. The Taba crossing is open 24hrs. If the Taba Hilton, which is just across the border in Egypt, is your destination, you need only show your passport. The Rafah crossing is open from about 9am to 5pm. If you only want to visit Sinai, then there is a Sinai visa which is issued on the spot at Taba and is valid two weeks. There are defined limits to the area covered by the visa: as far south as Sharm-es-Sheikh (the divers' mecca), St Catherine's monastery and Mt Sinai. If you overstay the two weeks' validity you are liable for a swingeing fine.

Bus travel to Egypt is relatively inexpensive and buses run daily. Buses leave for Cairo from Jerusalem, Tel Aviv and Eilat; the trip takes approximately 12 hours and there are fares from $40/$60 return for the night bus (departs midnight). Day departures are at 9am from Tel Aviv and 7.15am from Jerusalem and are more expensive than the night bus at about $75 single and $80-90 for a return. There are a number of tour/travel agencies with offices in both Tel-Aviv and Jerusalem including Nitza Tours (03-5102832), Egged Tours (03-5271212) and Masada Tours (02-6235777), also ISSTA (Israeli student travel organisation) offices (central tel 03-5220666) etc. where you can book tickets.

From Eilat, you can take bus 15 to the border, and take an Egyptian bus or a sherut to the Sinai or Cairo. Sheruts also leave for the border from the Damascus Gate in Jerusalem and the Central bus station in Tel Aviv. The border taxes to cross into Egypt and back total about $30.

Although flying to Egypt (Cairo) saves the trouble of border crossings and getting an Israeli stamp in your passport (see travel to Syria), it is expensive. Two airlines make the flight, El Al and Air Sinai.

You can also join an organised tour of Egypt from Israel, Galilee (03-5466333; fax 03-291770), Egged, and Neot Hakikar (03-5228161) are some of the companies that organise various packages to suit most budgets. As well as organising fare only (one-way and round trip) coaches from Eilat to Cairo, Neot Hakikar specialise in adventurous trips to the Sinai from Eilat and are cheaper than Galilee and Egged. Alternative Tours (Jerusalem Hotel, Nablus Road, Jerusalem; tel/fax 02-628 3282) also have trips to Sinai from US$55 organised by Palestinians.

For information on visas for Egypt see *Egyptian Visas* above.

Getting to Jordan

Nowhere is the peace dividend more evident than in the rush of companies to organise tours to Jordan from Israel and combined Israel and Jordan tours. While several companies operate ex-UK, there are also tours which you can arrange once you are in Israel or Jordan. Typical are: Tracks Adventure Tours (10 Kaplan St, Tel Aviv, tel 03-6916103; fax 03-6952226) which offers a 15-day Israel/Jordan programme of which the last two days is a tour of Petra and the Wadi Rum in Jordan, via the Arava border crossing near Eilat; Amiel Tours (03-5388444; fax 03-5336174), and Galilee Tours (03-5466622; fax 03-5466343) offer tours from Israel to Petra and Aqaba.

The Allenby Bridge point of contact has been supplemented by two other crossings between the two countries. The Allenby Bridge (called *Jisr al-Malek Hussein* or King Hussein Bridge by the Jordanians), 10km east of Jericho, is mainly used by local Arabs, and foreigners. You can get there by shared service taxi from opposite the Damascus Gate in Jerusalem. Alternatively you can take a sherut from Jericho. You must obtain a visa *in advance* from the Jordanian Consulate in the Ramat Gan district of Tel Aviv (see *Jordanian Visas* above). On the whole, Israelis do not use the Allenby Bridge crossing.

If you turn up at the Allenby Bridge without a visa you will not be allowed to cross into Jordan. By the same token, you must retain the entrance slip given you by the Jordanian border police if you want to re-enter Israel by the same route. The distance from the Allenby Bridge to Amman, Jordan's capital is about 40km. The Bridge is ostensibly open from open from 8am to midnight Sunday to Thursday, but times are liable to change without warning especially for Jewish and Muslim holidays.

Two new border crossings used by Israelis and foreigners were opened in 1994. One is the Arava crossing 4km north of Eilat at Wadi Araba. This crossing is the route taken by tour buses to Petra which is a couple of hours' drive from the border.

The other, Peace Bridge or Jordan River crossing to the Israelis (*Jisr Sheik Hussein*, Sheik Hussein Bridge to the Jordanians), is near North Shona and east of Bet She'an in the north of Israel. Visas can be obtained at these border crossings but to avoid delays it is still advisable to get a visa in advance, either in Israel or from the Jordanian Embassy in your own country. You can reach the Jordan River Crossing by bus from Beit Shean. Once over the border you can take a sherut to Irbid, the nearest Jordanian town of any size and then get other transport south to Amman.

It is likely that you can also get a visa arranged through one or two travel agents when booking tours to Jordan. For additional information you can contact the Jordanian Tourism Board, P.O.Box 224, Amman, Jordan; tel. +962 06-4642311 or +962 06 4642312; fax 64648465.

Useful Addresses

Alternative Tours: c/o Jerusalem Hotel, P.O. Box 20754, Jerusalem; tel/fax 02-628-3282; www.jrshotel.com Palestinian organised tours to Jordan and Egypt (from US$139 and US$159). Also trips to Sinai from US$55. All tours leave from the Jerusalem Hotel, Jerusalem.

Budget Travel Consultants: BTC, 1 Ha-Soreg Street, Jerusalem; tel 03-623 39 90; fax 03-625 78 27. Trips of one to four days in Jordan, four-day itineraries in Egypt.

Masada Tours: 9 Koresh Street, Jerusalem; tel 02-6235777; fax 02-625 5454. Trips to Jordan and Egypt. Travel service to Amman (Jordan) and Cairo.

Neot Ha-kikar: 5 Shlomzion Ha-Malka Street, Jerusalem; tel 02-623 62 62; fax 02-623 61 61. Specialises in Sinai. One day or longer.

Peltours: 28 Ahad Ha'am Street, P.O.B. 394, Tel Aviv; tel 03-5170871; fax 03-5160060. British based company Peltours have been organising tours in the Holy Land since the 1920s. Their Tel-Aviv office will book tours with Egged Tlalim or United bus companies to Jordan and Egypt as well as in Israel.

Youth Travel Bureau (1 Shezer Street, P.O. Box 2001, Jerusalem 91060; tel 02-6558400; fax 02-6558432), part of the Israeli Youth Hostel Association have a ten-day tour which includes Sinai and Jordan.

ACCOMMODATION

Youth Hostels

There are thirty-two Youth Hostels, situated throughout Israel, six of them in Jerusalem, operated by the Israel Youth Hostel Association. There is no age limit, nor is membership obligatory, although non-members pay slightly higher charges. In 1999 costs for one night ranged from $16.50 to $32 (£11 to £22) including breakfast. Youth hostel members also enjoy reduced fees for most historical sites and national parks as well as museums, buses and trains. International Youth hostel cards are accepted and can be obtained from the YHA in your own country.

A few hostels have a maximum stay of three nights. Unfortunately theft can be a problem in hostels: do not leave valuables lying around when you are asleep. The standard facilities include dormitories for males and females with mostly two-tier beds, mattresses, linen sheets and blankets and sanitary installations. A few hostels have guest houses with double, family rooms. Each hostel has a resident warden. Breakfast, lunch and supper are available in all hostels.

Some of the hostels are in interesting buildings. One of the best is the former Turkish governor's headquarters in the ancient walled Arab town of Acre (Akko). The rooms have high, carved wood ceilings and the first floor has stunning views of the sea.

Hostel Time Table

Check in 4-9pm; Breakfast 7-8am; supper 7-8pm; lights out at 11pm (except in some city hostels). Telephone for reservation only at 7-9am and 5-9pm.

Maps in English, German and French with all addresses and telephone numbers are available from all Goverment Tourist Offices. Youth Hostel Membership, from the Israel Youth Hostel Association in Jerusalem (see address below), or the Tel Aviv hostel (36 Bnei Dan Street, PO Box 22078, Tel Aviv; tel 03-5441748; fax 03-5441030). Applications will require a passport photograph.

Youth Hostel Package Tours

The Israeli Youth Hostel Association also organises package tours for individuals and groups under the banner *Israel on the Youth Hostel Trail*. Tours are in Israel, Jordan and Egypt including a six-day circuit in the Sinai with camels for $450 (does not include tips or border taxes). There are seven, 14, 21 and 28-day, go-by-yourself trips which include half-board in youth hostels, unlimited travel by Egged buses and entrance to nature reserves. A travel kit including vouchers, maps and information material is included. Prices are $320, $625, $890.

Further details from Israel Youth Hostels Association (1 Shezer Street, P.O. Box 6001, Jerusalem 91060; tel 02-655 84 00; fax 02-655 84 30; e-mail iyha@iyha.org.il).

Private Hostels and Rooms

Most large towns and cities also have privately-run hostels. It is usually possible for friends to share rooms or sleep on the roof in summer, at a lower price, and come and go at any time. Such hostels tend to be concentrated in the tourist places: Tel-Aviv, Jerusalem, Tiberias, Eilat etc. In other towns and cities there may be cheap hotels, religious hospices open to tourists (see below) or rooms in private houses.

Some of the hostels are listed below. Many are well-established; others come and go, and you can always find others by asking around the cheaper parts of town, looking for signs, asking in bars and cafés, and by word of mouth. Remember to exercise some caution in using unregulated hostels or rooms in private houses, as not all of them will be friendly and safe. If possible check with the tourist office or find an honest-looking local, or other travellers who can recommend somewhere. If you don't like the look of the place when you see it, because it is filthy and there are no locks on the dorm/room/street doors; don't feel obligated to stay there.

Rooms in private houses are available in many smaller towns. Rural kibbutzim and moshavim, always looking for a way to supplement their finances, by cashing in on tourist booms, have starting offering rooms, some of them in caravans, for rent at reasonable prices. Information about both town and rural private rooms can be obtained from Israeli Tourist Offices in Israel.

Private Hostels

Akko (Acre)

Walied's Gate Hostel (Salah ad-Din Street; tel/04-9815530; located next to Land Gate. Old and new sections; former has dorms and latter has hotel type rooms. From NIS 25 without breakfast. Has kitchen facilities, mixed and single-sex dorms, double-rooms and patio.

Paul's Hostel (also souvenir shop); (tel 04-9912857). Small hostel situated at the southern end of Ha-Hagana St towards the lighthouse. Hostel is behind the souvenir shop which takes the bookings.

Haifa

Beit Skandinavian Hostel: 49 Pinchas Margolin St; tel 04-8512470.
Bethel Hostel: 40 Hageffen Street; tel 04-8521110.

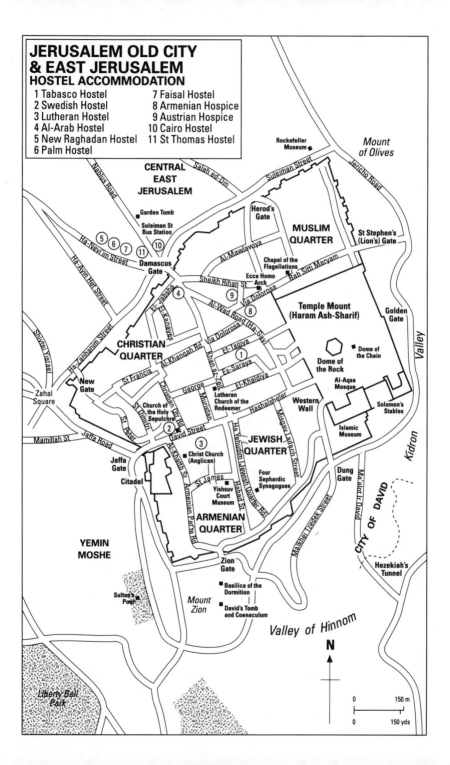

Jerusalem

The following are all in the Old City:

Al-Arab (Khan az-Zeit; tel 02-6283537). Near Damascus Gate. Free tea, coffee, safe. Arranges trips to the Palestinian camps. Very popular, particularly in summer and at Christmas.

Al-Ahram Hostel (64 Al Wad Rd; tel 02-6280926). Near Damascus Gate and opposite the third station of the Via Dolorosa. Kitchen, sitting room. Roof (NIS10) and dorm (NIS20)beds. Also doubles.

Black Horse Hostel: 28 Aqabat Darwish; tel 02-6286039; fax 02-6286039. Near Herod's Gate, Muslim Quarter.

Hashimi Hotel: Souk Khan Beir El-Zeit St (02-6284410). Refurbished by the American owner. Double rooms from about £20.

Petra Hostel: (1, David Street; tel 02-6286618). Near Jaffa Gate. Roof NIS15 (additional NIS5 for a blanket), dorms (NIS 23).

Swedish Hostel (29 David St, tel 02-6264124; fax 628 7884). Located near the Jaffa Gate. Not very Swedish, but always busy. Offers cheap tours.

Tabasco Hostel and Tea Room (8 Aqabat at-Takiyah; tel 02-628 11 01; fax 02-6283461). Near Damascus Gate. Offers free trips to the Palestinian refugee camps and Bethlehem. Free tea, cheap food. Roof beds, dorms, kitchen, dining room and showers.

The following are in Arab East Jerusalem:

Cairo: 21 Nablus Rd; tel 02 6277216. Also organises trips to Palestinian West Bank and camps.

Faisal: 4 Ha-Nevi'im Street; tel 02-628 75 02). View of the Damascus Gate. Free tea, storage, use of an iron. Generally friendly and hospitable.

New Raghadan (10 Ha-Nevi'im Street; tel 02-6283348). Popular and bustling.

Palm (6 Na'Nevi'im Street; tel 02-6273189). Very popular and international. Kitchen facilities. Roof beds, dorms and doubles.

St Thomas Hostel: 6 Chaldeen Street, off Nablus Road; (tel 02-628 26 57; fax 02-628 42 17. Pilgrim hostel complete with chapel. From $24 shared room with breakfast.

Also worth trying is the British School of Archaeology in Jerusalem (POB 19283, Jerusalem 91192; tel 02-5828101 & 02-5815028; fax 02-5323844; e-mail bsaj@vms.huji.ac.il) which was offering affordable hostel accommodation close to both the Old City and the Hebrew Mount Scopus Campus.

There are hostels also in West Jerusalem, but although they are very acceptable they cannot compete for atmosphere with the Old City and they are not usually as cheap. An exception is the Backpackers' Hostel (37 Jaffa Road) which is very lively and noisy with a disco downstairs which is not however, for those wanting a good night's sleep.

Tiberias

Maman Hostel (Atzmon St; tel 06-792986). Has kitchen facilities, dorm beds and private rooms with bath.

Nachum (Tavor St (tel 06-6721505). Near the bus station. Lively rooftop bar.

Hostel Aviv (66 Ha-Galil St; tel & fax 06-6723510). Quiet. Dorm beds, singles

and doubles.
Toledo (Bibas St; tel 06-6721649). Very popular and clean.

SPNI Field Study Centres

As an alternative to Youth Hostels you can stay at the Field Study Centres of the Society for the Protection of Nature in Israel (SPNI), a non-profit organisation founded in 1956 and dedicated to the preservation of the natural and historical aspects of the environment. Their residential FS Centres (see below), tend to be situated outside towns, in areas of outstanding natural beauty, and so are not suitable for those who prefer shops and nightlife. The buildings of the Centres which include a communal dining-room and kitchens, are extraordinarily well laid out, making the most of the views by adopting the most appropriate facing position and architecture.

FS Centres are also the perfect way to meet the Israelis who visit them for family weekends, i.e. the Sabbath plus another day or two, or they may arrive in groups from the kibbutzim, to explore the area. Their hospitality is at a peak on these occasions. The Centres provide facilities for self-catering and groups prepare huge, healthy meals from what would appear to be mainly the produce of their settlement, that are a nutritionist's dream.

The accommodation charge is approximately $30 a head per night. This is for a shared room of three or more beds with a shower, wash-basin and a separate w.c. If you are a member of the SPNI which costs £20 yearly, you will be entitled to a 20% discount on this charge.

The staff of the centres are keen to help you plan tours to observe the flora, fauna, geographical and archaeological aspects of the locality. Next to En Gedi FS Centre, beside the Dead Sea, is a nature reserve around the oasis of that name which is supposed to have inspired the writer of 'The Song of Songs'. It also contains animals such as the Ibex, a rare antelope, and a moderately tame leopard called 'Babta'.

Although there has been no Sinai FS Centre since the Sinai was handed back to Egypt, the SPNI staff in Eilat can still give advice to those planning tours and sporting activities both in Eilat and Sinai.

The Eilat FS centre is one of the most popular. It is hardly surprising considering the range of phenomena to see there. The colours of the coral and fish are stunning and even a non-diver can go on a trial dive with a qualified diving instructor; or you can make do with a snorkel. There is little danger if you take sensible precautions and the advice of the knowledgeable staff of the FS Centres.

Accommodation can be booked with individual centres or through the central reservation centre (tel 03-6388691).

Field Study Centres

The twelve Field Study Centres below offer accommodation similar to youth hostels.

Alon-Tabor: Mobile Post Galil Tachton 14101; tel 06-6766250; fax 06-6766272.
Carmel Coast: D.N. Maagen Michael, Menashe 37805; tel 06-6394166; fax 06-6391618.
Golan-Katzrin: P.O. Ramat HaGolan 12900; tel 06-6961352; fax 06-6961947.
Ein Gedi: Mobile Post Yam HaMelah 86980; tel 07-6584288; fax 07-6584257.
Eilat: P.O. Box 204, Eilat 88101; tel 07-6371127; 07-6371771.

Ha'Meron: Mobile Post Merom Hagalil 13870; tel 06-6980024; fax 06-6987723.
Har Gilo: Mobile Post North Judea 90907; tel 02-6768678; fax 02-9932644.
Har Hanegev: Mitzpeh Ramon 80600; tel 07-6588615; fax 07-6588385.
Hatzeva: Mobile Post Ha'arava 86815; tel 07-6581546; fax 07-6581558.
Hermon: Mobile Post Upper Galilee 12240; tel 06-6951480; fax 066951480.
Sde Boker: Sde Boker College 84990; tel 07-6532721.
Western Galilee: Mobile Post Galil Ma'aravi 22817; tel 04-9823762; fax 04-9823015.

Non-Residential FSCs
Ayalon, Beer'sheva, Carmel, Har Hanegev, Jerusalem, Kinnarot, Poleg, Soreq and Yarkon.

SPNI Offices Outside Israel
In addition to their head office in Israel (3 Hashfela Street, Tel Aviv 66183; tel 03-6388677), there are SPNI offices in:
The Netherlands: Hertellplein 5-6221ZB, Maastricht; fax 043-3261192.
Germany: Am Sonnenberg 14, 61279 Gravenwiesbach; tel 06086/695.
USA: 89 5th Avenue, Suite 800, New York 10003 N.Y.; tel 212-6458732.

Christian Hospices

There are about 65 Christian hospices in central and northern Israel which have long since diversified into a wider clientele than their once mainly pilgrim guests. However, they are liable to be booked up with the faithful at Christmas and Easter. They offer various standards and types of accommodation. Some have set meal times, while others do not serve meals at all. Price ranges: from $12 for a dormitory bed, $25-$50 for a single room with breakfast.

Some of the more popular hospices are:

Akko

Religious Sisters of Nazareth: P.O.Box 1009 (infront of the lighthouse) Old City (Akko el Atikha), Akko 24110.

Bethlehem

Abu Gubran, Lutheran Guest House, Paul V1 Street, P.O. Box 162; tel 02-2742312; fax 02-6470048.
Franciscans of Mary: (White Sisters), Milk Grotto St, POB 11; tel 02-2742441.
Saint Joseph's Home: Manger Street, POB 199 Bethlehem; tel 02-2770155; fax 02-2770334.

Jerusalem

Christian guest houses of the Old City have long welcomed non-religious guests. They charge similar prices to other hostels for dormitory beds, but their private rooms are at hotel rates. The Lutheran hostel costs about double the normal hostel rate for dorm beds. The following have dormitory accommodation in addition to private rooms.
The Armenian Catholic Patriachate Guest House: Via Dolorosa Street, Old City

Jerusalem; tel 02-6260880; fax 02-626 12 08.
Austrian Hospice: Via Dolorosa 37, P.O. Box 14037, Jerusalem 91140 (in the Old City); tel 02-6274636; fax 02-6271472.
Casa Nova: PP Franciscans, Casa Nova Road 10; New Gate, P.O.Box, Jerusalem 91013. In the Old City; tel 02-6271441;fax 02-6264370.
Christ Church Guest House: Jaffa Gate, P.O. Box 14037, Jerusalem 91140; tel 02-6277727; fax 02-6277730.
Lutheran Hospice: St Mark's Road 7, Old City, POB 14051; Jerusalem 91140; tel 02-6285105; fax 02-6285107. More expensive than others listed here.
St Andrews Scots Memorial Hospice: (David Remez St. 1, P.O. Box 8619, Jerusalem 91086 (near the Railway Station); tel 02-6732401; fax 02-6731711.
St George's Cathedral Hostel: 20 Nablus Road, POB 19018, Jerusalem 91197; tel; 02-6282627; fax 02-6282253.

Nazareth

Casa Nova Hospice: POB 198, Casa Nova Street, opp. the Basilica, POB 198, Nazareth 16101; tel 06-6571367; fax 06-6579630.
Christian Encounter Centre: P.O. Box 1508, Nazareth 16115 (next to Greek Catholic Seminary and Grand New Hotel), POB 1548; tel 06-6566762; 06-6576410; fax 06-6562470.
Monastère des Pères de Bet-Haram; tel 06-6570046.
Religious Sisters of Nazareth: Casa Nova Street, Nazareth 16101,(opposite the Basilica), POB 274; tel 06-6554304; fax 06-6460741.
St Gabriel Monastery Hotel: tel 06-6567349; fax 06-6554071.
St Margaret's: tel 06-6573507; fax 06-6567168.

Tiberias

YMCA Peniel by Galilee: Guest House, (Western Shore of the Galilee), POB 192, Tiberias 14101; tel 06-6720685; fax 06-6725943.
Sea of Galilee Centre (guest house): Safed Road, P.O. Box 104, Tiberias 14100; tel 06-6723769/6721165; fax 06-6790145; e-mail scottie@rannet.com. Run by the The Church of Scotland. Has special off season rates for B&B.

Haifa

Bethel Tourist Hotel 40 Hagefen St (Nr. French Consulate); tel 04-8521110.
Stella Carmel: Abu Khoury Street, Isfiya, (nr Carmel), POB 7045 Haifa; tel 04-8391692; fax 04-8390233.

Tel Aviv

Baptist Village: Petah Tikva, Mobile Post, Central Sharon 45875; tel 03-9311965; fax 03-9306624.
Beit Emmanuel: Auerbach Street 8, P.O. Box 2773, Jaffa, Tel Aviv 61027; tel 03-6821459; fax 03-6829817.

An up-to-date list of all Christian hostels can be obtained from: The Christian Information Centre (Jaffa Gate, POB 14308, Jerusalem 91140, Israel: tel 02-

6272692; fax 02-6286417; e-mail cicts@netmedia.netil.

Camping

There are about 40 well-run camping sites around Israel all of which are accessible by public transport except for Dor and Ashkelon. Sites are situated in scenic areas along the coast, near Jerusalem and by the Dead Sea, the Galilee regions and the Golan Heights. They can provide an economical way of touring the country compared with hotel accommodation. However, they are not as cheap as travellers hostels. All camping grounds have special areas for pitching tents and cabins for hire. Most of them have caravans available and some offer rooms to let. Facilities include showers, toilets, drinking water and often a restaurant and shop. You can buy camping vouchers for 7,14,21, and 28 day programmes which can be used at any camping site in Israel for tents, cabins, caravans or vacation cottages. The vouchers also entitle the holder to a continental breakfast and discounted car rental and unlimited bus travel.

Further information from the Israel Touring and Camping Union/Igud Ha'-Camping be'Israel (112 Moshav Mishmar Hashiva 50297; tel 03-9604524; 03-9604350; fax 03-9604712).

You can also get camping leaflets from IGTOs or Municipal Tourist Information Offices in Israel.

Scenic Israeli Camping Sites

Hamapalim Camping Site: Moshav Avnei Eitan, 12925; tel 06-6762151; fax 06-6762044. Waterfalls camping site.

Carolines-Almog Beach: P.O. Box 1582 Eilat 88115; tel 07-631911.

Ein Gedi: Outdoor Events & Tours
M.P. Dead Sea, Ein Gedi 86980; tel 07-6594726; 07-6594958; fax 07-6584125.

Field School Eilat:- Almog Beach, 88101; tel 07-6372021; 07-6371127; fax 07-6371771.

Gofra Beach Camping: Kibbutz Tel Katzir, 15165; tel 06-6731942; fax 06-6756870. S.E. Sea of Galilee.

Golan Camping Site: P.O. Box 120 Qatzrin 12900; tel 06-6961234; fax 06-6921104.

Hurshat Tal – National Park: Northern Galilee; tel 06-6942440; fax 06-6959360.

Ma'yan Baruch – Camping Site, Kayaking and Rafting: Kibbutz Ma'ayan Baruch, 12220 Upper Galilee; tel 06-6954601; fax 06-6954601.

Magdala Beach: P.O.Box 151 Migdal; tel 06-6722230, 06-6723684. Sea of Galilee, north of Tiberias.

Neve Yam Camping: Kibbutz Neve Yam, 30885; tel 04-9844827; fax 04-9844871. On the coast, south of Haifa.

Sleeping Out

All over Israel the main beaches have showers, toilets and drinking water, so, if you hitch-hike and can take a food allowance from the kibbutz, it is possible to have a cheap week-end or holiday on the beach.

Although completely legal you should however, not attempt sleeping out unless you are experienced in outdoor living and are travelling with several friends.

Particularly in the south, it is quite common to have some or all of your possessions stolen. For women, the persistent attentions of groups of males can be annoying and sometimes dangerous.

Although crimes of violence and muggings are rare, minor sexual assaults are common. The police are efficient, and generally very helpful but not at all sympathetic if you have been taking obvious risks. In the north, conditions are safer but it is still advisable to be very careful.

The wonderful climate in summer makes a tent unnecessary, but an essential piece of equipment is a sleeping bag with sheet. If you are going on a trip to Sinai you will need a specially insulated sleeping bag as the desert nights are freezing.

CITY LISTINGS

Tel Aviv

Accommodation For budget accommodation see *Cheap Accommodation in Tel Aviv* in *The Kibbutz* chapter.

Airport: Ben Gurion Airport, 22km southeast of Tel Aviv at Lod. Recorded flight info in English tel 03-9723344. Egged bus 475 from the 6th Floor of the New Central Bus Station in Tel Aviv leaves for the airport every 20-30 minutes. Also: United Tours bus 222 stops at various hotels on Hayarkon St.

American Express: 32 Ben Yehuda Street; tel 03-524 8862 (near Sheraton Hotel). Poste Restante Service for card holders only. Lost am-ex cheques only call toll free 177 440 86 94.

Car Rental: Avis (03-5271752); Budget (03-5621292); Eldan (03-6382525); Hertz (03-5622121).

Dan Buses: 39 Sha'ul Ha-Melekh; tel 03-693 33 33; bus information 03-6394444 for buses within Tel-Aviv.

Egged Bus Information: 03-6948888. Inter-city bus services.

Israel Student Travel Association: 109 Ben Yehuda Street; tel 03-5210555.

Main Post Office: 132 Allenby Street: Open Sunday to Thursday 7am to 6pm and Friday 7am to midday.

Magen David Adom: tel 5460111. Emergency medical aid.

Poste Restante: 7 Mikve Y'Israel Street with the International Telephone bureau. Open Sunday to Thursday 8am-6pm and Friday 8am-2pm.

Solan Telecom: 13 Frishman Street (03-5229424; fax 03-5229449). Discount international telephone calls and faxes open every day and night of the week 24-hours.

Tourist Office: 6th Floor, New Central Bus Station, Livinsky Street; tel 03-6395660; fax 03-6395659.

Trains: train station on Arlozerov Street. Buses to train station from Central Bus Station. Train information tel 03-693 7515.

Visa Office: Jaffa Shalom Tower; tel 03-651941/6517758.

Meeting Places and Pubs:

Buzzstop: pub/travellers meeting place next to Planet Hollywood in Yamit Park complex.

Joey's Bar: 42 Allenby Street (tel 03-6179277). American bar for late night swinging.

Mash: 275 Dizengoff St; tel 03-6051007. 24-hour bar/restaurant. Must be one of Tel Aviv's oldest travellers' meeting places. Stands for More Alcohol Served Here.

Shakespeare Café: British Council, Hayarkon Street. A quiet place to catch up on English newspapers and gossip.

Jerusalem

Alternative Information Centre: 6 Koresh Street, P.O. Box 31417; tel 02-6241159. Widely used by the foreign press, but accessible to non-journalists who want to learn more about the politics of the Middle East, the centre is non-sectarian and is run by Palestinians and Israelis. If you wish for discussion and insight, this is the place. The centre also carries its own publications.

Alternative Tours: c/o The Jerusalem Hotel, Nablus Road, P.O. Box 20754; tel/fax 02-6283282; e-mail raed@jrshotel.com Contact Abu Hassan. Tours organised by Palestinians to Palestinian cities and to Jordan, Egypt and Sinai. All departures from Jerusalem. For tour details see *The Palestinians and the Palestinian Governed Areas – Contact with Palestinians.*

American Express: 19 Hillel Street; tel 02-6254171; fax 02-6231520.

Bookshops with English books: Steimatsky's: 39 Jaffa Road; 9 King George Street; Cardo (Old City). The Society for the Protection of Nature (SPNI) has a book shop in its offices at 13 Heleni Ha-Malka Street where you can get excellent maps and guides and books on Israel's flora and fauna. You can also book tours (tel 02-6252357).

Car Rental: Avis (02-6249001); Budget (02-6248991); Eldan (02-6252151; Eurodollar (02-6235466); Hertz (02-6251851); Netz Harel (02-6382044).

Christian Information Centre: Al Khattab Square (Old City, just inside the Jaffa Gate); tel 02-62726 92; fax 02-628 64 17. tel 02-287647. Provides lists of church services, accommodation, information on Christian sites, maps and books.

Egged Bus Information: 02-5304555.

Egged Tours: 44A Jaffa Road; 02-6253454.

El Al: 12 Hilel St (02-6246725).

King David Hotel: 23 Hamelekh St; tel 02-6208888; fax 02-6208882. One of the world's famous hotels.

Israel Student Travel Association: 31 Ha-Nevi'im Street; tel 02-6257257.

Jewish Student Information Centre: 5 Beit El; tel 02-6282634; fax 02-6288338. Organises hospitality with Orthodox families, tours and Judaism classes.

Libraries British Council libraries are found at 4 Abu Obeida Street (tel 02-6282545) in East Jerusalem and 3 Shimshon Street (tel 02-6736733). Open hours are 11am-4pm Monday to Thursday and Fridays from 9.30am-1.30pm. Closed at weekends.

Main Post Office: 23 Jaffa Road; tel 02-6290898; open Sun-Thurs 7am-7pm; Fri 7am-noon; closed Saturday. Parcel Office: Sun-Thurs 8.30am-1.30pm; Fri 8.30am-noon. Closed Sat.

Main Post Office East Jerusalem: corner of Salah-el-Din and Suleiman St. Open Sun-Thurs: 8.30am-12.30pm and 4pm-6.30pm. Mon, Wed, Fri: 8.30am to 12.30pm. Tues 8.30am-2.30pm. Closed Sat.

Magen David Adom: Israel's emergency medical service; 6523133 or dial 101.

Masada Tours: 9 Koresh St; 02-6235777. Tours to Jordan and bus tickets for Cairo.

Municipal Tourist Information Office: Municipal Hall complex (3 Safra Square; 02-6258844). Leaflets and maps.

Telephones: telecom company, Solan Communications' branch at 12 Luntz Street (tel 02-6258908; fax 02-6258879) offers phone, fax and telegram services. There is also a branch inside the Jaffa Gate.

Tourist Information: Jaffa Gate (02-6282295). Open Sun-Thurs 8.30am-5pm; Fri 8.30am-2pm. Closed Saturday.

Sherut Taxis: for shared taxis on routes beyond the city try the Central Bus Station.

Taxi Services: Jerusalem Taxi (4 Histradut St; tel 02-6255253); Nesher (21 King George Street; tel 6257227 – offers shared taxi service to Ben Gurion Airport.

Meeting Places and Cafés
Backpackers' Tearoom: Aftimus Street in the Old City's Christian Quarter.
Blue Hole: 12 Salomon St; tel 02-6256488. Popular bar.
Mike's Place: Horkanos Street, Russian Compound. Tiny place with guitarist.
Netcafé: 9 Heleni Hamalka Street; tel 02-6246327; e-mail info@netcafe.co.il. Soon internet cafés like Netcafé will no doubt have proliferated.
Tabasco Tea Room: off Suk Khan Ezeit, Old City; tel 02-6284954. Well-known meeting place for travellers. Underneath the Tabasco Hotel.
The Underground: Zion Square. Probably the most popular pub/disco, if that is a recommendation.

CONSULATES AND EMBASSIES

Israel claims Jerusalem as its capital. However, Israel's annexation of East Jerusalem in 1967 has never been accepted internationally and remains controversial. Israel's claim to Jerusalem is disputed, with some justification, by the Palestinians who also regard it as partly (or wholly) theirs. Foreign embassies, being necessarily diplomatic, are therefore nearly all based in Tel Aviv; some also have consulates in Jerusalem.

Tel Aviv
Australia: 37 Shaul Hamelech; tel 03-6950451.
Belgium: 266 Hayarkon St; tel 03-6054164.
Canadian Embassy: 3 Nirim Street (across Ayalon Road, nr. the basketball stadium); tel 03-6363300.
Denmark: 23 Bnei Moshe St; tel 03-5442144.
Egypt: 54 Basel Street, off Ibn Givrol; tel 03-5464151-2.
Finland: 2 Ibn Givrol St.; tel 03-6950527-8.
France: 122 Herbert Samuel Blvd; tel 03-65245371.
Germany: 3 Daniel Frish St.; tel 03-6931313.
Greece: 35 King Saul Blvd; tel 03-6959704.
Italy: 4 Weizman Street; tel 03-6964223.
Jordan: 14 Aba Hillel Street; tel 03-7517722.
Netherlands: 4 Weizman; tel 03-6957377.
Norway: 40 Nemal Tel Aviv; tel 03-5442030.
Portugal: 4 Weizman (Beit Asia); tel 03-6956372.
South Africa: 50 Dizengoff St (16th Floor); tel 03-5252566.
Spain: 3 Daniel Frisch Street; tel 03-6965218.
Sweden: 4 Weizman (Asia Centre); tel 03-6958111.
Switzerland; 228 Hayarkon St; tel 03-5464455.
United Kingdom: 192 Hayarkon St; tel 06-5249171.
USA: 71 Hayarkon St.; tel 03-5197575; fax 03-516 0315; e-mail acs.amcit-tela-viv@dos.us-state.gov

Jerusalem
USA: 27 Nablus Road; tel 02-628 7200.
United Kingdom: 19 Nashashibi St, East Jerusalem; tel 02-5828281.

COMMUNICATIONS

Telephone and Post

There are public telephone booths in Post Offices, main bus stations, hotels and in streets. Public pay phones use telecards of 20, 50 or 120 units, which can be bought almost anywhere you'd expect: post offices, shops, bars, news-stands an so on. The off peak time (50% cheaper) is between 1am and 8am (i.e. when most people are asleep). The rate is also reduced by a quarter on Sundays. Given this minimal cheap time it is hardly surprising that discount companies are springing up. The best known is Solan Telecom which offers discounted international calls from its offices in major cities and large towns which are open 24 hours. Don't expect a huge saving with their prices or you will be disappointed. Look out for other international services including Barak and Golden Lines which offer substantial discounts on overseas phoning. The cheapest time is usually from midnight to 7am.

Over recent years telephone numbers in Israel have undergone nationwide revision to cope with increasing demand for telephone, internet and fax lines and not least because kibbutz members now tend to have a phone each. If you have any problems the Directory of Assistance should be able to help you – dial 114.

Main Area Codes
02 Jerusalem & the West Bank	07 Negev to Eilat, Gaza Strip and the
03 Tel Aviv	Dead Sea area
04 Haifa & North Coast	08 Coastal Plain (south of Tel Aviv)
06 Galilee & the North incl. Golan	09 North of Tel Aviv (Sharon)

Telephones may also be used in shops and hotels, but using non payphone telephones (i.e. without a pay slot) usually costs double.

English language directories, which are published every three years, are available at main post offices and hotels. Long distance calls can be booked at the International Phone Centres in the central post offices. If you need assistance, or want to call collect, or with a credit card, dial 188 for an international operator.

International Phone Centre, Jerusalem (3 Koresh St; open Sunday to Thursday 8am to 9pm; Friday 8am to 2pm).
International Phone Centre, Tel Aviv (13 Frishmann St; open Sunday to Thursday 9am to 11pm; Friday 8am to 2.30pm; Saturday 6.30pm to midnight.)

Post Offices
Post offices are identified by a blue sign with a white, leaping deer. Most post offices are open from 8am to 12.30pm and 3.30pm to 6.30pm. On Wednesdays they are open from 8am to 1.30pm and Fridays and the eves of major holidays from 8am to 12 noon. All main post offices offer Poste Restante.

All post offices are closed on the Sabbath and religious holidays.

Fax
Faxes can be sent from post offices and Solan offices. It is also possible to arange to receive faxes at Solan.

Internet and E-mail
Israel is a high tech nation and internet cafés are proliferating. In Tel Aviv, In Bar (tel 03-5282228; fax 03-5282225 website www.isralink.co.il), seems very expensive so check out their prices and then shop around. Also try Strudel Café. The British Council Library allows members only to access the net. A possibility open to all is Momo's Hostel (28 Ben Yehuda Street) which has different prices for guests and non guests. Guests pay NIS15 for 30 minutes and NIS25 for an hour (non-guests pay NIS20 and 30 respectively). One minute costs NIS10, just long enough to send your e-mail.

Television and Radio

As well as the three regular Israeli TV stations: Israel One, Channel Two and Reshut Hashidor, it is possible to tune into the usual array of channels via cable and satellite TV. If you want to hear news in English then you are spoilt for choices. Jordanian television station JTV2, has daily French and English news as does Palestinian television. There are also subscription, cable networks accessing dozens of channels including Sky, CNN, BBC World etc.

Israeli television's Channel One offers educational, information and entertainment programmes in Hebrew, Arabic and other languages. The commercial Channel Two (innaugurated in 1993) is divided among several private producers with some hours reserved daily for educational programmes. Many programmes on Israeli television are in English with Hebrew and Arabic subtitles. Channel One broadcasts news in English daily at 6.15pm (earlier on Fridays and Saturdays) and Channel Two has a American news bulletins.

As for radio, Kol Israel (The Voice of Israel) operates eight networks in 17 languages. The Israeli Defence Forces have their own radio station Galei Tzahal. The Israeli radio also puts out short-wave multi-lingual transmissions to listeners abroad providing up-to-date news and information about Middle-Eastern and Jewish affairs. Kol HaMuzika is Israel's version of the British radio *Classic FM*. The *Voice of Peace* radio ship, beloved of travellers and most Israelis, broadcasts non-stop popular music. Behind it is Abe Nathan, the colourful peace campaigner. Its broadcasting range is limited though, and you may not be able to hear it all over Israel.

Listings of TV and radio programmes can be found in the *Jerusalem Post* newspaper.

Newspapers

Major magazines and newspapers (often a day old) from all over the world are available at main news-stands, at a price. *The Jerusalem Post*, Israel's only daily English language newspaper worthy of the name, has up-to-date information on entertainments (Friday supplement), flight arrivals, situations vacant, goods for sale, emergency services and of course local and international news. Unfortunately, its news coverage is generally recognised as expressing right-wing views. You can check it out on line at (www.jpost.co.il).

The Israeli press produces over a dozen Hebrew Newspapers and eleven in other languages daily. In addition there are over a 1,000 periodicals and specific interest magazines – not a bad output for a small country but useless to travellers who do not speak Hebrew or Arabic.

The Palestinians have a weekly English-language weekly newspaper, *The*

Jerusalem Times, published in East Jerusalem. The paper gives information on Arab affairs and a view of the Jewish-Arab problem from their angle.

Languages

The official language of Israel is an updated version of biblical Hebrew. Arabs will speak their own language. English is the most commonly spoken second language as it is mandatorily studied in Israeli schools. Other widely spoken languages include French, Spanish, German, Russian, Polish, Hungarian and Yiddish.

Learning Hebrew or Arabic

It is possible to study Hebrew through the study programmes organised by Ulpan Akiva Netanya. The courses last from three to 20 weeks and comprise several hours study daily and evening cultural activities. Non-Jews are welcome and the minimum age is 18. Further details from Ulpan Akiva Netanya POB 6086, Netanya 42160 Israel; tel 09-8352312/13/14; fax 09-865 29 19; e-mail ulpanakv@netvision.net.il   website www.ulpan-akiva.org.il   Americans can contact JCC Ulpan Center, 12 W.65 St, 8th Floor, New York, NY 10023; tel 212-580 0099.

Learning Arabic can sometimes be fraught as Birzeit University north of Ramallah in the West Bank, has a history of being closed every time Israel feels threatened. Bir Zeit runs a Palestine and Arab Studies (PAS) Programme which includes courses in Arabic (standard and colloquial). Courses are for one semester and the cost of $500-$600 includes board and lodging.

Further details from The Student Affairs Department (Birzeit University, P.O. Box 14, Birzeit, West Bank, Palestine (tel 02-998 20 00; fax 02-995 76 56; e-mail pas-isp@admin.birzeit.edu   website www.birzeit.edu/pas

There may also be other possibilities for learning arabic elsewhere in the West Bank and in East Jerusalem; these should be given on Birzeit's website.

Useful Hebrew Words and Expressions

Numbers

One	eh-HAD	Six	shaysh
Two	SHTA-yim	Seven	SHEV-vah
Three	sha-LOSH	Eight	sh-MO-neh
Four	AR-bah	Nine	TAY-shah
Five	cha-MAYSH	Ten	ESS-er

50	cha-MAYSHEEM	1000	Elef
100	MAY-ah	2000	Al-Pah-YEEM
200	mah-tuh-YEEM	3000	schlosh-ET-elef-EEM
300	Schlosh-may-OAT	5000	cha-maysh-ET-elef-EEM
500	cha-MAYSH-may-OAT		

Days and Time

Sunday	YOM-ree-SHON	Thursday	Yom-cha-mee-SHEE
Monday	YOM-shay-NEE	Friday	Yom-shee-SHEE
Tuesday	YOM-shlee-SHEE	Saturday	Yom-sha-BAT
Wednesday	YOM-reh-vee-EE		

What's the time?	MA ha-sha-AH
birthday	yom-hu-LAY-det
day off	yom huf-SHA
holiday	HO-fesh
working day	yom avo-DAH
today	ha-YOM
tonight	ha-LIE-ah
minute	da-KA
hour	sha-AH
seven o'clock	ha-sha-AH SHEV-ah
day	Yom
week	sha-voo-ah
month	CHO-desh
Year	sha-NAH

Useful Words and Expressions

hello/goodbye	sha-LOM
please	be va ka-SHA
thank you (very much)	to-DAH (rah-BAH)
yes/no	ken/lo
excuse me	sleecha
good morning	BO-ker tov
good evening	erevtov
good night	lie la tov
see you later	le-HIT-rah-OTT
you're welcome	al low da VAR
I don't speak Hebrew	AHNEE lo m'dah BEHR eeVREET
Do you speak English?	ahTAH m'dah BEHR ungLEET?
How much is it?	KA-mah zeh?
England	AN-glia
Israeli	sa-BRA
Money	KES-sef
postcard	gloo-yah
stamp(s)	bool(im)
letter	mich-tav
Is there any mail for me?	yesh DO-ar bishvi-LI?
my name is	She-MI
Where's the letter box?	ey-FO fey-VAT ha-DO-ar?
Wait	REG-gah
What?	mah
When?	mah-tiee?
Where is...?	AY-fo
right (correct)	na-CHON

Transport

station	ta-cha-na
airport	sde t'uFAH
plane	mu-TOS
railway	rah-KEH-vet
bus	autoboos
taxi	mon-NIT
docks	nu-MAL

boat	sir-RAH
Which bus goes to?	EH-seh autoboos no-SAY-ah le..?
Stop here	ah-TSOR-kahn
Near	ha-ROV

Food and Accommodation

to eat	le-eh-CHOL	cold meat	ba-SAR ka-FU
to drink	lish-tot	salami	nak-NIK
food	OCHEL	dates	tema-RIM
fruit	py-ROTE	wine	YAH-yin
water	my-im	beer	Beer-AH
apples	tapuh-IM	ice-cream	glee-DAH
orange	tapuz	menu	taf-REET
cheese	g'VEE-nah	breakfast	ah-roo-CHAT BO-ker
bread	LECH-em	supper	ah-roo-CHAT erev
butter	chem-AH	bill/tab	CHESH-bon
milk	cha-LAV	hotel	mah-LON
yoghurt	LE-ben	room	chedar
egg	bay-TSA	toilet	sherrooTIM
rooms to let	haderim l'haskir		

Post and Shopping

Post Office	dough-are	lipsalve	mi-SHA lasfa-TA-yim
letter	mich-tav	soap	sa-BON
envelopes	ma-ata-foth	sun cream	krem SHIZ-uf
telegramme	miv-rock	talcum powder	talk
pharmacy	bait merkah-CHAT	toothpaste	mis-HAT shi-NA-im
shop	cha-NOOT	toothbrush	miv-RE-shet shi-Na-im
shampoo	ha-fee-FAH	towel	ma-GE-vet
cotton wool	TZE-mer GE-fen	expensive	ya-KAR

The Countryside

excavations	hafi-ROT	road	ke-VISH
desert	mid-BAR	dunes	ho-LOT
farm	ME-shek	tree	etz
field	sa-DE	valley	E-mek
plain	mi-SHOR	vineyard	KE-rem
plantation	ma-TE	wadi	na-HAL

Useful Arabic Words and Expressions

Numbers

0	sifr	1	wa-hid
2	tinen	3	talatay
4	arbaha	5	khamseh
6	sitteh	7	sabah
8	tamanyeh	9	taisah
10	ahsharah	100	miyyah

Words and Expressions

hello	MAR-haba	yes/no	ay wah/la
please	min fadlach	thank you	SHUK-raan

how much is this?	ah-desh hadah?	why not	laish ma'a
tonight	laile	tomorrow	boo-khra
get lost!	rooch min-hon	go away!	imshi
coffee	cha-hawy	Jerusalem	al-Kutz
pilgrim hostel	ribat		
good morning/evening	sabah el-kheir/masa'al-kheir		
goodbye	salaam aleicham ma-ah salemeh		

ELECTRICITY

The electrical current is 220 volts A.C. single phase 50 cycles. Kibbutz volunteers' accommodation will have points suitable for personal electrical equipment including portable music centres and hair-dryers, but an adaptor is needed as two-pin round plugs are the norm in Israel.

HEALTH

There are no vaccination requirements for Israel but typhoid and polio are recommended. Before leaving home, you should consult your doctor as to the advisability of injections against hepatitis and tetanus.

Since AIDS is still a fatal illness, Kibbutzim health authorities may insist on an HIV test on arrival at the kibbutz. This is normally free of charge.

All medical, dental and hospital care must be paid for, so an insurance policy to cover these eventualities is essential. On the kibbutzim and moshavim, such a policy is obligatory and can be purchased from the Kibbutz Representatives and Moshav Offices in Israel, or in your own country. If you decide to arrange your own policy before arriving in Israel then you must ensure that the insurance company has an office in Israel. The British company, Home and Overseas, provides the cover sold by the Kibbutz Representatives in London.

The general water supply in all major towns and cities is perfectly safe as are taps marked as drinking water. Any other source of water should be treated with care.

Consider that we receive dire warnings of the sun's power in the northern reaches of Britain, and then work out how much fiercer is the sun over Israel. Simple precautions including sunblock, hats and scarves, and tanning progressively, can all help prevent the misery and dangers of over exposure: heatstroke and sunburn, permanent damage to the skin's DNA, and worse. Follow local dress habits and cover up exposed areas with loose, cotton garments which will also help you to keep cooler. Always drink plenty of water (even if you do not feel thirsty) to prevent dehydration. Get into the habit of wearing sunglasses to protect your eyes instead of as a fashion item, and a hat, or even a keffir (arab) head-dress, to prevent sunstroke.

You will find the following items useful and on sale in Israel, but if you have room in your backpack, they will probably cost less to buy at home: insect repellent, water bottle, medication for stomach upsets, toilet paper, torch and a pocket knife.

Israel does not possess much infamously deadly flora and fauna but there are a few unfamiliar hazards to watch out for. Large rocks, particularly in desert areas can conceal scorpions: large black ones which give a nasty and dangerous sting and the smaller, light-coloured ones which also give an unpleasant but less dangerous sting.

There are also several types of snake, mostly harmless, but some extremely dangerous and potentially deadly. On the kibbutz they can be in roof areas, unused irrigation pipes, bales of cattle food and generally in quiet, warm areas. They are usually quite timid if left alone and should be avoided. If you disturb one accidentally and are bitten, try to get help immediately. Wasps' and bees' nests, which are quite commonly found on kibbutzim, should obviously be avoided.

If you are unlucky enought to need a chemist, doctor or dentist in an emergency, a telephone call or visit to any Magen David Adom first aid station (marked by a red Star of David on a white background) will bring either practical help or advice.

In the sea, particularly around the coral reefs, it is essential to wear shoes while swimming to protect yourself from the deadly stone fish, which is indistinguishable from the coral it uses as camouflage. There are several other nasty but non-deadly species to avoid contact with including the lion fish. There is a chart available in the Eilat Field Study Centre, and diving centres for indentifying these in advance of any possible encounters. It is also inadvisable to swim if you have cuts and grazes as there are bacteria in the water that can aggravate these and cause delay to the healing process.

Magen David Adom is Israel's version of the Red Cross. Emergency stations are open 24-hours a day.

SOS Doctors will make emergency home visits and can be reached in Tel-Aviv on 03-503 3939.

Information on duty hospitals and emergency chemists is printed daily in the *Jerusalem Post*, but if all else fails, a phone call to the police will bring information.

The police emergency number in most parts of the country is 100.

EATING AND DRINKING

Food
The Hebrew word *kashrut* (kosher) means clean or fit according to Jewish dietary laws and covers not only the types of food but also their preparation. There is no difference in taste between kosher food and food prepared in other ways. Observant Jews do not eat or drink dairy products together with meat dishes, nor are they allowed to eat certain fish, fowl or animals listed in the Book of Leviticus as unclean. Shellfish are non-kosher so you will have to look out for non-Kosher or Arab restaurants where they are served.

As Israeli eating establishments are on the whole, kosher, except in tourist areas like Eilat or in the Arab areas and towns, you should bear in mind that at Kosher establishments you will not, after a meat dish, be served cheese, or milk in your coffee.

In the Palestininian areas including the West Bank, Gaza and parts of Jerusalem, many restaurants close for the month of Ramadan, though some may be open after sunset.

There is a wide variety of cheap foods available in restaurants and at take-away stalls. They are a mixture of Middle-Eastern and European dishes.

More expensive restaurants fall into three groups:

European, which are mainly Polish, French, German, Viennese and Hungarian and lately Russian.

Dairy-vegetarian including traditional Jewish dishes.

Oriental, that is Middle-Eastern.

There are also hamburger joints (including McDonalds), pizza and Chinese restaurants in the large cities.
Some of the cheap foods available throughout Israel are:

Pitta – a flat, pancake-shaped Arab bread, hollow in the middle and opened like an envelope. Arabs and Iraqi Jews often serve pitta with olive oil and a mixture of herbs and spices into which you dip the pitta.

Felafel – Possibly Israel's best known fast-food, felafel is a meal in itself and inexpensive. Sold at stalls and kiosks everywhere. Small balls of deep fried, ground chick peas stuffed into a pitta along with salad, coleslaw and pepper; help youself to a large selection of sauces – one of the best is *charif* which is hot and peppery.

Humus – a soft paste made from ground chick peas, garlic and olive oil eaten by dunking a pitta.

Tchina – looks the same as Humus but is made with sesame seeds and has a consistency like peanut-butter.

Eshel – like sour cream but thinner.

Shemenet – like thick sour cream.

Kebab – chopped and spiced lamb, grilled on a skewer.

Shashlik – pieces of lamb or beef, grilled on a skewer with onions and tomatoes.

Schnitzel – veal slices or turkey breasts, beaten flat, breaded and fried.

Bamia – a Middle-Eastern vegetable (okra) cooked in a thick tomato sauce.

Koosa – a vegetable similar to aubergine (egg-plant) and served stuffed with rice and spices.

Shawarma – grilled lamb or turkey, served in slices with salad stuffed into a pitta.

Burekas – filo pastry, usually triangular, containing potato, cheese, spinach and or meat.

Drink
Coffee: in Israel coffee comes in many forms: a thimbleful of strong and sweet coffee is called Turkish. There is also espresso, instant and café hafuch which is three-quarters milk and one-quarter coffee. Arabs and Yemeni Jews often serve coffee flavoured with cardamom, a spice.

Beer: imported and local beers and spirits are available in restaurants, supermarkets and liquor stores.
There are two good quality lager-type local beers Macabbi and the more expensive Gold Star while the Palestinian version is called Taybeh. These are comparable in quality and price to cheaper, European, beers.

There is also a non-alcoholic beer called Nesher. This comes in two types: a shandy style and a dark, sweet malt drink. Nesher beer is very cheap by European standards, and if you drink enough on a hot day you can get slightly high.

Wine: most wine produced comes under the Carmel Cooperative label. There is a variety of locally-produced wines and spirits, mostly of the sweet variety. Prices are comparable to cheap Spanish and North African drinks but more expensive, better quality drinks are available. Imported brands are also available but at 50-100% more expensive than in their country of origin.

SHOPPING

The opportunities for shopping in Israel range from sophisticated department stores where good quality goods from all over the world are available and Tel-Aviv designer boutiques, to Bedouin tribesmen sitting with their wares under a palm tree.

Interesting things to buy, originating in Israel are generally best found in bazaars, and flea markets. Hand woven and stitched goods such as shirts, belts, bags, waistcoat-jackets, rugs, wall hangings, camel saddles and trappings, leather-wear, sheepskin coats and jackets are best found in Arab, Druze and Bedouin villages and towns. Of particular interest to women, may be the traditional, and if you are lucky antique, Bedouin dresses in dark colours and heavy with embroidery. Also primitive hand-made old and new jewellery in silver, copper and tin often with old coins.

All these things along with objects in olive wood, copper and brass are best bought at the Druze villages near Haifa, the bazaars in Jerusalem's Old City and in Nazareth, Acre, Bethlehem and Hebron. In Beer'sheva, there is a regular Bedouin market every Thursday, starting very early in the morning. There you will see tribesmen and their families gather to sell and buy camels, goats, sheep and hand-made goods.

Stores and Jewish shops are closed Friday afternoon and all day Saturday. Jewish shops and businesses also close for the main Jewish holidays (Rosh Hashanna, Simhat Torah, Independence Day, Shavuot). During Sucoth and Passover weeks, shops close on the first and last days and in between open in the mornings only.

Arab shops and bazaars close on Fridays and Christian shops close on Sundays.

Bargaining

For any transaction involving money it is always worth trying to bargain, as generally this is the usual way for most small traders to do business. The main exceptions are large stores and better quality shops that are obviously run on European lines.

All small shops, markets, bazaars, taxi-drivers, etc., will bargain; even the price of a beer can be negotiated.

The procedure where bargaining is obviously the accepted method of business is very simple. First you ask the price, then, make an offer of half that and gradually work upwards until you can either agree on a price, or negotiations break down. A good ploy if you cannot agree is to walk determinedly away; often a small boy will come running after you to call you back.

If what you wish to buy is available at several stalls in the same market it is advisable to negotiate a price with the other traders as well and in this way you can obtain a true picture of the real price.

Despite lots of shouting and long faces the whole procedure is usually great fun and when a successful deal is concluded you may be asked into the 'inner sanctum' for coffee or mint tea and refreshments to seal the bargain.

If you return to the same trader at a later date to make further purchases it will be possible to get an even better deal as you will then be a regular customer.

With such things as taxi-fares, meals, drinks, etc., it is essential to fix the price *before* you make your order. It is no use trusting or relying on price lists or even the price you paid on a previous visit. It is also very important, even in quite smart places to check your bill. Waiters often get paid by commission and their addition of your bill can sometimes be quite amazing.

General Shopping Hours
Sunday-Thursday 8am-1pm and 4pm-7pm.

On the Sabbath, as with everything else in Israel, shops close about 2pm on Fridays and don't re-open until Sunday morning.

PHOTOGRAPHY

It is possible to buy all kinds of film in Israel, although specialist film may only be available in large cities. Films are substantially more expensive in Israel than elsewhere so it is advisable to take some stock with you.

If you decide to take exposed, undeveloped film with you, pack it in your hand luggage as a precaution against damage from airport security inspections. Video equipment such as a camcorder or VCR cannot be bought into Israel without declaring it to customs on entry and paying a deposit refundable when you leave Israel.

Developing is usually of a satisfactory standard but check the prices before leaving your film.

You should bear in mind that the sun in Israel is particularly bright, and in some areas, to obtain good photographic results it may be worth thinking of using special filters.

There are some restrictions on picture-taking in Israel. It is forbidden to take photographs of any military area, equipment or personnel on duty, civil or military airstrips, airports or any seafront installations. All these areas ar usually clearly marked in several languages as no-photography areas. It is also forbidden to take any photographs from the air without special permission. Photography is not allowed at Jewish holy places on the Sabbath and may be restricted at other times.

Some inhabitants of Israel, particularly Arabs from remote areas, can take extreme offence at being photographed. Sometimes their displeasure can be violent and take the form of verbal abuse or stone-throwing. Usually, this is because of religious interpretations or a superstition that the camera can capture or control the spirit, but it can also be because they are insulted that you have not asked permission. It is in any case courteous ask first (sign language will do it). You may find some expect you to make a small payment for the privilege, while others will pose for the hell of it.

DRUGS

It won't be written in your tourist visa, but you should know that Israel can be bad news if you are busted for drugs. If convicted of possession, buying, selling or smoking hash, or any dangerous drugs, the penalty can be ten years in jail. Dangerous drugs include opium, morphine, cocaine, cannabis satvia (hashish and marijuana), LSD, mescaline and amphetamine.

The preparation, possession, use, export, import, transportation or sale of these drugs is illegal. This is so whether one commits such acts for profit or otherwise. It is also forbidden to allow premises for which you are responsible, to be used for any of these activities.

A non-Israeli citizen who is convicted or even merely accused of a drugs violation may, in addition to any other punishment, be subject to an expulsion order. This can compel him to leave Israel and, under certain circumstances, forbid his return. A person convicted in Israel who returns home may face additional charges if a court in his home country deems that he committed part of the offence there, such as conspiracy, providing or sending the money for its purchase or possessing or receiving the drugs.

First offenders, and those convicted of possession of small quantities – up to an ounce or so – may receive a suspended prison sentence or probation and a fine. Their chances are better if they are young, not too hippy-looking and there are no aggravating circumstances. Promising to leave the country immediately and showing the judge a valid ticket may sometimes prevent imprisonment.

The district attorney or the police generally ask the court to impose severe sentences. Judges tend to accept their arguments that prison sentences and heavy fines are necessary in order to deter what is now considered here to be an alarming type of crime.

A conviction in Israel on a drugs offence can turn up to haunt a young American or Canadian when he or she returns to University or makes a job application. It may have been a conviction for only a single joint, but his or her criminal record in the States or Canada will read 'conviction of narcotics laws in the State of Israel'. The American, Canadian and some other embassies in Israel keep advised of such cases and usually report them to their home authorities.

Persons appearing to be hippies can expect to be stopped and searched now and then by Israeli police. They do not require a search or arrest warrant. You can also be arrested for having no obvious means of support or reasonable explanation.

The police can search any person, their possessions, home or place of lodging. Even if the court decides at a trial that the police's arrest, search or seizure was unjustified, the evidence can still be used for conviction.

If arrested, you have the right to remain silent and to refuse to make any statement. You also have the right to make one telephone call. If you know of a lawyer you can call them or your Embassy. The police must allow the lawyer to visit you. You should only give statements in English unless you are fluent in Hebrew, and you can insist on all proceedings and documents at the police station and the court being in English.

On the kibbutz all the laws relating to drugs are observed and if it is thought you are violating those laws you will be immediately expelled and the police will be informed.

It is possible that young, plain-clothes police may occasionally visit the kibbutz on some pretext to obtain information about possible drug law violations.

WEATHER

Winter is from November to March. The range of temperatures during this time allows winter sports on Mt. Hermon in the north and skin diving and swimming in the Red Sea in the south.

All over the country at this time there is a regular cold, heavy, rainfall. In the north sleet and hail is possible at times. In between, however, there can be quite warm sunny periods.

If you are visiting a kibbutz or moshav at this time it is worth taking practical rainclothes that are suitable for farm work in conditions of rain, sleet and mud. The kibbutz will provide you with working clothes, but they will not always be waterproof. Relatively cheap rubber boots are available in Israel.

Although in the south, it is possible to spend days on the beach, the nights are cold and sometimes wet, so sleeping out is difficult.

Spring in March and April is incredibly beautiful all over Israel with mountains, valleys and even the desert covered in a profusion of wild flowers and greenery, some quite exotic. This is the perfect time of year for walking.

It is possible to swim and laze on beaches comfortably from the end of February onwards, particularly in the south, but even on the northern, Mediterranean coast it is possible to swim enjoyably at this time. The Israelis wait until much later in the year before they flock to the beaches, but cold-blooded Europeans will find it very pleasant most of the year round.

Summer is from April to October and from the beginning of April, the weather starts to get very warm until the peak in July and August. During the summer it almost never rains so days on the beach and sleeping out are perfect.

Mean Temperatures in Centigrade

	Jan	March	May
Jerusalem	7.5-13.9	11.0-18.0	16.2-26.2
Tel Aviv	8.8-19.0	11.2-21.7	15.4-26.1
Haifa	10.6-16.6	12.8-20-9	16.9-24.6
Tiberias	12.0-20.4	14.1-26.3	19.7-33.1
Eilat	10.9-22.0	19.0-28.3	22.8-36.3

	July	September	November
Jerusalem	19.4-28.3	19.0-27.9	12.4-18.9
Tel Aviv	21.5-30.5	21.2-31.3	13.0-23.9
Haifa	21.7-28.1	22.4-28.4	15.9-21.1
Tiberias	24.7-36.6	25.1-36.2	16.8-24.9
Eilat	28.9-39.8	26.3-37.6	15.1-27.6

HOLY DAYS AND HOLIDAYS

Israeli and Jewish Holidays

There are three kinds of holidays in Israel: religious, national and agricultural festivals.

These holidays fall on different dates each year because of the different calendars that are operated. Officially there are two calendars, the Jewish and Gregorian. There are also two unofficial calendars, the Julian and Moslem. These combinations make for instance four different New Year Eves.

Like the Jewish Sabbath, holidays commence at sunset on the preceding day and end at sunset on the day itself. On all important holidays all activities will stop as on the Sabbath.

Here is a list of the Jewish holidays celebrated in Israel:

Tu B'Shevat (The New Year for Trees) – Israeli schoolchildren plant saplings, and traditionally fifteen species of fruit are tasted.

Purim (Feast of Lots) – Commemorates the casting of lots by Hamam, a wicked chancellor in ancient Persia, to decide which day to slay all the Jews in his territory. Fortunately the plot was foiled by Queen Esther and her uncle Mordechai. Nowadays the book of Esther which tells this tale is read in the synagogues and children wear fancy dress and eat triangular pastries which are called Hamam's ears.

Pesach (Passover) – This is one of the main festivals for Jews worldwide, and recalls the Exodus of Jews from slavery in Egypt. It lasts a full week and commences with the *Seder*, a special meal accompanied by a reading about the miracle of Passover when a plague which took the first born sons of Egypt 'passed over' the Israelites. Only unleavened bread (*Matza*) is eaten during this time and Jews make pilgrimages to the Western Wall in Jerusalem. During this festival Jewish shops keep limited hours and public transport stops on the first and last days.

Yom Ha-Atsuma'ut (Independence Day) – Commemorates the founding of the State of Israel in 1948. Celebrated with picnics, parties and letting off steam in the streets of Tel-Aviv, against a background of fireworks. Shops and offices close but public transport operates.

Lag B'Omer – A religious holiday which succeeds 33 days of mourning. Hasidic Jews make a pilgrimage to Meiron in Galilee, an area holy to Jews for over 1,700 years, where they light candles and bonfires. Three-year-old boys have their first haircut and the shavings are thrown onto the fire.

Shavuot (Pentecost) – Feast of the Giving of The Law – This commemorates the handing down of the ten commandments to Moses on Mount Sinai, from whence the Israelites received them. However the main celebration is based on a harvest festival (the in-gathering of the wheat). In ancient times an offering of the first fruits would be taken to the Temple where they would be burned. Shavuot is usually lavishly celebrated by kibbutzim and moshavim with people dressing in white and eating milk products and honey. Shops, offices and public transport close down.

Tisha B'Av (Fast of the 9th of Av) – This marks the destruction of the First and Second Temples, and is commemorated by mourning, fasting and pilgrimages to the Wailing Wall in Jerusalem. Banks close.

Rosh Hashana (Jewish New Year) – Together with Yom Kippur this is one of the most solemn festivals or 'Days of Awe', when Jews are called to give an account of themselves before God, and is observed by two days of prayer and the blowing of the *Shofar* (horn) to remind the faithful to obey God. Shops, offices and public transport closes down.

Yom Kippur (The Day of Atonement) – Ten days after Rosh Hashanna comes a day of fasting and prayers. All public and commercial services in Israel shut down, including radio and television stations. The Arabs launched an attack on this day in 1973, (The War of Yom Kippur) thus hoping to catch Israel off guard.

Sukkoth (Feast of the Tabernacles) and *Simchat Torah (The Rejoicing of the Law)* – During this festival most Jews, religious or not, live in shelters they put up in their gardens, to symbolise the wandering of the Israelites in the wilderness following the Exodus. Simchat Torah is the eighth day of Sukkoth observed by ending the annual cycle of readings of the Law *Torah* and beginning a new one.

Hannuka (Festival of Lights) – This is an eight-day celebration of the victorious Maccabean revolt of 167 B.C. Hannuka is symbolised by the eight-branched candelabra, the Menorah, on which a new candle is lit every night, representing the miracle of the oil (see Maccabees 4: 52-59). Doughnuts and potato pancakes are traditionally eaten at this time. Shops and banks close and there are no buses.

Jewish Holy Days & Israeli National Holidays

	2000	2001	2002
Tu Be'Shevat	22 Jan	8 Jan	22Jan
Purim	21 Mar	9 Mar	26 Mar
Shushan Purim	22 Mar	10 Mar	27 Mar
Pesach	20-26(27)Apr	8-14(15) Apr	3 Apr-28 Mar
Independence	10 May	28 Apr	17 Apr
Lag Ba'omer	23 May	10 May	30 Apr
Shavuot	9 June	28(29) May	17 May
Tishah B'av	10 Aug	29 July	18 July
Rosh Hashana	30 Sept-1 Oct	18(19) Sept	7(8) Sep
Yom Kippur	9 Oct	27 Sep	16 Sep
Sukkot	14-20 Oct	22-28 Oct	21-26 Oct
Simhat Torah & Shmini Azeret	21 Oct	9 Oct	26 Sept
Hanuka	22-29 Dec	10-17 Dec	30 Nov-7 Dec

DEPARTURE

It is wise to check and confirm your flight at least 72 hours before you leave. Most flights in and out of the country are booked up in peak seasons like Christmas, and your place will probably be allocated to someone else if you don't confirm; also departure times are frequently postponed or changed.

There is an airport tax, payable on departure. The amount of this tax is constantly changing, so check the amount you will have to pay when you confirm your flight.

When flying El Al you can check in your luggage at their offices in Jerusalem, Tel Aviv and Haifa the evening before departure, except on Fridays, holidays or the eve of a holiday. It will be taken straight on to your plane and you need only arrive at the airport one hour in advance of departure instead of the normal two hours.

If you have flown to Israel you may decide to return home overland or by sea. It is very important when buying your air ticket to make sure the return half can be cashed in or exchanged for alternative travel. Some airlines, particularly El Al, are un-cooperative in these circumstances, and interpretations of regulations vary from office to office.

When buying a ticket, it is essential to retain all receipts and if possible to obtain written instructions, on headed paper, as to cashing-in procedures.

When attempting to cash-in you must be able to produce passport, ticket, receipts and cashing-in instructions.

Getting to Ben Gurion Airport

From Jerusalem:
Egged buses 945 and 947 to Ben Gurion Airport leave from the central bus station roughly every half an hour from 6.30am to 8.30pm, Fridays from 7.30am to 3.30pm and Saturdays from sundown to 10.30pm. Further information on 03-6948888.

Nesher Sherut taxi service: book a day in advance at 21 Rehov Hamelekh George (tel 02-6257227 or 6231231; fax 02-6241114). Collects you from your door for an extra charge..

From Tel Aviv:
The 222 United Tours airport bus (tel 03-6916256) runs hourly from 4am till midnight and picks up passengers at major hotels including the Palace, Dan and Sheraton on Hayarkon Street.

Egged bus 475 from the new central bus station, sixth floor, every 25 minutes. Sunday to Thursday 5am-11.35pm, Friday 5am-1.30pm.

From Haifa:
Egged bus from the central bus station, every hour from 6.30am until 6pm.
Aviv Sherut taxi service at Rehov Nordav (tel: 666333), every hour from 6am until 5pm.

Israel's Regions & Cities

THE COAST

All the main beaches have modern facilities with showers, toilets, drinking water, refreshments etc., and for many of them there is a charge for entry. It is also possible to find more isolated simple beaches which are free and may also have some facilities. Some are signposted and others the locals will tell you about. Nude bathing is inadvisable anywhere except south of Eilat where it is accepted practice or on designated nudist beaches (see below). South of Eilat, it is possible to camp under palm trees a few feet from the Red Sea beaches, where the coral, fish and diving are perfect.

There are certain hazards on the beaches however. On some Mediterranean beaches strong currents can be very dangerous. Shoals of jellyfish can also be a problem. There is a system of flag warnings on main public beaches in summer: black means no swimming, red means conditions may be dangerous, and white is *carte blanche* to go ahead. Lifeguards watch over the main beaches and some have giant shrimp nets with which to scoop up any jellyfish that may wander into the bathing area.

Other hazards are outcrops of coral that can tear your skin, spiky sea plants that your feet get impaled on and camels or goats eating your clothes while you swim.

For women, the most unpleasant feature of some beaches is however not the wildlife but the local life. The behaviour of some Israeli males can range from helping themselves to your cigarettes to making crude advances. Age or looks are no barrier, as long as you are female and an obvious tourist, you are certain to get their attentions at some time.

The approach is always the same, a request for a light, the time or direct questions such as 'what's your name?', 'what country are you from?'. If you show the slightest interest or response, in no time, you will be surrounded by several men and nothing, no matter how rude or angry you get, will make them go away.

The only answer is to stay near to other people, go to the beach with male companions and always ignore even the most innocent-seeming requests.

You may find these adventures amusing and interesting but be very careful not to get yourself into a situation that you cannot control. The police will be helpful if any of your belongings are stolen but tend to think sexual offences result from the behaviour of the female, and are not always sympathetic in what is after all, still a pretty chauvanist country.

Finally remember the sun can burn your skin badly and very quickly, so be careful what you wear, don't fall asleep in the sun, carry a water bottle and wear a hat when hitch-hiking.

Obviously, most of Israel's beaches are on the Mediterranean coast and the Red Sea. There are however lakeside beach resorts from which you can swim and windsurf, around the Sea of Galilee. The Dead Sea is impossible to swim in because of the excessive salt content; but you can float in it and emerge out of the water encrusted with the stuff.

Tel Aviv and North

Tel-Aviv: the arrival point in Israel for most visitors arriving by air is Tel Aviv, a financial and cultural centre and a hedonistic beach resort with a non-stop night life. Tel-Aviv has a five-mile long stretch of white sand, partly divided into beach fronts for the main hotels: Sheraton and Hilton and three other sections. The southern beaches tend to be quieter but all are subject to random and rampant thieving. On the beaches you will find showers, toilets and places to change. Other popular hotels include the Dan with rooftop swimming pool (tel 03-520 2525) and the three star Basel Hotel (tel 03-520 7711). For budget accommodation including the IYHF Youth Hostel, see *Cheap Accommodation in Tel Aviv* in the Kibbutz section.

There is much to see and do in Tel Aviv whatever the time of day or night. Make the most of the daytime by strolling along the seafront promenade to Old Jaffa where you can wander around the heavily restored cobbled streets with their artisanal and artists workshops. Every Wednesday morning at 9.30am there is a free guided tour in English, setting off from the Clock Tower.

Back in the city hubbub, Dizengoff and Schenken Streets are the main café area, where is an endless choice of places to eat and drink. Whatever your taste, you will find something to suit you from felafel stands, burger joints, or upmarket restaurants, to ice-cream parlours and tea-shops.

Herzliya: 15km north of Tel-Aviv is the up-market suburb and resort of Herzliya with its luxury apartments, hotels, marina and spotless, gorgeous beaches. There are buses there from the central bus station (nos 501 and 502). As you would expect from the surroundings there is no real budget accommodation in Herzliya.

Netanya: Netanya is known as the Miami of Israel because of its concentration of affluent oldies. The authorities have been trying to promote Netanya as a chic resort having become aware of its image as 'God's luxury waiting room.' Efforts are ongoing to make it attractive and appealing to a wider age group by providing free entertainment year round, and good waterskiing, paragliding and windsurfing facilities. You can get there by bus 605 from Tel Aviv. There are usually people camping on the beach but it is not particularly safe, especially for women on their own. The further north in Netanya you go, the less crowded the 11 km beach becomes. Just south of Netanya, not far from Kibbutz Ga'ash, the cliffs offer a modicum of privacy for one of Israel's more popular nudist beaches. Netanya's tourist information is off Ha'Atzma'ut Square (tel 09-8827286). The Youth Hostel is off the same square (tel 09-8822562).

About 6km south of Netanya is the Kfar Vitkin Emek Hefer Youth Hostel (tel/fax 09-8666032), set in a leafy grove and in easy walking distance of some great beaches. You can take buses 901 and 921 from Haifa to get there, or from Tel Aviv central bus station take 702, 852 or 901 buses.

Haifa and beaches nearby: Israel's third city Haifa, dominated by Mt. Carmel, has its share of well-patronised beaches despite being the main industrial centre and port. Towards the north, sandy spots include Ha-Hof Ha-Shaket a short (no 41) bus ride from the Hadar district. Hof Bat Galim is another popular beach, also to the north.

Nahariya and Beaches North of Haifa: Nahariya is one of the smaller and quieter Israeli resorts easily reached by bus or train. Both the bus and train station are at the southern end. The main beach Galei Galil is very popular with Israelis and is Israel's northernmost resort. There is another beach, Akhziv, about 4km north of Nahariya which is also very busy. There is nowhere cheap to stay in Nahariya though you could ask the tourist office (tel 04-9879800) for rooms in private houses and haggle over the prices. Failing this, there is camping at Akhziv; try Eli Avivi Hostel, Akhziv (tel 04-9823250; fax 04-9829998) or Club Med in summer only (tel 03-5212525; fax 03-5271345) and also the SPNI Field Centre (tel 04-9823762) which is however pricey even though the NIS120 for a shared room includes all meals.

Rosh-Hanikra: Rosh Hanikra lies 10km north of Nahariya and has magnificent white chalk cliffs and some massive caves. Nature has been enhanced a little with additional tunnelling to produce easier access, and there is a cable car from the roadside up to the cliff top. Rosh Hanikra is also the Israeli border with the Lebanon and is swarming with Israeli and UN military personnel. Swimming in the clear blue sea looks inviting, but it is banned because of strong undercurrents, not to mention security reasons.

South of Haifa: South of Haifa, the beaches tend to be less packed: there is Hof Carmel, 4km out of town (site also of the Haifa Carmel Youth Hostel; tel 04-8532516; fax 04-8532516), right at the foot of Mt Carmel. Take buses 43 or 45 from the central bus station in Haifa to get there. Further south is another beach Hof Dado. From there to the remains of the crusader fortress of Atlit, the coast is just one long beach. Near Atlit you can camp at Kibbutz Neve Yam (30885 Neve Yam; tel 04-9844827; fax 04-9844871)) about 20km south of Haifa and just opposite the beach. 29kms south of Haifa, on the coast road is Dor, a modern settlement of mainly Greek Jews. Nearby is the ancient site of Tel Dor and the beautiful sandy beach of Tantura. You can pitch a tent in the vicinity or pay to use the proper campsite on the Moshav Dor (Merom-Hagalil 13825; tel 06-6399121). To get to Dor ask the bus driver of any Egged bus on the Haifa-Hadera road to drop you off there.

Caesarea roughly midway between Tel Aviv and Haifa, Caesarea is one of Israel's most important archaeological sites and it dates from the end of the first century BC. The city and port of Caesarea were built by King Herod the Great to magnify himself, but he bowed the knee to Augustus Caesar and called it after him. Caesarea is also the location of some terrific beaches, smart hotels, an 18-hole golf course and a diving centre.

There is an infrequent bus service to and from Caesarea; the most practical option is to set off from Hadera, the nearest town, from which there are several daily number 76 buses. Food is very expensive in Caesarea, so if you are planning to stay, camping or sleeping on the beach, try to take some supplies with you. If this is impractical there is a reasonably priced cafeteria at the nearby Kibbutz Sdot Yam, which also has accommodation (tel 06-6364470) comprising private apartments or dormitories. The latter cost from NIS17 and the price varies according to season. The other budget accommodation is the Caesarea Sports Centre (tel 06-6364394) which has all-in daily rate for dormitory accommodation and meals.

Camping on the beach (illegal in any case) is not recommended but diehards do it anyway.

South of Tel-Aviv

Bat Yam: Bat Yam is just south of Tel Aviv-Jaffa and is a modern resort with a popular long sandy beach. You can walk there from Tel Aviv.

Ashdod: once a Philistine city, and reputed burial place of Jonah (of whale fame), the modern port and industrial city of Ashdod may not be most people's idea of a beach resort but the beaches are pleasant, have showers and facilities and you can pitch a tent nearby. The main beach is the Lido, but with industrial edifices visible all round there are many more beautiful beaches in Israel to aim for.

Ashkelon: Ashkelon, another Israeli town with antique origins, has never been fully excavated. It has a population of nearly 89,000 including a large Russian enclave. It has five, fine, sandy beaches, part of a national park and all of which are very popular with Israelis. The national park is littered with interesting bits and pieces of ruins from former eras' habitations. There is no cheap accommodation so a daytrip from Tel-Aviv (about an hour by bus), or camping at the Bustan Ha-Zeitim campsite in the National Park at the southern end of town, (tel 07-6736777) or wild camping in the same park without facilities, are the options.

Gaza Strip
South of Ashkelon is the 40km long, 6km wide Gaza Strip, now mostly under the control of the Palestinian Authority except for the Gush Katif area in the south near Khan Yunis. There is a youth hostel at Gush Ketif and the Israeli run Palm Beach hotel on the nearby coast, all within the Israeli settlement zone and surrounded by wire fences and army checkpoints. Coming from Ashkelon the nearest checkpoint entrance into the Gaza Strip is Erez. Rafah is the checkpoint nearest Khan Yunis and the Egyptian border.

Eilat and the Red Sea

Eilat is Israel's southernmost and number one resort with year round swimming, snorkelling and diving and an international clientele. The town has a 5km strip of beach, dozens of luxury hotels and all the tourism paraphernalia that goes with a world class resort. 10km south of Eilat is the international border with Egypt at Taba. No visa is needed if you cross the border just to reach the Taba Hilton which has a great snorkelling beach. However, you will have to show your passport. It is very inadvisable to sleep on the beach at Eilat as theft is endemic. Unfortunately, the cheap accommodation which is found quite easily in Eilat is not very secure either, but marginally more so than the beach. The Coral beach is probably the best spot if you are going in for camping. The SPNI FS Centre has a year-round campsite there (tel 07-6372021/1127; fax 07-6371771); Caroline's – Almog Beach just south of the SPNI, has chalets, and Zefahot Camping (tel 07-6374411; fax 07-6375206) provides camping and shower and toilet facilities. You can snorkel from the beach.

For casual work possibilities in Eilat (which is one way to get free board and lodging) see the section on *Other Work in Israel*.

Eilat's best sites are probably the underwater ones. You can snorkel or dive for close encounters, or you can watch from behind glass (who is watching whom?) at the Coral World Underwater Observatory and Aquarium. If you want to swim with dolphins you can visit Dolphin Reef (bus no 15) and cavort with semi-captive ones. Twitchers and nature lovers can take advantage of the jeep and walking tours arranged by the International Birdwatching Centre, P.O.Box 774, Eilat 88106 (tel 07-6374276) or visit the SPNI (their Field School is opposite the Coral Beach – see above) where good advice is free but you have to pay for the maps.

If you need accommodation, a good place to start your search is at the tourist office. Cheap hostels chop and change and prices are according to supply and demand and the season. The tourist office can put you in the picture and give you an idea of what you should expect to pay and where to go. Two goodies which are also usually very busy are the Youth Hostel (5835 Mizrayim Road; tel 07-6370088; fax 07-6375835) which costs about NIS17 for a dorm bed and the pricier Spring Hostel (126 Ofarim St; tel 07-6374660; fax 6371543) from NIS 27.

Useful Addresses
Tourist Information: Yotam Road (tel 07-6372111).
Egyptian Consulate: 68 Ha Efroni Street (tel 07-6376882). Sinai only visas are
  available at the border but for visiting elsewhere in Egypt a visa is required.
Eilat Youth Hostel: Ha-Arava Road (tel 07-6372358).

South of Eilat South of Eilat you are in Sinai, part of Egypt since 1982. The crossing is straightforward but lengthy at the Taba border point. If you are not planning visiting elsewhere in Egypt, you can get a 14-day Sinai visa at the border. There is an idiosyncratic bus service from Taba down the Red Sea Coast to Sharm ash-Sheikh, the end of the Sinai. Stopping off sandy places include Dahab and Nuweiba. Down south of Eilat the air is hot and so dry, your skin will cry out for moisture and you will feel you are in Africa which is where Sinai really belongs.

INLAND (North to South)

The Golan Heights

In September 1994 the then Israeli Prime Minister Yitzhak Rabin offered to negotiate over the return of the 770 sq.km of the Golan Heights that Israel conquered, in return for peace with Syria. At the time of press there is no report of a breakthrough in progress over this proposal. There are about thirty Israeli settlements located on the volcanic plateau of the Golan, and both the settlers and Israeli military strategists are fervent about wanting the Golan to remain Israeli. In the real world however, a deal will have to be struck involving concessions to Syria. In time therefore, visitors can expect to need a Syrian visa to visit the region. This is as good a reason as any for visiting there now. Others are: it is scenically stunning, underpopulated and unspoiled. You can get a whiff of a breeze there on the hottest day and take a refreshing dip in the water courses and waterfalls of the area. Disincentives are equally apparent: once the region was a frequent target for Syrian gunners on the opposite heights, the the area is scattered with Israeli army outposts and minefields. The other inhabitants are the Druze, a breakaway Arab sect with representatives also in Syria and the Lebanon with whom they strongly identify.

Bus services to this remote region are inadequate. Egged buses go there from Kiryat Shmona and Safed, but really the only sure way, apart from organising yourself for a major expedition with maps, a local guide, tent and supplies of food and water, is to take a coach tour. Unfortunately, most tours (like Egged's from Tiberias) are daytrips, which are too brief, whetting your appetite without satisfying it. SPNI hiking tours lasting several days are well-organised and get you to the remote spots. The settlement of Katzrin has an SPNI Field School (tel 04-6961234), and will advise on where you can stay in the Golan with Israeli settlers.

Safed

On the route to Katzrin is Safed (population 23,000), Israel's highest town built atop several hills including Mt. Kenaan (Canaan), Israel's third highest mount. Its name probably derives from Saphet, the name given to the fortress built there by a Crusader king. It is known variously as Safat, Safed, Zefad and Tzfat according to which map you look at. In the fifteenth and sixteenth centuries it was a centre of Jewish learning. During the declaration of Israeli independence, the arab inhabitants were driven from the town by the Jews, and the former arab quarter contains art galleries and studios as well as new immigrants from Russia and elsewhere.

Cheap accommodation is not immediately obvious in Safed but there are rooms in private houses advertised on signboards in the old city. The following were offering rooms at the time of press: Ahuzat Binyamin at Arlozorov St 107 (tel 067929163), House Rubingar, P.O. Box 40 (tel 06-6920085) and Kadosh Tali at Yud Alef 34 (tel 06-6920326).
Useful Safed Contacts
Egged Buses: Central Station; tel 06-6921123.
Tourist Office: (tel 06-6927485) is on the ground floor of the Wolfson Centre.
Youth Hostel: 1 Lohamei Ha-Geta'ot Street; tel 06-6921086.

Gamla

Near Katzrin is Gamla whose hilltop ruins bear witness to a Roman seige which ended in the slaughter of some 9000 Jews who had taken refuge there in 67 BC. Many of the beseiged flung themselves into the ravine rather than surrender. Further information from Gamla Reserve (P.O.Box 1143 Safed; tel 06-6762040).

Galilee

Main towns: Haifa, Kiryat Shemona, Nahariya, Akko (Acre), Haifa, Nazareth, Beit Shean, Afula, and Tiberias.

The Galilee region in the north of Israel excluding the Golan Heights, contains the Sea of Galilee, the Jezreel Valley, Mts Hermon, Canaan, Carmel, Tabor and Meron. Meron, is the highest mountain in the Galilee (1208m). There are also several nature reserves including Mount Meron, Carmel, Mt Hermon (Banias), Horshat Tal Natur and Hula: a combined entry ticket is available for these from an y nature reserve. The region borders Lebanon in the north and Syria to the north east and reaches south as far as Caesarea in the west and Beit Shean (near the new border crossing with Jordan) in the east.

Tiberias

The main resort on the Galilee is the low lying and (in summer) humid Tiberias. The area is an an ideal base for exploring as there is a wide choice of accommodation there of which some examples are given below. There are also lots of unlicensed rooms in private houses though you should be aware that there is no vetting system for these and you will be taking pot luck.

The 'beaches' of the Galilee are mostly sandless. The ones in Tiberias are owned by the hotels and charge an entry fee. There are more beaches north and south of Tiberias. These include the municipal beach (south) which has the cheapest entrance charge and Lido Kinneret, Shell Beach, Quiet Beach and Blue Beach. If you want to swim for free, you will have to hike until you find a suitable spot or work on one of the kibbutzim with private beaches. Every now and again there is an alligator scare (alligators from the nearby alligator farm are occasionally rumoured to make their getaway in the Lake). If you prefer to camp there are several possibilities around the lake's shores. However, this being one of Israel's prime tourist spots the campsites are pricey. Most are run by the various kibbutzim.

The bad news for swimmers is that the waters of the Galilee are shrinking fast, owing to drought and the heavy toll exacted by using it as a national reservoir. Things could get even more dire if the Syrians who are claiming the eastern side of the lake along with the Golan which it borders, get it in the proposed settlement for peace. The Syrians, who are short of water themselves will cause additional strains on the lake.

About 3km south of Tiberias are the Hot Springs where you can have a mineral bath said to cure skin ailments. Local buses can also take you to Karnei Hittim (the Horns of Hittim) site of the crusader defeat by Saladin in 1187. You can walk to the top of the hill in 45 minutes and view the panorama reaching from the Mediterranean to Jordan. At the southern end of the Lake, where the River Jordan flows out is Israel's oldest kibbutz, Degania, founded in 1909.

Nightlife swings around the *midrahov* and the promenade and there is a range of eating places that offer more than just loaves and fishes. They range from Maman's (corner of Ha-Galil and Bibas streets) for pitta bread with hummus and tahina dips to Pagoda, which claims to be the biggest kosher Chinese restaurant in the world.

Useful Tiberias Contacts

Egged Information: Central Bus Station; 06-6791080.

Tourist Office: Habanim Street; tel 06-6725666; fax 06-672 44 89). Very handy if you are staying at the International Hostel Meyouhas in the same building.

Car Rental: Autorent; Eldahif St 12; tel 06-6725688; Reliable Cars; 9 Eldahif St; tel 06-6724112

Central Post Office: Hayarden Street; tel 06-672 09 94. Poste Restante and Western Union facilities.

Aviv Hostel: 66 Hagalil St; tel 06-672 00 07. Same price as Maman for dorms.

Maman Hostel: Ha-Shiloah Street; tel 06-679 29 86. Dorm beds NIS25 low season (September to June), near double that in high season (July and August).

Meyouhas International Youth Hostel: corner of Ha-Banim and Ha-Yarden; tel 06-672 17 75; fax 06-672 03 72. Beautifully restored nineteenth-century building. Cost from US$18 for dorm bed including breakfast; discount for members.

Scottish Guest House: corner of Ha-Yarden and Gdoud Barak (near the Meyouhas Youth Hostel); tel 06-672 37 69; e-mail scottie@rannet.com Cheapest single is US$65.

Sherut Taxis: Haemek Taxis (06-6720131); Hagalil Taxis (06-6720353).

Solan Communications: 06-6726470.

Akko (Acre)

Akko is a gem of a place. It is a museum town inhabited by real people. Its origins are literally lost in antiquity. It was known to the Egyptians in 1900BC, it was a mint in the time of Alexander the Great, and the main base of the Crusaders in the seventh century. When Napoleon attempted to take it by sea in 1799 he was driven off and the port of Akko remained part of the Turkish Empire until the British took in 1917 during the Palestine campaign. The Jews captured it in 1948 but since then have left the old walled town to the Arabs, preferring to live in a modern part to the north. Apart from the promenade on the sea walls which date from the 12th century, the underground Crusader city, excavated in recent times is a must see. Consisting of a series of underground passages and halls and chambers it was not always subterranean. When the Mamelukes razed the city, it was easier to built the new one on top of the old rubble and so the city to-day is several metres higher than it would have been when the Knights Hospitallers entertained their guests, who included Marco Polo, in their great dining hall. Excavations are still going on. Great care has to be taken to ensure that the parts of the town above the re-hollowed out chambers do not collapse into them.

Places to stay:

Akko Gate Hostel: next to the Land Gate, (tel 04-991 0410; fax 04-981 5530). Dorm beds from NIS32. Tour operator in the hostel.

The Light House Hostel: (tel 04-981 5530; fax 04-991 1982). The Light House Hostel used to be the Youth Hostel and is housed in a gracious Turkish mansion. Dorm beds cost from NIS25 without breakfast. Pick-ups from the bus station can be arranged with advance warning.

Paul's Hostel: (tel 04-9912857). Dorm beds from NIS25. Kitchen facilities.

Haifa

Israel's main port and third city (population 250,000) is not a prime tourist trap. However, its surrounding landscape (it lies on the wooded slopes of mount Carmel) are worth seeing. The upgraded beaches south of the city are another possibility though they are not Israel's finest. Haifa docks are the jumping off point for ferries to Greece and vice versa. The train station (trains to and from Tel-Aviv and Jerusalem) and the Central Bus Station are interlinked by underground walkways. Built more or less in three districts on as many levels, the topmost area (Carmel Centre) is the expensive bit. There is is a one line subway (six stops) which shuttles up and down the hill to Carmel centre in about six minutes. There is also a scenic cable car up to the Carmelite Monastery from the coastal (Bat Galim) promenade. While there may not be much cheap accommodation in Haifa, cheap eating is available at the many felafel stands.

Haifa's main site is Elijah's Cave off Allenby Street near the coast. In the Bible, Elijah sheltered from the wrath of King Ahab (Elijah had called down the wrath of God upon the king's subjects who were worshippers of Ba'al and who were promptly consumed in heavenly fire) in the caves at the foot of Mt. Carmel. Arabs revere Al-Khadar (Elijah) as a prophet and Jews believe he will precede the second coming of the Messiah.

Useful Addresses

Tourist Information: 48 Ben Gurion Street; tel 04-8535606 and also on the base level of the Central Bus Station (tel 04-8512208).

SPNI: 18 Hillel St (tel 04-8664135). Israel's nature protection society organises tours and hiking in the Carmel Mountains.

Ferry tickets to Greece: there are several possibilities: Caspi Travel at 76 Ha-

Atzuma'ut Street (tel 04-8674444), Mano at 2 Shar'ar Palmer Street (tel 04-8667722) and ISSTA, Israel's student travel organisation at 2 Balfour Street (tel 04-8669139). A ferry arrives early Sunday morning from Greece and leaves at 8pm the same day. There is another ferry company running ferries on Thurday evenings departing 8pm. There is also a weekly ferry to Cyprus. The terminal is next to the train station and you have to be at the docks at least two hours before departure. Tickets cost about US$100.

Bethel Hostel: 40 Geffen Street; tel 04-8521110. Christian hostel with dormitory accommodation for about US$12.

Carmel Youth Hostel: tel 04-853194; fax 04-8532516. Situated a long way out of the city centre at Hof Carmel (Carmel beach).

Nazareth

The Arab town of Nazareth (population about 170,000), roughly mid-way between Haifa and Tiberias is not what you might imagine from biblical imagery depicting Jesus in his home town, or the Annunciation (Mary's visit from the angel Gabriel, which is taken to have happened in Nazareth). It is a vibrant, brash town where lethally driven BMWs have long replaced dromedaries and donkeys. The Nazarenes who are Israeli (as opposed to Palestinian) Arabs hung back a bit during the intifada for fear of jeopardizing their rather obvious prosperity. The town is about 30 per cent Christian Arabs and the rest are Muslims.

Nazareth anticipates a windfall in 2000 with the visit of the Pope to Israel, and a consequent rise in the number of tourists, many of them bent on a tour of the Holy Land's Christian sites. There is also the much publicised Nazarene biblical 'theme park', a rencontruction of a village at the time of Christ, based on biblical descriptions and stories and utilising archaeological ruins for construction materials and techniques. Work on completing the village will go on for several years, but it should be open for business at the time of publication, complete with locals dressed in first century attire performing traditional village tasks such as weaving and winemaking. Visitors will be given the option of dressing up and joining in. Funds to create a lasting village have been pressed from all over the world including such unlikely sources as ex-US President Jimmy Carter.

At the time of press there is an unholy row brewing between the Muslim and Christian citizens over the proposed siting of a new mosque overlooking the Basilica and Grotto of the Annunciation (where Christians hold that Mary lived and where the messenger Angel Gabriel told her she would give birth to the Saviour). All the Christian sites are in the the old (Arab) town including St. Joseph's Church (supposed site of Joseph's House), The Church of St. Gabriel (Greek Orthodox), built over the town's ancient water source and supposed place where the Angel Gabriel appeared, and Mary's Well to which healing powers are attributed.

Har Tavor (Mount Tabor), site of Christ's Transfiguration is a short bus ride south-east.

Useful Addresses/Websites

www.nazareth.muni.il   website of Nazareth and municipality listing religious sites.

Nazareth Tourist Office: IGTO, Casa Nova Street; tel 06-6573003; fax 06-6573078.

Sisters of Nazareth: P.O. Box 274, 306 Casa Nova Street, opposite the Basilica; tel 06-6554304; fax 06-6460741. Probably the cheapest accommodation at about US$8 for dormitory. Breakfast is extra, or you can use the self-catering facilities.

The Dead Sea and the Negev Desert

Main towns and sights: Ein Gedi (oasis and nature reserve), Qumran (caves of the Dead Sea Scrolls), Beer'sheva (capital of the Negev), Arad, Dimona (home of the black Israelites), Mamshit (Nabatean city).

The large (65km long) salt water lake known in Hebrew as Yam Ha-Melah (Sea of Salt) is the lowest point on planet earth at about 400 metres below sea level, and is getting lower by the minute as development and drainage of the Sea of Galilee (which provides it with a constant top-up) take their toll. The shrinkage is evident at the northern and southern tips where sandbars and creeping land exposure are visible.

At 30% salinity, its salt content is eight times that of oceanic salt water and the only living things that can survive in such conditions are micro-organisms. Human organisms often enter it spurred on by medical belief in the curative powers of the water, said by some to soothe the nervous system and stimulate glandular function. Anyone bathing in the Sea (or more precisely floating on it) comes out encrusted with salt, hence the handy fresh water showers provided on most beaches.

On the Dead Sea shores is **Qumran** where the famous 2000-year-old Dead Sea Scrolls were found. The most important of these ancient Hebrew texts is a version of the the book of Isiah, now displayed in Jerusalem at the Israel Museum.

Ein Gedi
Also near the shores of the Dead Sea is En Gedi. The beautiful oasis full of lush vegetation and waterfalls is in what is now the Nature Reserve and claims to be one of the inspirations for the *Song of Songs* in the book of Solomon in which it is mentioned. Today Ein Gedi is primarily a touristic hotspot, but it is still possible to appreciate the beauty of the oasis if you can manage to be there at the crack of dawn. The area also has a very popular SPNI Field Study Centre (07-6584288). Accommodation can be found at the Beit Sara Youth Hostel, (07-6584165; fax 07-6584445), the Field Study Centre (tel 07-6584350; fax 07-6584257 usually very busy) or the Ein Gedi Camping (fax 07-6584342).

Massada
About 20km south of Ein Gedi is the vast, inspiring fortress of Massada built over a hundred years BC as a defence against the Greeks and the Syrians. In 66AD a whole community of nearly 1000 Judean rebels lived behind its strong walls and held out against a Roman seige for five months. The Romans finally built an enormous earth ramp with which to scale the walls and used Jewish slave labour so that the Judeans would not attack them as the worked. When it became apparent Massada would fall, the inhabitants collaborated in a mass suicide rather than be taken as slaves. When the Romans entered the handful of survivors told them the story of the martyrs. Such powerful history has made Massada a do or die symbol for the Israeli Army. New recruits in the Israeli forces are taken there to swear an oath that Massada will never be allowed to fall again. There is a Massada Youth Hostel (tel 07-6584349).

The Negev

Be'er Sheva (population 157,000) is one of Israel's main cities. It is located west of the Dead Sea on the northern plane of the triangular Negev region of which it is the adminstrative capital. In 1948 when the Israelis seized it from the Palestinians it was a small, if historic town. The city name translates as 'well of seven', a reminder that Abraham's well is the star biblical attraction there. He is assumed to have paid in sevens whatever produce he had, for the right to use it. Nowadays, far from being the Turkish outpost that it became in 1906, **Be'er Sheva** is a large, ugly, modern metropolis packed full of new immigrants from a range of countries including, Russia, Albania and Ethiopia. Its aesthetic attractions are few. However, the Bedouin market on Thursday mornings (near the bus station on Eilat Street) is definitely one of them and a stroll around the old city centre is enjoyable. Budget accommodation is difficult to find. There is a youth hostel (Bat Yatziv, 79 Ha'Atzma'ut 6277444). Most people come to Beer'sheva for the day, in transit to the Negev desert or elsewhere in Israel.

Going west from the Dead Sea to Be'er Sheva, the chances are you will pass through either Arad or Dimona. **Arad** (35km east) is a new town built on a high plateau. With a history going back a mere 40 or so years, there is not much of interest to see. Arad's main highpoint is the annual, four-day Hebrew Music Festival held in July which is a must for all youthful Israelis and not a few tourists.

Dimona (population 32,000) is a new town named after a biblical one. The desert environment is harsh and the surroundings not preposessing: high-rise blocks, factories and Israel's nuclear power plant, now synonymous with Israel's 1986 spy scandal, when the technician Mordechai Vanunu, blew the whistle on Israel's nuclear weapons programme to *The Sunday Times* for which heinous crime he is still languishing in solitary confinement in an Israeli prison.

Dimona is also the adopted town of 1,500 Black Hebrews, a black sect from the United States (Chicago and Detroit) who believe their roots can be traced back to Israel. Their spiritual leader is the charismatic Ben-Ami Carter. They live their own vegetarian, home-spun life-style and visitors to their community on the outskirts of Dimona can, by prearrangement (call 07-6555400) visit them, discuss their beliefs (which include wearing only natural fabrics and worshipping the God Yah) and see around their community. If you like it so much you want to stay the night, there is a guest house (US$20 including food) but you have to book ahead as there are only a couple of rooms. If you can't get a room but love vegetarian food, you can always dine at their village restaurant. They have other eateries in Tiberias and Tel-Aviv.

Mamshit (note that the name applies both to the modern town and the ancient ruins nearby) is 6km from Dimona. The ruins are Israel's answer to Petra, the Nabatean city in Jordan. When the Nabatean power over the spice routes crumbled, the city was taken over and improved by the Romans. Unfortunately for those who like to exercise their imaginations, the Israelis have not stopped with merely reconstructing it, but have created a Nabatean theme park with live actors doing everyday Nabatean tasks like offering Nabatean baked bread to 21st century tourists. There is even a Nabatean restaurant amongst the ruins.

The marked trails of the Ein Avdat Nature Reserve somewhat further southwards into the Negev, are popular with hikers. The entrance to the reserve is 10km from the Kibbutz Sde Boker (home to the late David Ben Gurion).

The real wonder of the Negev desert though is considered to be Makhtesh

Ramon, the largest of four enormous natural craters in the Negev. Ramon is 40km long by 9km across and about 400m deep. Despite the harsh, arid surroundings of the desert it is worth spending some time absorbing the grandeur of the sweeping geological formations which are now the basis of a national park with marked trails and awesome views. The base for visiting the park is Mitzpeh Ramon a small town (population 4,800) on the edge of the crater. There is a Youth Hostel (07-6588443; fax 07-6588074) on the edge of the crater or the SPNI Field School (07-6588615; fax 07-6588385) which costs less than the YH for dorm beds and can help with hiking plans but it is rather isolated. The SPNI do organise tours and these are best enquired about in advance. Other local tours by foot, 4x4 and camel can be arranged through Desert Shade (tel 07-6586229; fax 07-6586208). If you are going to hike on your own, you should get advice and maps from the SPNI and also leave them a plan of your route. The desert demands respect and can be deadly without sensible precautions against its heat and harshness.

The Palestinians & The Palestinian Governed Areas

Since the last edition of this book, considerable concessions have been made by the Israelis towards granting the Palestinians within Israel's self-declared borders, some measure of self-rule. The peace process began with the acceptance of Yasser Arafat as the leader of the Palestinians and the signing of a peace process outlining the stages of the handover of certain territories to Palestinian government. These included Jericho and the Gaza Strip from which Israel withdrew in 1994, and the withdrawl plan for the West Bank which began in October 1995. The Palestinians see real hope that the West Bank will provide a basis for an independent Palestinian state to be established within the next two years. However, the estimated 144,000 Jewish settlers remaining in the West Bank appear to threaten the aspirations of the Palestinians, not least because they are likely to create their own private army. The Israelis have tried to diffuse the situation. They have offered any settlers wishing to leave, compensation and they have built an elaborate network of new roads, i.e. 'security roads' to access the settlements without passing through or very near Palestinian towns and villages. They have arbitrarily expropriated land without reference to the Palestinians, in order to build these roads.

The peace process has so far proceeded according to plan. The main stumbling block, apart from the Israeli settlers in the West Bank, is Jerusalem itself. Israel is adamant that Arab East Jerusalem which was also seized by Israel during the 1967 Six-Day War is not negotiable. According to many recent newspaper reports Israel's policy towards East Jerusalem is one of making it Israeli by stealth. Arab land and buildings within and near the city are simply seized 'in the public interest.' Furthermore, it is deliberate policy to make it virtually impossible for Arab citizens to acquire building permits in East Jerusalem. Meanwhile an unprecedented spate of Israeli building has taken place in East Jerusalem and on the huge tracts of land in the West Bank near Jerusalem which the Israelis claimed were part of Jerusalem when they seized them, along with East Jerusalem in 1967. They have created whole new suburbs and tens of thousands of new dwellings for Jewish citizens with the obvious aim of creating a Jewish majority in East Jerusalem-a goal which has now been achieved. The Arab areas are now encircled and dwarfed. Thus the Arabs are being literally squeezed out.

The Palestinian population of Israel, and the Palestinian ruled territories (The Gaza Strip, West Bank, Jericho) is an estimated 3.2 million. About 1.2 million Palestinians live in the West Bank which includes about 154,000 thousand in East Jerusalem. An estimated 900,000 live in the miserable and overcrowded conditions of the Gaza Strip to which self-rule has brought very little in the way of material compensations. There is very little infrastructure and virtually no employment opportunities in the Gaza Strip and only embryonic versions in the West Bank which desperately needs to promote tourism as a source of income.

The granting of limited autonomy to the Palestinians of the West Bank and the Gaza Strip ended 27 years of Israeli military rule. During the late seventies, the policy of Begin's *Likud* (Labour) government was to strengthen Israel's claim to the West Bank by declaring it part of Eretz Israel, removing the territorial boundaries which marked the Gaza Strip and West Bank as Occupied Territories from all maps so that they appeared part of Israel. Waves of settlers were sent in to colonise the West Bank and the Israeli government steadfastly refused to consider the Palestinian claim for a homeland of their own or even their claims to the land which the Israeli settlers were building on. The resentment caused by the policies of Begin's and successive governments eventually reached crisis point on December 9th 1987 when the Palestinian Uprising began in the West Bank and Gaza. Apart from the Palestinian stone-throwing at Israeli soldiers, this took the form of strikes, leaving many Arab businesses closed for most of the day. This policy of non-cooperation and retaliation was known as the *Intifada*. Israel responded by sending all Palestinian workers from the Gaza Strip back there from their jobs in Israel in May 1989, and issuing them with identity cards, thus ensuring even tighter control. Even with self-rule in the West Bank and Gaza it is very difficult for Palestinians to move around freely, especially between the West Bank and Gaza and Israel. Furthermore, Israel retains an armed presence in the West Bank for guarding the Israeli settlements still based there and a larger force for the troublesome Israeli fanatics in Hebron.

Not all Palestinians live in the Palestinian-ruled territories. There is a sizeable Arab population in Tel-Aviv Jaffo and in various towns and villages near Haifa. The beautiful walled-town of Akko (Acre) is an Arab town. There, you are likely to find yourself with several impromptu Arab guides who will take you via the most circuitous route to the Youth Hostel, just so they can practise their English. There are other Arab towns strung out between Haifa and Jerusalem, including Taibeh, Tira and Daburiya. Palestinians are also to be found in the Galilee region. There are also bedouin Arabs who comprise about ten per cent of the Palestinian Arabs. It is still possible to see them tending their herds of goats in the Negev Desert with their black goats-hair tents in the background; but some have become permanently settled, especially in the Galilee region. In all about 800,000 Arabs (called Israeli Arabs by the Israelis) live in Israel excluding the former occupied territories.

Cultural and other information regarding the Palestinians can be obtained from The Palestinian Academic Society for the Study of International Affairs (PASSIA) in East Jerusalem. For PASSIA's address see below. In the UK there are several organisations which can help with contacts for voluntary work, cultural events etc with the Palestinians in the Palestinian ruled territories and East Jerusalem. For voluntary work see *Voluntary Work with the Palestinians* in the section *Moshav and Other Work*.

Contact with Palestinians

Al-Arab Tours: c/o Al-Arab Hostel; tel 02-6283537. Al-Arab tours can arrange
   visits to the Palestinian Refugee Camps, also to Gaza.
Alternative Information Centre: 6 Koresh Street, P.O. Box 31417; tel 02-
   6241159. Widely used by the foreign press, but accessible to non-journalists
   who want to learn more about the politics of the Middle East through discussion. The centre is operated by Palestinians and Israelis and is non-sectarian.
Alternative Tours: c/o The Jerusalem Hotel, Nablus Road, P.O. Box 20754;
   tel/fax 02-6283282; e-mail raed@jrshotel.com Contact Abu Hassan. Tours
   organised by Palestinians. Regular day tours of Jerusalem (3hrs), Bethlehem
   (3hrs), Hebron (6hrs), West Bank Refugee Camp (3hrs), Jericho and environs
   (^{1}/2day), Gaza (via Eretz checkpoint 1 day), Nazareth and Tiberius (1 day),

Masada and Dead Sea Sunrise Tour (11 hrs). Cost from NIS35 to NIS130 (Gaza). Also regular tours to Jordan and Egypt from US$139 and Sinai from US$55. The aim of the tours is to reveal Palestine's attractions and provide information about the life and history and the current political situation of the Palestinian people. All tours depart from the Jerusalem Hotel.

Also check out the following Palestinian travel websites: www.visit-palestine.com and www.palestinehotels.com

The National Palace Hotel: 4 Zahra Street; tel 02-6273273; fax 02-6282139. For those interested in the Holy Land, The National Palace Hotel in East Jerusalem has an Information Centre for Christians which can arrange meetings with Palestinian Christians.

Palestinian Association for Cultural Exchange: based in Ramallah (tel 02-9958825). Produces information booklets on Palestinian towns and cities and all things Palestinian. Also arranges historical and informative tours all over Palestine.

PASSIA: (P.O. Box 19545, East Jerusalem; fax 02-6282819; e-mail passia@mail.palnet.com). The Palestinian Academic Society for the Study of International Affairs, was set up in 1987 by a group of Palestinian academics in East Jerusalem.

It is an independent organisation whose aim is to present the Palestinian question in its national, Arab and international aspects through academic research, dialogue and publication.

Anyone interested in the question of Jerusalem as a capital of two states or in any occupied Jerusalem issues including access to information, holy sites and Israeli settlement can ask about PASSIA's public information programme including workshops and seminars.

The PASSIA Diary, published annually is a directory of local/international institutions/organisations operating in the West Bank, Gaza and Jerusalem, a year's calendar, and an agenda with useful information about all vital aspects of the Palestinians including health, education, economy, refugees and so on.

UNRWA (United Nations Relief and Works Agency for Palestinian Refugees)
UNRWA was set up in 1950 when it became clear that the Palestinians made homeless by the creation of the State of Israel in 1948, were unlikely to be able to return to their former homes. UNRWA administers eight refugee camps in the Gaza Strip, twenty in the West Bank as well as others in Jordan, Syria and the Lebanon.

In the Gaza Strip, over 70 per cent of the Palestinians are living in refugee camps. In the West Bank, three-quarters of the refugees live outside the camps. It is easy to be completely unaware of the existence of such camps as they do not figure on any tourist map. However, visits can be arranged, and are welcomed by UNRWA. Visits should be arranged a few days in advance through the Public Information Office, UNRWA, PO Box 19149, Nablus Road, East Jerusalem; tel 02-5890409/9; fax 02-6322842. For Gaza, contact the Gaza Public Information office: tel 07-6876044; fax 07-6867044..

Arab Travel Agencies in Jerusalem:
Alternative Tours: c/o Jerusalem Hotel, Nablus Road (near the Garden Tomb and bus stop), P.O. Box 20754; tel/fax 02-628 3282; www.jrs.hotel.com
Arab Tourist Agency: 25 Salah Eddin Str; tel 02-6277442; fax 02-6284366.
Bible Land Tourist Bureau: 23 Zahra Str.; tel 02-6271169; fax 02-6272218.

Nawas Tourist Agency: 2 Zahra St; tel 02-6282491; fax 02-6285755.

Gaza (The Gaza Strip)

The 35km long, overpopulated and impoverished coastal strip, is not the first place you'd think of for a holiday. There are nearly 3,000 people per square kilometre living there and barely a third of homes are connected to a mains sewer. However, Gaza now has over ten hotels with others under construction. The Strip's potential for beach holidays, and the facility for landing commercial jets at the recently opened Gaza International Airport mean that tourism can now be promoted there. Tourists can get information about the Strip's attractions at the Erez checkpoint between Gaza and Israel. The sites include a restored arab mansion with Napoleonic connections in Gaza City.

However, even this piece of over-populated Palestinian governed territory, is not what it seems. You might be surprised to find that there are no fewer than eighteen Jewish settlements within the borders of Gaza in spacious compounds with modern facilities including plumbed water, a luxury most Palestinians there do not enjoy.

It may be easier to enter Israel from Gaza than to reach the West Bank from there. Despite the opening of a new 'safe road' between the two Palestinian areas of Gaza and the West Bank in October 1999, the route is intended primarily for Gazans wanting to work or visit family in the West Bank. The Israelis provide two buses weekly and the service is subject to heavy restrictions: special passes have to be obtained and border crossing restrictions may be reimposed at any time by the Israelis. In any case, being stopped at checkpoints and searched for over an hour by Israeli soldiers is still a way of life here if you are Palestinian or a stranger.

The West Bank

Main towns: Jenin, Nablus, Tulkarm, Qalquiliya, Ramallah, Bethlehem, Hebron, Jericho.

At the time of going to press, the staged Israeli withdrawal of troops from agreed Palestinian areas of the West Bank was ahead of schedule, which might have pleased the assassinated Yitzhak Rabin, who gave his life for it. None the less, the process is problematic and the fact that thousands of Israeli settlers are remaining in the West Bank guarded by Israeli soldiers, is a potential touchpaper for yet more violence. The town of Hebron will retain its Israeli population of 450 (amongst 120,000 Palestinians) who will be guarded by Israeli security forces which makes it the most potentially explosive place in the West Bank. Sacred to both Jews and Muslims, it was the scene of a massacre of 30 Arabs by an Israeli settler apparently in a sound state of mind, in 1994.

The other settlers are isolated in their settlements accessed by brand new roads built by the Israelis to bypass habited Palestinian areas. All the settlers are armed. They have declared their intention to ignore any dictates by the Palestinian police in the West Bank. In fact, according to their leaders, they will most probably shoot them. The settlers very presence in the West Bank is seen by many as the biggest threat to the entire peace process.

When you actually study the terms of the handover it amounts to a rather piece-meal deal for the Palestinians, who will have control over about 40 per cent of the West Bank as represented by the main towns. In the rest of the West Bank including the 450 smaller Palestinian towns and villages (comprising about

60 per cent of the West Bank), the Israelis will still have final control. In unpopulated areas of 'strategic importance' to Israel and Jewish settlers in the West Bank, Israel will have full control. Palestinian police will not have power of arrest over Israeli settlers.

Control over holy sites such as Bethlehem, in the West Bank have passed to the Palestinian authorities and special arrangements have been made to guarantee Jews access to the tombs of the Patriarchs in Hebron, Rachel in Bethlehem and Joseph in Nablus.

The peculiar nature of the West Bank means that normal life, is liable to be disrupted at short notice. In particular the economy of the West Bank is so dependent on Israel that it can be crippled by Israeli sanctions and restrictions on Palestinians movements. The area has very little infrastructure and is in desperate need of tourism, and a viable economy. Pretty large sums of aid are finding their way to the West Bank, unfortunately they are inclined to end up in the wrong place like some officials' bank accounts.

Travelling in the West Bank is likely to be less organised than in Israel and with more hassles generally. However, the area has so much that is of interest that it will more than repay any extra effort and patience needed. As the tourist infrastructure is embryonic, expect few hotels and little advertised tourist accommodation. The Palestinian Authority is still establishing tourist offices and soon it may also be possible to find budget accommodation too to supplement the gaudy new hotels. For the time being most visits will probably have to be on a day basis from Jerusalem or an organised tour (see below). If you go on your own it is advisable to have a guide, who you can engage in Jerusalem (see below), or Bethlehem etc.. You will almost certainly be bombarded with offers from the locals to guide you if you do not and which could impede your progress. On the other hand going without a guide is certainly one way of getting to meet the locals and helps to establish your reason for being there. However because of the difference in status between western, and many muslim women, western women will just have to put up with being pestered, or take a male companion.

When using Arab buses be aware that the concept of a fixed timetable does not exist. Buses usually leave when they are full or when the driver feels like it.

Jericho
Reputed to be the oldest city in the world and certainly at 367m below sea level, the lowest. Jericho is an easy 40km trip from Jerusalem going eastwards. Buses and service taxis regularly ply the route to and from Jerusalem's Damascus Gate.

The ruins of the ancient town of Jericho and Hisham's Palace are a few kilometres south of the Arab town of Jericho where 7000 Arabs live. If your budget does not stretch to a hired guide and jeep, you can rent a bicycle in Jericho. Your first visit should probably be the Tourist Office (run by the Palestinian Authority and located out of town) where you can get a free map and some advice.

Nablus
An ancient town that has seen off many invaders including the Turks, the British and the Israelis, Nablus (its Arabic name Jabal an-Nar means hill of fire), is the West Bank's largest city (apart from East Jerusalem) and, compared with many other West Bank towns, has a prosperous air reflecting its commercial importance and the fact that it is home to some of the wealthiest Palestinian families. Nablus, like Jericho is an easy day trip from Jerusalem from which it is 63km distant. You can travel to Nablus from Jerusalem on a Tamini bus which leaves

from Nablus Road, or get a shared taxi. As with most Arab buses, they leave when full. As there is little in the way of budget accommodation in Nablus, it is probably cheaper to stay in Ramallah about an hour away from where you can get a Sherut to Nablus.

The old part of the city is very atmospheric and the pilgrim sites include Jacob's Well (3km east) now incorporated into a Greek Orthodox shrine, near which is the other main sight: Joseph's Tomb. Olive oil soap is produced locally and there are some Turkish baths (men and women on separate days).

Ramallah

The Arab hill town of Ramallah is 16km from Jerusalem. Situated at 900m above sea level, the air tends to be cool and refreshing and was once a great attraction for summer residents from Jordan and the Lebanon. The Intifada put a stop to such halcyon days. Ramallah and nearby Bir Zeit University play a hectic part in Palestinian politics. The city is rapidly becoming the base of the growing world of Palestinian officialdom as the Palestinian Authority takes on increasing responsibilities. It is already the home of several ministeries. Not surprisingly, it is a progressive place where the women tend to dress in western-style casual clothes. There is plenty of opportunity to meet the locals – unofficial guides and Arab hospitality abound in Ramallah. There is a lively daily market and a visitable chocolate factory.

Buses for Ramallah leave from the Damascus Gate in Jerusalem, or from the bus station on Nablus Road. Service taxis also ply the route regularly between Jerusalem and Nablus.

Near Ramallah is the biggest Palestinian University, Bir Zeit, scene of much Palestinian political activity which led to its suffering regular shut downs by the Israeli authorities. The new campus of Bir Zeit is 12km from Ramallah.

Bethlehem (Beit Lahm)

Probably one of the most significant events in Bethlehem's history since the birth of Christ, was the ending of Israeli military rule there in 1995. However, there is an Israeli military checkpoint and roadblock just outside the town which inevitably causes bottlenecks both in and out of the town. A transformation of this Palestinian town of 125,000 inhabitants (split between Muslims and Christians) is being effected in the name of Millennium festivities. There is an ambitious renovation and building programme. Manger square is now a pristine plaza, historic buildings like the Franciscan church of St Francis are getting a facelift, and sorely-needed upgrading of sewers and utilities is taking place. There will be upwards of 600 new hotel beds in Bethlehem by the time this book is published – a five star Intercontinental hotel located in a former grand arab house lords it over the Hebron road near Rachel's Tomb, and another new hotel is scheduled for Solomon's Pools in the same vicinity. Several new hotels are due to open at the end of 2000, and no doubt there will be others after that. Suave tourist police and licensed, professional tour guides offer professional service to bemused tourists.

While being a spiritual magnet for countless Christian pilgrims, Bethlehem's popularity with tour buses, mainly from Jerusalem six miles away and the profusion of gaudy souvenirs on sale, gives a first impression of a mega tourist trap. Even tourism however, brings some benefits. The town is well used to strangers and makes them welcome, and there is no shortage of spotless accommodation, of the Christian hospice type (except at Christmas!). The experiment of offering bed and breakfast accommodation in hundreds of inspected and approved houses and apartments to accommodate the Millennium crowds, may continue.

The (Palestinian) Ministry of Tourism in Bethlehem has ambitious plans for guided tours including a life of Jesus tour to include the River Jordan (Christ's baptism), Temptation Mount (Christ's Temptation by the Devil), Burquin (miracle cure of the lepers) and Jerusalem (Crucifixion and Resurrection).

The downside of this tourist honeypot, apart from the tourist shops, is that prices for many things are higher than in other Palestinian towns and bargaining is essential. It is also said that considerable amounts of the foreign aid provided for these improvements has found its way into the pockets of the Palestinian establishment.

Manger Square is the focal point of the town as far as tourists are concerned. Avoid Bethlehem at Christmas if you are uncomfortable in crowds. It will be packed out, especially for the the Midnight Mass in St Catherine's Church, which is broadcast live worldwide. Accommodation for Christmas has to be booked a year in advance. Also in Manger Square are the Tourist Office, Post Office, The Police Station and the stopping place for minibuses and service taxis which ply between Jerusalem and Bethlehem. The Grotto of the Nativity is under the basilica. Other sites include the Milk Grotto Church (in Milk Grotto Street) where the Holy Family is reputed to have taken refuge on their flight from Herod; the Well of David (in the King David Cinema car park) and Rachel's Tomb (sacred to Jews) and located on the edge of Bethlehem.

Getting there: from Jerusalem arab buses leave from the Suleiman Street bus station (near Damascus Gate), and also from the Damascus and Jaffa Gates) and cost about NIS 2.5. Shared taxis are quicker, leaving from the Damascus Gate and cost about £4. The distance from Jerusalem is only 8km/6miles, but be prepared for hold-ups at the Israeli checkpoint outside Bethlehem (see above).

Useful Addresses

Ministry of Tourism & Antiquities: P.O.Box 534, Bethlehem, Palestine; tel +972 2 274 1581; fax +972 2 274 3753. Located above the Al Andalus Hotel in Manger Square. Source of maps, and accommodation and touring information.

Tourist Police Office: (tel 6477050) on the ground floor below the Ministry of Tourism.

Franciscan Convent (tel 742441): the attached pension located in Milk Grotto Street has a few rooms costing US$18-25 with breakfast.

Casa Nova (tel 743981): slightly more commodious and off Manger Square. Bed and breakfast cost US$20-25. Other meals available.

Hebron

Hebron (Al Khalil ar-Rahman in Arabic) is probably the West Bank's most notorious town). It has been labelled a new Berlin on the West Bank. There are about 400 Jewish settlers living in Hebron, who are armed themselves and heavily guarded by Israeli soldiers and they are free to move between the West Bank and Israel as they wish. They are living amongst nearly 200,000 Palestinians who need to obtain a permit even to visit nearby Jerusalem. The Israeli presence is a taunt to the Palestinians. The settlers believe that Hebron is the heart of the ancient Jewish kingdom. It is after all the burial place of the Jewish Patriarchs, starting with Abraham. The settlers believe that the land is theirs by right now and forever. Against such a rock all reason founders. Much the same belief is shared by the orthodox Jews living in the makeshift settlement of Bat Ayn, 5km from Hebron, on land belonging to Palestinian farmers and also by the settlers of Kiryat Arba a mere 1km northeast of Hebron where a Jewish population of 5,000 think that there should be room in Hebron for them too.

If you visit Hebron you will see the rooftops bristling with Israeli soldiers. Meanwhile the Palestinians of Hebron brood on the unprovoked massacre of 30 Palestinians there by Baruch Goldstein in 1994. Jewish settlers in Hebron have put up a shrine to Goldstein.   Despite the tensions, it is possible to visit Hebron which is 35km south of Jerusalem. Arab buses leave for there from the Damascus Gate or Alternative Tours of Jerusalem (tel/fax 02-628 3282) run day trips there (NIS60) from the Jerusalem Hotel in East Jerusalem.

The main sites in Hebron include the Tombs of the Patriarchs; nearly all of them rest in the Cave of Makhpela. Hebron also has one of the best markets in the West Bank.

Maps and Guides
There are a number of specialist Israeli guides, who offer to chaperone tourists in the West Bank and excel in explaining and promoting the Israeli line on the West Bank. After a short while such propogandising becomes surreal, especially as the facts tell another story. If you want an Arab guide, try the Arab hostels in Jerusalem (see 'City Listings'), or ask travel agents in Arab East Jerusalem or see *Arab Travel Agents* above.

Palestinian Maps of Gaza and the West Bank do exist but are elusive and you may find that they are only obtainable periodically and on the spot. At the time of press there was mention of a new Palestinian guidebook, produced by the Palestinian Association for Cultural Exchange dealing with Palestine only: *The Tour Guide to the West Bank and Gaza* is published in Ramallah (tel 02-9958825 for further information) . For the dedicated tourist, it might be annoying as all mention of Jewish sites is excluded. A weekly publication of entertainments and what to do listings is also planned to be available free to tourists.

Also at the time of press, Bradt Publications (01753-893444) had just published *Palestine with Jerusalem* a 230 page historical and practical guide book for independent travellers; price £12.95.

Further Reading on Israel and Palestine

From the Holy Mountain byWilliam Dalrymple published by Flamingo 1998 (£8.99).

A Golden Basin Full of Scorpions – The Quest for Modern Jerusalem by Con Coughlan published by Warner 1997 (£7.99).

The Innocents Abroad Mark Twain's original 1871 account of being a tourist in the Holy Land republished by Oxford University Press (USA) 1997 at £19.99.

In the Land of Israel by Amoz Oz published by Random House USA.

Israel ,a History by Martin Gilbert, published by Black Swan 1999 (£14.99).

Israel, Palestine and Peace: essays by Amos Oz the famed Israeli novelist published by Vintage in 1994 (£6.99).

Jerusalem: City of Mirrors: Amos Elon (Flamingo £6.99). May be out of print. Enquire to Harper Collins 0141-772 3200.

Like Water in a Dry Land – The Journey to Modern Israel: by Bettina Selby published by Fountain 1996 (£7.99).

The Question of Palestine and Peace and its Discontents by Edward Said, the well known American Palestinian academic and intellectual.

Soldier of Peace: by Dan Kurzman, published by Harper Collins (USA) 1998 (£20). Biography of the late assasinated (prime minister of Israel, Yitzhak Rabin.

The Weekend that Changed the World: Peter Walker published by Marshall Pickering 1999 (£9.99).

Online and UK Travel Booksellers

www.amazon.com

www.amazon.co.uk

Blackwells Map & Travel Bookshop: 50 Broad Street, Oxford, OX1 3BU; tel 01865-792792; www.blackwells.co.uk   Very comprehensive range of maps and travel guides.

Daunt Books: 83 Marylebone High Street, London W1M 3DE; tel 0207-224 2295. Specialised travel bookshop with up to date maps and guides, second-hand, out of print travel books and political history. Will try and get anything for you; email enquiries@dauntbooks.com

Stanfords: 12-14 Long Acre, London WC2 9LP; tel 0207-836 1321. Britain's world renowned seller of maps and guides. Huge selection of maps, charts, atlases, etc.

The Travel Bookshop: 13 Blenheim Crescent, London W11 2EE; tel 0207-229 5260. Specialises in maps and guides and associated literature past and present to do with travel. Very helpful staff.

The Kibbutz

'To everyone according to their need, and from everyone according to their ability'

BACKGROUND AND ORGANISATION

A mere 2.4% (125,000 people) of Israel's population of nearly five million are kibbutzniks. The kibbutz is a communal, socialistic society, in which all means of production are owned by the community as a whole. Back in 1909 when the first kibbutzim were being formed everything was owned, everything was produced and all profits were shared equally by all the members. It was, and to a limited extent still is, an honest, committed attempt to live a life based on co-operation, equality and democracy. On the first kibbutzim literally everything was communal, even the clothes. However, there is a considerable gap between the strict ideology and austerity that characterised the first kibbutzim and life on a kibbutz in the 21st century. The kibbutzim generally have become less communal and increasingly materialistic. Members of most kibbutzim have their own homes and all mod cons. Some have even committed the ultimate heresy of demanding private incomes while the final nail in the coffin of the pioneering dream, looks like being the government's declared intention to privatise kibbutzim. There is still however a nugget of idealism in a number of these settlements.

According to Yehuda Harel, author of *The New Kibbutz* there has been a cessation in the founding of new kibbutzim. One of the youngest kibbutzim, and therefore an example of the New Kibbutz (which is far removed from those conceived by the Zionist pioneers) is Neot Smadar. Described as a 'New Age' kibbutz, it was founded in the southern Negev in 1990 by city dwellers who felt that modern Israel has lost its way in an orgy of materialism. There are other 'unusual' kibbutzim: Kibbutz Harduf (founded 1980) in the Galilean hills is a anthroposophical kibbutz based on the ideas of the Austrian Rudolph Steiner, while Kibbutz Samar not far from Eilat describes itself as 'an anarchist' kibbutz (see *Kibbutz Directory* for full details). In 1992, one kibbutz, Ein Zivan in the Golan Heights voted to pay its members salaries according to the value of their work. This is regarded as the ultimate heresy as it defies the accepted definition of kibbutz.

At present there are 250-70 kibbutzim throughout Israel which are organised into three movements. There is some co-operation between their movements on various projects of mutual aid and common interest, both economic and cultural.

HaKibbutz HaDati, is the minority religious movement, which has a membership of sixteen kibbutzim. There are two main movements: HaKibbutz Ha'artzi and Takam, the United Kibbutz Movement of HaKibbutz HaMeuchad and Ichud HaKevutzot Ve'HaKibbutzim, which merged in 1980. Help given to their members includes advisory services for agricultural planning, industry, building and architecture, cultural and social matters, medical problems, education and so on. Each movement has facilities for making loans to individual kibbutzim, and the larger ones have building contracting operations which can undertake major building projects in Kibbutzim and outside.

There are various committees in each of the movements to help settle any disputes between kibbutzim and also to help kibbutzniks if they have a grievance against their kibbutz.

The differences between the movements are almost imperceptible to an outsider and a mystery even to many kibbutzniks. They each have varying political alignments, mainly left-wing. There are also some religious differences.

The Kibbutz has often been described as 'the purest form of communism.' It is generally accepted that the kibbutz as a purely socialist organisation has had its day, but despite many changes adherance to their communist roots is still strong on a number of kibbutzim. Even after the fall of communism in one country after another in Europe, kibbutzim in Israel were still celebrating May Day. But along with tributes to their past, kibbutzim are carrying on daily life and planning for the future in ways that would have been unthinkable to their founders, who eschewed paying salaried workers or appointing bosses of any kind, let alone floating kibbutz company shares on the Tel-Aviv stock market as has now happened. Many kibbutzim employ professionals including accountants, financial advisors and medical staff to perform work for which kibbutz members do not have the appropriate skills and knowledge. This concession is also regarded as a heresy by traditionalists.

The kibbutz was once regarded as unique to Israel. However, it does have rivals in other commune movements worldwide. Geof Bercovich of Kibbutz Ammiad went two years running to a 'kibbutz-type commune in San Francisco' and says there are many similar types of commune, some of which may be interested in taking volunteers like kibbutzim, while others want to be 'left in peace.'

From the volunteer point of view, many aspects of kibbutz life may be difficult to understand, and as many of the older kibbutzim are very much rooted in their history, a little knowledge of their origins and ideals may help to make more sense of what is clearly a very different culture.

In the late 19th and early 20th centuries, eastern and central Europe were facing enormous political and social upheavals as liberalism, socialism, nationalism and communism developed into mass movements. It was through the rejection of the old order that the romantically inspired youth movements of central Europe were born. The Jewish Youth Movement, formed from young, middleclass intellectuals, was dissatisfied with the Jewish existence in exile, and determined to break away from the ghetto life of their forefathers, and they preferred agriculture to traditional careers in business. The young pioneers desired to create a way of life through a return to nature and simple values such as loyalty, brotherhood and truth.

Optimism turned to dismay when the tide of pogroms and other forms of anti-semitism swept through Europe and Russia at that time. It was from this growing adversity that Zionism was born. Zionism produced the desire to create a Jewish revolution, an ideal Jewish homeland, and the return to the promised land of Palestine (then part of the Ottoman Empire) and to reclaim it through labour.

It was from this background that the first group of farmers joined forces in 1909 to form Degania – the first kibbutz. Their very strong beliefs enabled the early pioneers to overcome the most appalling conditions, and indeed many more gave up the struggle than stayed. The State of Israel was not founded until 1948 and the kibbutzim played an important part in defence when conflict erupted between the various communities laying claim to the land. A measure of the importance of the role the kibbutz has played in Israeli life is that many high ranking army appointments and ministerial positions in the Knesset (Israeli parliament) have been filled by kibbutzniks. However, their influence has waned considerably in political and military life. In the last twenty or so years kibbutzim have been marginalised as force in Israeli life. Their government subsidies have ceased, most have severe debts and as already mentioned, the government wants to see them privatised.

Estimates of those still taking individual volunteers vary; in 1999, the Kibbutz Representatives put it at 50+, while another organisation, Project '67 put it at 80+. Other estimates reach 100. It is important to remember that not all of the kibbutzim that still take volunteers have them all of the time. There are kibbutzim taking organised groups of foreigners, lately many of them Koreans who may also pay the kibbutz for English lessons. Volunteers are expected to work longer for their keep; the working week is up from 36 to 48 hours. The Kibbutz Representatives in London send about 1,000 British volunteers are year to work on kibbutzim.

From an historical perspective, we can see that from its difficult birth in circumstances of great adversity, the kibbutz movement grew to strength, and played an important part in the development and security of the nation. In some cases sheer physical effort and ideological commitment became the foundation of prosperity which is evident today, despite the enormous debt and question mark which hangs over the next phase of kibbutzim existence.

The State of the Kibbutz Today

As already indicated, there are still a host of problems for the kibbutzim. On paper most are bankrupt from borrowing huge sums of money from the state in the 1980's with which to expand, and which they now find themselves unable to repay in the forseeable future. In many cases the original debt has more than doubled despite the fact that banks made a deal with the Israeli government in 1990 to write off a quarter of all kibbutz debts. As more and more compromises are made to capitalism and pragmatic financial management in order to combat this predicament, the original ideals of the movement are diluting, while the kibbutz works out its new role in a society more individualistic and materialistic than that of eighty, or even thirty years ago.

The economy of the kibbutzim is broadly based on industry although most retain diverse agricultural elements. Virtually the only kibbutz which is still based mainly on agriculture is Alumim near Palestinian Gaza and even it has branched into the tourist business. In fact letting holiday flats or running motel-style accommodation has provided an additional source of income for kibbutzim for the last couple of decades, while in 1999, several kibbutz timeshares were on offer for £5,000 for 25 years of visits. About 30% of most other kibbutzim's production is agricultural.

Since the 1950's kibbutzim have had factories and over the intervening decades they have become increasingly industrialised. Diversification and co-operative ventures with other kibbutzim, and lately with outside companies means that kibbutzim now produce everything from underwear elastic to microcircuits, for the home market and export. Since Israel has become more 'respectable' through trying to bury the hatchet with the arab world, tourism to Israel has surged and then dropped again depending on the various international and internal crises which have afflicted it. The kibbutzim have not been slow to exploit tourism as a money spinner and increasingly kibbutzim offer guest rooms on a bed and breakfast basis. Many of these rooms were previously used for housing volunteers. This means the number of volunteers taken by many kibbutzim has been reduced to make way for this more profitable practice. For instance Kibbutz Ammiad has reduced its volunteer capacity from 30 to just ten.

Another factor causing a reduction in the number of volunteers from abroad was the huge influx of immigrants (approximately 800,000) from the former Russian Empire and eastern Europe in the last decade of the twentieth century. The Israeli government has insisted that the kibbutzim play their part in absorbing this new wave of immigration. Despite the allocation of volunteer housing to tourists and despite the influx of immigrants from eastern Europe and the fact that kibbutzim have an increasingly mechanised regime, some of them do still face periodic labour shortages. However a large number of kibbutzim have had to trim their budgets to cope with their economic straits and many jobs previously done by volunteers are now done by the kibbutzniks, or cheap labour from Romania and Thailand, and this further reduces the demand for outside volunteers.

Each volunteer costs the kibbutz about NS 250 (about $125) in administration charges. When the volunteer starts work there is the additional cost of bed and board and the customary volunteer trips for long service. Thus most kibbutzim think carefully before taking volunteers and they have nearly all reduced their intake or ceased using volunteer help completely.

In 1999, a final blow seemed to have been dealt to the kibbutz ideal with the news that the Israeli government's plan to privatise the kibbutzim was about to be finalised. This means that kibbutzim will officially be privately-owned and profit-making enterprises.

With all the changes in the kibbutz system taking place it is difficult for the prospective volunteer to know what type of community he or she will discover on a placement. Are they political, right wing, left wing, industrial, agricultural, old or new, traditional or innovative? For those who like to do their research so they can request a certain type of kibbutz, it may be possible to discover more by contacting the International Communes Desk at Yad Tabenkin Research and Documentation Centre (Ramat-Efal, 52960; fax 03-534 637; e-mail yadtab@act-com.co.il).

Despite its phenomenal pioneering example, not everyone in Israel has benefited from the kibbutzim. For an alternative view of kibbutz culture ask the London Friends of Palestine (21 Collingham Road, London SW5 ONU) for their leaflet *The Kibbutz: Who Benefits Who Suffers?* A SAE is required.

THE KIBBUTZ AND THE MEMBERS

The early way of life on a kibbutz was of necessity austere and basic. In those early days, the kibbutz was common property, the showers were for everyone. In the clothes store even the underwear belonged to everyone. The kibbutznik did not even own a watch and had no time that was his own. There was no room on the kibbutz for the expression of personal style or taste. Everyone was too busy combatting the land, the heat, disease and marauding arabs reacting to the unilateral expropriation of their land, to think of their personal needs. Everyone belonged to the collective and the collective belonged to everyone, in every way and at all times.

Work

The kibbutz member can be assigned any job on the kibbutz; his status is not affected by the work he or she performs as everyone is regarded as equal and all jobs are considered to be of equal importance; ultimately the member will be given a permanent job to which they are best suited.

Most service work is rotated on a temporary basis, everyone taking their turn; however it has gradually become usual for the volunteers to do most of the worst jobs, at least until they have proved that they are well-behaved and/or show skills that could be utilised in more interesting work.

Technical training and education are available to those with an aptitude and interest.

Members wishing to work at occupations or professions for which there is no room on their kibbutz, such as lawyers, doctors, teachers and social workers, can usually work outside the kibbutz (many do) where high fliers can earn as much in a month as their fellow kibbutzniks earn in a whole year. The catch is that they have to turn over their income to the kibbutz and they do not profit in any way from their expertise and talent. Their accommodation on the kibbutz is of the same standard as a manual worker's or a nurse's. This makes a major contribution to kibbutz income for the 80% of kibbutzim which are now in the situation of having high earning kibbutzniks working outside the kibbutz while much of the donkey work on the kibbutz is done by cheap outside labour, usually arabs.

Small wonder perhaps, that the youngest generation of educated kibbutzniks are increasingly choosing to leave the kibbutz for good to enjoy the fruits of their labours as individuals, in marked contrast to their selfless forbears.

Personal Budget

The division of wealth in the kibbutz is decided according to the basic principle 'to each according to his needs'. The kibbutz takes care of its members supplying virtually all needs in housing, services, clothing, food, education, healthcare, care of the elderly and so on. For personal transport members fill in a form to book a communally-owned truck or car.

It is usual for kibbutzniks to have personal budgets in lieu of wages for consumer goods and luxuries which they now consider part of their daily life. The budget is meant to cover furnishing, extra clothing, time off, foreign travel and even cars. Individual electricity meters are now becoming commonplace on many kibbutzim as the personal budget is also meant to cover running costs of a personal dwelling. As one kibbutznik put it 'It means that no-one leaves the lights on any more if they are paying for their own electricity.'

Leave of Absence

Frequently a member, particularly if young, feels a need to explore the opportunities and experience the life of the outside world. Once such a move meant leaving the kibbutz for good as permission to return was not automatically given. Kibbutzim usually allow an absence of one or two years to allow the kibbutnik to experience life not only outside the kibbutz but outside Israel if they wish. This means that if they decide after such an absence that they still wish to settle on the kibbutz permanently, it is more meaningful and they are more likely to be dedicated kibbutzniks. More and more young people are however choosing to leave for good after their military service.

Housing and Children

Members live in single or double accommodation incorporating a bedroom (or bedrooms depending on family circumstances), sitting room, small kitchen, bathroom and lavatory. Although modest in size it will almost certainly contain most of the consumer durables considered essential to modern life. Radio, stereo unit, television, video-recorder, cooker, refridgerator and air conditioning/central heating.

Some of the most radical changes on the kibbutz have happened in the sphere of child-rearing. No longer do kibbutzim maintain the once standard practice of communal child-rearing which involved separating very young children from their parents for most of their waking hours and every night. Infants and children were cared for by 'kibbutz mothers' in special children's houses. The practical reasoning behind this arrangement was that it freed the parents, and particularly mothers from the drudgery of bringing up babies and children. Eventually, deprived maternal instincts led to a clamour for parents to be able to have their children living with them in the parental home, at least until puberty when they would be transferred to 'youth houses' where they could learn the art and skills of living communally with their peers – sound preparation for future kibbutzniks.

However, even the age at which children move to the youth house has been raised, from early to mid-teens, to combat the likelihood of drug addiction and sexual problems which have infiltrated even the idealistic society of the kibbutz.

Kibbutz children usually attend the kibbutz school where the education includes an element of the philosophy of kibbutz life as benefiting the community as a whole. Teachers encourage children to organise their own affairs and older children may have a small farm to run and usually spend a few hours each week working alongside their parents. All children have the opportunity to go on to higher, technical and university education.

Healthcare and the Elderly

The kibbutz takes care of all aspects of medical and dental care for its members. Facilities include dispensaries, ambulances and trained nurses. Regular visits are made by doctors, dentists and eye specialists which ensure a high standard of care for everyone.

The sons and daughters of the first kibbutz pioneers of eighty years ago, now constitute the largest proportion of members on some of the oldest kibbutzim like Afikim. For the elderly on the kibbutzim retirement at some stage is not compulsory. Many take pride in working for a short period each day in factory or farm well into their eighties. The kibbutz provides them with free medical care and every device possible is used to ensure that mobility is not a problem for those with disabilities. The elderly have the security they have earned, and the comfort of knowing that the kibbutz will look after them until they die.

Clothing

All clothing on the kibbutz is handled by the laundry and repair department. Deposited laundry is returned at the end of the week, washed, ironed and mended. Many kibbutzim keep a record of clothing owned by each member and certain items are replaced automatically when they are seen to be worn out.

Members can buy extra clothing with their personal allowance either in the kibbutz non-profit store or in town.

Women in the Kibbutz

The kibbutz principle of equality means that women enjoy equal rights and status in the kibbutz.

At work however, women themselves often choose to do the 'traditionally female' jobs, i.e. those connected with food, clothes and children. Where once their foremothers clamoured for the right to be freed from child rearing to work alongside the men in the fields, kibbutz women now expect more time to spend with their children. Women do work temporarily in 'traditionally' male jobs, but it is unusual to find them working permanently in spheres other than education, health and social services or in the professions.

Culture

The variety of cultural, educational and sporting activities available to the average kibbutznik is almost endless: folk-dancing, drama and dance groups, pottery, photography, art, music, films, as well as lectures on a variety of subjects including history, literature and politics. Concert artists and theatre groups make regular visits to the kibbutzim, and many kibbutzim have their own arts festivals.

Sometimes a study month is arranged and members are released from work every afternoon to attend. Adult education classes may be held in the evenings and most kibbutzim have well-stocked libraries.

There is an inter-movement orchestra and choir which gives regular concerts, sometimes with internationally famous guest conductors and soloists.

Collectively just about every conceivable sport is practised with kibbutz teams competing in national leagues and championships; there are even cricket and rugby teams. Gymnasiums, swimming pools, sports fields, ball courts and horse riding are provided with all equipment on the kibbutz or shared with nearby kibbutzim.

There are always opportunities for members to introduce new sports and activities.

Summary

It can be seen that the kibbutz is not afraid to change, to try out new ideas or to rethink the ideals of the past. In the past the kibbutz has founded new settlements, defended borders, absorbed new immigrants and was once responsible for the bulk of the agricultural production of the country (now this virtue is claimed by moshavim). As the demands have changed, the kibbutzim have turned to other fields; industry, and most recently tourism to boost their financial status.

It is the kibbutzim's ability to maintain strong basic principles yet adapt to challenges that holds the greatest promise for the future.

THE KIBBUTZ AND THE VOLUNTEER

To be a visitor, a guest, a volunteer on a kibbutz can mean many things. Kibbutz society is a strict, rigidly structured system.

On a kibbutz all members are equal, as long as you do not seriously offend the obvious standards, you can live how you please. Most volunteers tend to look back on a spell spent on a kibbutz as a mixture of the tedious and the enjoyable. One of the most fondly recalled pleasures is the mind-broadening aspect of working and living alongside volunteers from around the world. They may come from as far away as Mexico or as close as the Netherlands. Volunteers make their own fun whether it be organising a disco or a football match. Many kibbutzim offer a building that can be used as a bar/volunteer meeting place where younger members of the kibbutz will also come to socialise, as will most probably the young soldiers guarding the kibbutz.

There is however a complaint common among volunteers that they are treated as 'low life' and 'second class' citizens while on the kibbutz by all but those members with whom they have everyday dealings or who are of their own age. Although annoying, this is understandable in some ways. From the kibbutznik's point of view, there is a fast turnover of volunteers and the faces are always changing, so why bother to make the effort to get to know individuals. The younger members are more curious and generally welcome the chance to meet so many different people from around the world.

Working hours on a kibbutz are now generally eight hours a day, six days a week. The hours may vary slightly. For instance if the work is back-breaking and involves being in the fields in the mid-day sun the hours worked may be less than for a relatively light jobs in a factory. Shift work is usually the norm so that the free period will vary each week or even daily. There is generally sufficient leisure time to visit Israeli towns, Arab villages, cafés and bazaars, beaches; you name it, it's there. You may want to walk, borrow a bike (occasionally a horse) and see some of the most beautiful landscape you will find anywhere: there are mountains, deserts, oases, waterfalls and natural springs, fields, forests, valleys, hills, lakes and mountain pools; wherever you are in Israel there will be something ancient, or beautiful, or amazing, or all three and much to see or do outside or after the kibbutz.

Apart from the pleasures of being a volunteer with all your basic needs catered for, while surrounded by a usually sympathetic bunch of people to share the work with, there is the aspect of kibbutz life that is most important to the kibbutzniks themselves. For you, the experience is just a working holiday cum party, but for the kibbutzniks it is a commitment to an ideal, an experiment in a way of life that has in many ways been a success but which now faces a challenge for its survival in the present form. A great part of the fascination of your visit should be an appreciation and understanding of this commitment; to know why, for instance on some kibbutzim everyone eats together, why teenagers live together in special houses apart from their parents and how labour is organised, how profits are used and so on. There is also the human story of suffering and achievment, how and why did these people come to be here from all over the world, speaking seventy different languages.

With so much to experience and learn and so little restriction, one of the hardest parts of the volunteer's life can be imposing some kind of self discipline. You will be trusted by the kibbutzniks to give of your best at work and not to offend. Kibbutzniks are tolerant to a fault; they have to be to live with each other, but some of the behaviour of drunken volunteers in recent years has shocked even the most laid back kibbutzniks. Once expulsion of volunteers was a rare event, but sadly it has become a not infrequent occurence.

For those who wish to get involved more constructively in Israeli culture there is the Working Hebrew scheme which involves 36 hours of work and 12 hours study weekly on a kibbutz (see below for details).

What Can a Volunteer Expect?

As a volunteer you will be left largely to organise your own fun. Kibbutzim vary enormously in the commitment of their volunteer organiser towards his or her responsibilities in this area. Some give negligible attention and minimal effort while others (probably the minority), warm to the task and contribute much to the satisfaction of the volunteers with their stay. In theory at least, the volunteer organiser is responsible for everything from volunteer work schedules to their general welfare and is there to act as a liaison between the volunteers and the kibbutz.

The volunteer worker can expect to be able to join in many of the kibbutz social events and to be able to receive many of the benefits of members themselves: use of the sports facilities and laundry and so-on. A volunteer will not however, be allowed to take part in any committee meetings that concern the running of the kibbutz, or take part in any security or guard duties.

The Work

As already stated, work on a kibbutz by no means implies that of the outdoor, agricultural variety although it will almost certainly include it. Since virtually all kibbutzim have at least one factory and most have two or more the volunteer should at least anticipate the possibility of being assigned some light factory work even if it is only keeping the factory floor swept. Some kibbutzim do not give volunteers factory work at all, but if you want to work only, or mostly outdoors you will have to check with the kibbutz or the kibbutz representative in your own country whether they can select a kibbutz where your wishes are likely to be met. Otherwise, consider working on a Moshav (see section on Working on Moshavim) as they are mainly agricultural.

There is a great variety of work on the kibbutz, some of it seasonal. The volunteers will be expected to rotate their job with other volunteers as some of the work is boring and unpleasant. Volunteers can be found peeling vegetables, washing dishes, shovelling manure, working in fish ponds, cleaning, working in the kitchens, picking, packing, spraying fruit and vegetables, cutting flowers, pruning, doing mindless factory work (and generally putting up with it) all over Israel.

There are also more interesting jobs available and these are sometimes allocated after a probationary period, to longer-staying volunteers. Being 'promoted' to a more interesting job will depend on your own efforts. You must let the work organiser know what you want and also let the person in charge of the relevant department know of your interest and enthusiasm for this particular project. It is important not to be put off by what may seem a lack of response to your request, and if at first unsuccessful, keep trying. You will be judged on your work record and your general attitude.

You will be expected to accept your allocated job without complaint although if you have a particular problem, efforts will be made to give you more compatible work if it is available. Your work will be allocated each evening by the volunteers' organiser and a list placed on the volunteers' notice-board. The main categories of work are listed at the end of this chapter.

Working Hours and Time Off

The six-day, 42 to 48-hour week is broken by a free Saturday. After work the volunteers are free to do what they like. Most work takes place in the early mornings; The start may be as early as 5.00am in the south where it is hottest while 6.30am to 12.30pm is more usual in the north. Many volunteers therefore find themselves free from the afternoon through to the following morning.

aware of the possible dangers it is easy to make contact with and enjoy the friendship of Israelis and there will be no shortage of genuine invitations once you have made friends. Because of the national feeling of isolation, they are very interested to meet and talk to young people from overseas

HIV Tests

In 1988 a handful of kibbutzniks became infected with the HIV virus which it is assumed they caught from volunteers. Since then it has become standard on most kibbutzim to test volunteers for HIV on arrival. This is nearly always done free of charge.

Visiting Other Kibbutzim

If you have a close friends on another kibbutz, it may be possible to visit them for a short stay. Generally your friend will have to obtain permission first, and on arrival you will be expected for security purposes , to deposit your passport at the kibbutz office.

Long-term Stays

Generally, volunteers are not allowed to stay for long periods on the kibbutz. Experience has shown that long stay volunteers become so integrated that they feel they are due rights and a status to which they are not entitled; also long-stay volunteers have been known to form strong romantic attachments with the members and their final departure from the kibbutz can lead to emotional problems for the boy or girl left behind.

Duration of Stay

Most kibbutzim allow an official maximum stay of three months. Of course many volunteers stay for shorter periods of five to eight weeks. Some kibbutzim state that they prefer a minimum of eight weeks and each kibbutz may have its own conditions which it imposes to ensure volunteers stay the agreed period. Some, including Dafna, have taken to imposing a financial penalty of NS150. This sum is requested on arrival as a deposit and is not refunded (except in exceptional circumstances) if the volunteer leaves early.

Kibbutz Gan-Shmuel has a longer than usual minimum stay: a minimum stay of three months and preferably six months and only sometimes accepts volunteers if they can only stay two months.

Return Stays

If the volunteer wishes to make a return visit to the same kibbutz this is sometimes possible, especially if the volunteer has shown their value at work.

Visa Extensions

Please note that if you stay longer than three months in Israel your passport will be stamped with a visa extension which precludes travel afterwards to an arab country except (at the time of going to press) those of Egypt and Jordan with whom Israel has signed peace accords.

MAIN CATEGORIES OF WORK ON KIBBUTZIM

1. Service Jobs

Service work common to all kibbutzim:

Kitchens – girls and boys. Cleaning vegetables, preparing food, washing and cleaning equipment, cleaning and restocking store rooms and refridgerators.

Dining-room – girls and boys. Cleaning tables, washing walls, floors, windows; serving food, washing dishes either by machine or hand. Some work at weekends, evenings and holidays.

Laundry – girls. Ironing, mending and repairing, operating washing machines, folding clothes and sheets.

Children's Houses – girls. General cleaning, bedmaking, serving food, feeding small children, assisting nurses in minding and walking children.

Other Service Jobs – Boys and girls. Cleaning and restocking shops, supermarkets, clothes stores, toilets and showers, clubhouse, foodstore.

2. Farm Work

Cotton fields: weeding, operating planting machines, assembling and placing irrigation pipes, harvesting. Hard interesting work in hot conditions. Mainly boys.

Citrus (*Pardess*) Fruits: pruning trees, planting new trees, servicing irrigation pipes. Picking fruit in teams by climbing and moving ladders and operating fruit picking machines. Enjoyable work. Cold and wet in winter. Boys and girls.

Banana and date plantations: irrigation, spraying machines, picking. Routine work in hot conditions.Boys and girls.

Fruit packing houses: wrapping and packing fruit, usually on a conveyor belt. Competitive work in hot noisy conditions. Boys and girls.

Poultry: cleaning out manure. Cleaning feed and drinking equipment. Some night work packing live birds for market. One of the hardest jobs for those unused to farm life. Boys and girls.

Cows: milking, feeding, cleaning out manure, moving heavy feed bales, assisting at calving. Shift and night work only available to experienced teams. Hot, hard work. Boys and girls.

3. Factory Work

Most factories are modern, labour-saving operations making anything from underwear to microchips. The work normally entails operating simple machinery, cleaning and packing. For people with relevant skills, more interesting opportunities may be available.

Many factories are joint ventures between kibbutzim and so volunteers from more than one kibbutzim may be working there. Because factories normally run 24 hours a day you may be expected to work unusual hours and take your meals and breaks at the nearest kibbutz.

Garages and metal workshops. Servicing and repairing vehicles and equipment. Interesting work usually for boys with some experience.

Jewellery Workshops. Assembling jewellery in precious metals and semi-precious stones. Interesting work for girls with patience and aptitude for intricate work.

APPLICATION

Application From Your Own Country

Although it may not be necessary to fix up everything in advance from your own country, it is generally reassuring to do so especially if you are worried that by arriving in summer without a kibbutz place arranged in advance you risk being disappointed. If there is a glut of volunteers you could go instead to a moshav or look for other work in Israel (see *Moshavim and Other Work in Israel*).

There are kibbutz representatives in many countries to which prospective volunteers can apply for work. Sometimes they may be part of larger offices whose main task is to deal with *aliya* (immigration) to Israel, or they may be dedicated kibbutz placement offices like the Kibbutz Representatives in London. There are also ordinary travel agents like Felix Rejser of Fredericia, Denmark, or commercial operations like Project '67 of London and Tel Aviv which can arrange a place on a kibbutz through a personal contact with kibbutzim or their organisations. The age range for kibbutz volunteers applying through all these organisations is 18-32 years.

All the above organisations will offer a complete package including flights and insurance. Deals offered by different organisations may vary slightly in cost. If you arrange a package in advance it is likely that you will find yourself on the same flight with a group of prospective volunteers and will be met at the airport in Tel Aviv by a representative of the organisation, or someone from the kibbutz. Some of the arrangements for meeting at the airport have proved rather haphazard in the past.

Vacancies on any kibbutzim will depend on the workload. The kibbutzim will know in advance which times their existing labour force will need to be supplemented by volunteers. Once the kibbutz knows when it will need volunteers it will, through its movement's organisation, inform kibbutz offices abroad of its requirements.

To make an application through a kibbutz representative in your own country, you should first ask for an application form. When it arrives there will be a medical questionnaire to complete. You will need to have the latter completed by a doctor. Generally you will require two written references from persons of standing. Once the application, medical certification and references have been returned to the kibbutz representatives you will have to ring them to arrange a time for an interview. In Britain those applying through Kibbutz Representatives should apply to their London office address below, in the first instance although interviews may take place in London, Glasgow or Manchester.

Disabled Volunteers

It has been possible in the past for volunteers with some types of disability to work on a kibbutz. However, as always when you have a disability you have to convince the interviewer that you are as good as, if not better than, any volunteer without a disability. The private organisation Project '67 has been sympathetic in the past to deaf volunteers. No allowances are made for disabilities so you have to convince the interviewer (a) you can work as hard and fast as anyone else; (b) you will not be a hazard to yourself or anyone else. Insurance might be an additional problem as you would have to let the insurers know and they are almost certain to charge an extra premium.

Insurance

Whilst on the kibbutz you will receive free first-aid medical attention, but the kibbutz will not be responsible for the expense of hospitalisation, personal accident or loss of belongings. It is therefore essential to have private insurance. This can be arranged through the kibbutz application office or in Israel. If you are travelling independently, there are insurance companies which offer policies aimed at 'the backpacker market' and will cover you for casual work. However, most ordinary travel insurance bought from high street travel chains will not cover you for any kind of work. If you do not want the deal offered by Kibbutz Representatives you should check that any other insurance covers you (a) for working and (b) that they have a correspondent/representative office in Israel.

Club Direct: Dominican House, St John's Street, Chichester, W Sussex (01234-817766/www.clubdirect.co.uk). Work is covered provided that it does not involve using 'heavy machinery.' Year-long cover available.

Columbus Travel Insurance: 17 Devonshire Square, London EC2M 4SQ; tel 020-7375 0011. Detailed cover, or a basic medical cover only. Year-long available.

Downunder Worldwide Travel Insurance: 3 Spring Street, Paddington, London W2 3RA; 0800-393908. Backpacker policy which covers working holidays.

Leisurecare Insurance Services: Shaftesbury Centre, Percy Street, Swindon, Wilts.; tel 01793-750150. Policy includes working holidays.

Travel Insurance Club: 0800 163518; www.travel insurance club.co.uk Includes working holidays.

Wallach & Company: 107 West Federal Street, P.O.B. 480, Middleburg, VA 22118-0480; 1-800-237-6615; www.wallach.com A company which specialises in insurance for Americans living overseas.

Other Charges

In addition to the cost of the flights and insurance you will probably have to pay a small administration charge and all your expenses such as visiting London for the interview, the first night at a hostel in Tel Aviv, the costs of getting to the kibbutz and the fee for a working visa (currently $20 for up to three months' stay; plus $40 for an extension after three months).

Israeli Government Kibbutz Representatives Abroad

Britain

The Jewish Agency, Aliya and Kibbutz Department, Balfour House, 741 High Road, North Finchley, London N12 0BQ; tel 0208446 2266; fax 020-8446 4419. Ask for Sylvia Peleg, Aliya Department.

Kibbutz Representatives: 1a Accommodation Road, Golders Green,London NW11 8ED; tel 020-8458 9235; fax 020-8455-7930; e-mail enquiries@kibbutz.org.uk

Zionist Youth Movement (Takam), 11 Upper Park Road, Salford, Manchester M7 OHY; tel 0161-740 2864. This office no longer acts as a general kibbutz volunteer recruiter. It accepts only members of the Young Zionists organisation and arranges Ulpan for them on kibbutzim of the Takam movement.

United States of America

Kibbutz Program Center: Fourth Floor, 110 East 59th Street, New York, NY 10022, USA; tel 800-247 7852 (toll free USA); tel 212-318 6130; fax 212-318 6134; e-mail kibbutzdsk@aol.com Represents all kibbutzim in Israel.

Kibbutz Aliya Desk: 6505 Wilshire Blvd, 816, Los Angeles, California 90048; tel 213-782-0504; fax 213-655-1827.

Israel Aliya Center (Kibbutz): 4200 Biscayne Blvd., Miami, Florida 33137.

Israel Aliya Center: Suite 1020, Statler Office Building, 20 Providence Street, Boston MA 02116.

Kibbutz Aliya Desk: 6600 West Maple Road, West Bloomfield, Michigan 48033;

U.A.H.C.: 838 Fifth Avenue, New York 10021; tel 212-249-0100; fax 212-517 7863.

Canada
Kibbutz Aliya Desk: Israel Experience Centre, 1 Carré Cummings Square, Montréal, Québec H3W 1M6; tel 514-345-6444; fax 514-345 6418; e-mail MIEC@total.net
Israel Aliya Center: 950 West 41st Avenue, Vancouver B.C. V5Z 2N7; tel 604-257 5141.
Israel Program Center: 151 Chapel Street, Ottawa KIN 7Y2; tel 613-789-5010.

Australia
Israel Information Centre: Kibbutz Programme, 61 Woodrow Avenue, Yokine 6060, Perth, W.A.; tel 08 92768730; fax 08-92768330.
Kibbutz Programme: 146 Darlinghurst Road, Darlinghurst 2010, Sydney, New South Wales; tel 02-360 6300; fax 02-360 5124; e-mail szcnsw@tmx.com.au
Kibbutz Programme Desk: 308 Hawthorn Road, Caulfield 3162, Melbourne, Victoria; tel 03-9272 5531; fax 03-9272 5540; e-mail zfaaz@netspace.net.au

Austria
The Jewish Agency: Desider Friedmannplatz 1/2/a, 1010 Wien; tel 01 5330323; fax 01 4789437.

New Zealand
Wellington Zionist Society: Post Box 27156, Wellington; tel/fax 04-384 4229.
Kibbutz Desk; 528 Parnell Road, Post Box 4315, Auckland; tel 09-309 9444; fax 09-373 2283.

Other Agents

Below is a list of tourist offices/travel agents which are run by the Israeli government, or which are travel agents which cooperate with the kibbutz movements.

Austria
Amichai: Dollinergasse 5/2/16, 1190 Vienna.

Belgium
Desk Kibboutz: Bureau des Volontaires, 68 Ave Ducpetiaux, 1060 Brussels, Belgium; tel 02-538 10 50.

France
Objectif Kibbutz: 15 rue Beranger, 75003 Paris.
Hachomer Hatsair: 12 rue Mulet, Lyon 69000.
Dror-Habonim: 8 rue Idrac, Toulouse 31000.
Dror-Habonim: 32 rue Estelle, Marseille 13001.

Germany
Vereinigte Kibbutzbewegung: Savignystrasse 49, 6600 Frankfurt/Main 17; tel 069-740151; fax 069-745860.

The Netherlands
K-Tours Kastelenstraat 268, 1082 Amsterdam, tel 20-6463331; fax 20-6464655.

Oppenheim Travel: Cronenburg 154, 1081 GN Amsterdam; tel 20 4042040; fax 20 4044055.

Scandinavia
Felix Rejser; Korskaervej 25, 7000 Fredericia, Denmark; tel 75 92 20 22; fax 75 92 20 11. Organises kibbutz volunteer packages.
Svekiv: Svenska Kibbutzvänner, Box 14216, 10440 Stockholm; tel 08-6609393; fax 08-6630102. Organises kibbutz packages for volunteers.

To obtain the addresses of commercial organisations specialising in kibbutz volunteer groups in your country, you can enquire from any Aliya (immigration to Israel) organisation or the Israel Government Tourist Office. If neither of these exist in your country you may be able to obtain advice from the Israeli Embassy or Legation or by logging on to the kibbutz website (www.kibbutz.org.il).

Private Organisations in England

In England the main private organisations sending volunteers to kibbutzim are:

Project 67 Ltd.; 10 Hatton Garden, London EC1N 6AH (near Chancery Lane tube station); tel 020-7831 7626; fax 020-7404 5588. Project has been organising working holiday visits to Israel for about 33 years and in that time over 40,000 clients have passed through their office. They also have an office in Tel-Aviv which is essentially a travel agent that can arrange return and onward flights, additional information and advice such as how to reach the kibbutz or moshav to which you have been allocated. Their price includes return London/Tel Aviv flights, guaranteed kibbutz or moshav placement, initial registration fee and the facilities of the Project Office in Tel Aviv (94 Ben Yehuda Street, Ground Floor Shop; tel 03-5230140/5230845; fax 03-5247474). As well as arranging return flights, change of kibbutz or moshav (subject to availability), renewing insurance and giving general advice to travellers, the Tel Aviv office can be used as a forwarding address, baggage store and can arrange tours to Egypt and Jordan, and advice on onward travel and excursions throughout Israel and the Mediterranean. Once registered, the price includes the above services from the Tel-Aviv office for the duration of stay in Israel up to one year.

Transonic Travel: 10 Sedley Place, London W1R IHG; tel 020-7409 3535; fax 020-7409 0030. Transonic organises kibbutz and moshav places. There is a registration fee of about £35 and flights cost from about £100 one-way and from about £200 for an open return valid for a year. Volunteers can take a minibus transfer from the airport in Tel Aviv to an overnight hostel for an additional charge of about £7. Compulsory health insurance costs about £45 for up to a year's cover and is payable in Tel-Aviv. In addition there is a £25 administrative charge payable to the Volunteers' office in Tel-Aviv. This is refundable by the kibbutz. Total minimum cost with a one-way flight is just over £200; return flight to the UK from £200. Minimum volunteer stay is two months.
     Transonic will also arrange registration only with a kibbutz (i.e. without travel arrangements) for £35.

Bridge in Britain Programme; Friends of Israel Educational Trust, 25 Lyndale Avenue, London NW2 2QB; tel 020-7435 6803; fax 020-7794 0291; Sponsorship trust which enables 12 school leavers a year to go to Israel (including on a kibbutz working visit for five months) all for free. Bursaries are awarded to the writers of the best essays on the subject of why they want to spend time in Israel.

Application From Your Own Country Direct to a Kibbutz

Writing directly to a kibbutz is not encouraged unless you are a return volunteer. However, if you have a particular kibbutz in mind, and since neither the Kibbutz Representatives or the other organisations can guarantee a place on the kibbutz of your choice, it is worth trying. Where a kibbutz has indicated that it will accept written applications direct, this is indicated in the individual kibbutz listings at the back of this book. You should address your enquiry to the Volunteer Organiser, or that person's name if known, and the kibbutz address including the mobile post office and zip code. Once the kibbutz has replied accepting you for the dates requested, you can make travel arrangements through a specialist such as Project '67 or Transonic, or by looking for cheap flights from London to Tel-Aviv in *Time Out, TNT* and other London magazines and newspapers including *The Evening Standard*. The travel company WST (45 Vivian Avenue, Hendon, London NW4 3XW; tel 0208-202 800; fax 0208-202 0805) has links with the Israeli air company Arkia and since 1999 has been operating regular charter flights from Heathrow to Tel Aviv; also flights from Manchester, Gatwick and Luton. In 1999, by ringing around, the cheapest one way fare on offer in low season was £99. The Kibbutz Representatives will also arrange flight only deals. Remember that if you travel to Israel on a one-way ticket, you are likely to have problems with immigration unless you have a reasonable sum of money (£300/$450) on you in cash or travellers cheques. Even if you have a return ticket you are still strongly advised to take a sum of not less than £175/$260 as otherwise you are unlikely to be allowed into Israel, or at best only allowed to stay for two weeks.

On arrival in Israel, you should pay a visit to the Working Visitor office of the Takam and Ha'artzi movements (Kibbutz Programme Centre, Takam-Artsi, 18 Frischman Street, P.O. Box 3167, Tel-Aviv 61030; tel 03-524 6156; fax 03-523 9966) which is on the corner of Ben Yehuda Street; open from Sunday to Thursday from 8am to 2pm. You should take with you a letter of acceptance from the kibbutz, your passport and medical certificate and proof of funds (see above). You will have to take out the standard insurance policy which is valid for a year, is transferable between kibbutzim, and between kibbutzim and moshavim. You will also have to pay a registration fee currently about £35/$50. The Kibbutz Volunteer centre will also give you instructions on how to reach the kibbutz if these have not already been sent to you by the kibbutz.

Application in Israel

The ease or difficulty in finding a place on a kibbutz after arriving on spec in Israel has varied considerably over the years according to the various crises which seem to punctuate Israel's existence. The manager of the KPC, Rina Keren says they receive hundreds of e-mails and faxes from potential volunteers and 'all are answered.' According to Rina, volunteers are needed all year but that 'sometimes in July and August there are waiting lists, but only for a few days.'

As there so many variables influencing the vacancy situation, the most sensible approach is probably to contact the kibbutz in which you are interested and obtain the promise of a place. You can also consult the KPC on the general vacancy situation. Note that the KPC will not reserve a place on a specific kibbutz or in a specific region prior to your arrival in Israel.

In July and August kibbutzim take all kinds of organised groups of volunteers from abroad, Israeli high school pupils and older students, as well as those with a few months to spare before military service. Most of these take priority over the independent volunteer. The summer months are also the hottest, when many volunteers find the heat difficult to cope with and work in. The best time for vacancies is normally September through to May.

If you decide to turn up on the spot, it is advisable to visit or telephone the the kibbutz offices in Tel-Aviv as soon as possible as they will be able to give you up-to-date information on the vacancy situation. Remember that the office is obliged to give precedence to volunteers who have come through an overseas Kibbutz Representative. Another point to remember is that kibbutz and other offices in Israel open from Sunday to Thursday and are closed Friday and Saturday. So, if your flight arrives on a Thursday afternoon you will have to wait two whole days (and three nights) before turning up at the offices.

Volunteers who turn up on spec pay the same registration fee (120 shekels in Israeli money), as those who have come through a representative.

When you turn up at the Kibbutz Programme Centre in Frishman Street you will need:

1. A valid passport.
2. $52 for the registration fee (valid for 12 months).
3. $55 for health and hospitalisation insurance tailored to kibbutz volunteers.
Note that volunteers who already have their insurance arranged in their own country need to send evidence of this to the KPC in advance to make certain it gives appropriate cover.
4. Personal funds of $250 and a return ticket, or additional funds to cover a ticket. In the event that there is a sudden shortage of volunteers and the kibbutzim are desperate, it has been known for the amount of money a volunteer is, or is not carrying, to be irrelevant.
5. 2 passport photos. When you arrive at the kibbutz or the KPC you will need two passport photos for the working visa which currently costs $17 and will be arrange by the kibbutz or the KPC.

Turning up at the Kibbutz Gate

Officially this is not encouraged, but some prospective volunteers have found themselves passing a kibbutz and have called in to ask if they need volunteers. Security is strict in Israel and this is one reason why this practice is not encouraged. You stand the best chance if you know someone who is already working on the kibbutz or a former volunteer who has recommended you, but this may not always be an essential requirement particularly if the kibbutz is short of volunteers. If you do get taken on in this way, the kibbutz will square things with the kibbutz office in Tel-Aviv and may even send you there to register. In any case they will deal with your documents and send your passport to the nearest passport office for a working visa stamp for which you will be charged (see above).

If you want to move to another kibbutz you can enquire directly at other kibbutzim for a place. If possible get a letter of recommendation from the kibbutz you have been working on, otherwise you should have a plausible story as to why you have left.

The Kibbutz Movements

There are three main kibbutz movements:

Takam (United Kibbutz Movement) has its headquarters in Tel-Aviv and shares the volunteer recruiting office with the Ha'artzi Movement at The Kibbutz Program Center (Volunteer Department, 18 Frishman Street/Corner of Ben Yehuda, Tel Aviv 61030; tel +972-3 527 8874; fax +972 3 524 6156; e-mail kpcvol@inter.net.il).
Takam is the largest kibbutz movement representing about 70% of kibbutzim. Although a total of about 120 kibbutzim belong to Takam about 20 of these do not take volunteers. Ten kibbutzim take 170-220 volunteers a year, forty take from 100 to 150 volunteers; fifty take about 50 and the the rest fewer than 50 a year.
Most Takam kibbutzim support the peace movement and the necessary territorial concessions.

Hakibbutz Ha'artzi was established in 1927 and has a membership of 85 kibbutzim plus an additional ten or so kibbutzim which are not members but which have their affairs handled by this movement. Ha'artzi shares a volunteer recruiting office with the Takam movement (see above). The Ha'artzi are more left-wing than Takam, but like them are supporters of the peace process and territorial concessions.
About 80 kibbutzim in this movement take volunteers. The busy period is from September to the end of May. From September crops such as bananas, avocados, citrus fruits, winter vegetables and flowers are harvested and many volunteers are required. Whatever time of year you turn up, precedence is given to those who have made arrangements with the kibbutz or the Ha'artzi office in advance.

Hakibbutz Hadati is the minority religious movement, which has its offices at (7 Dubnov Street, 64732 Tel Aviv; tel 03-695-7231; fax 03-695-7039). Hadati represents the sixteen religious kibbutzim who will only take orthodox Jewish volunteers. These kibbutzim are: Alumim, Be'erot Yitzak, Beit Rimon, Ein Hanatziv, Ein Tzurim, Kfar Etzion, Kvutzat Yavneh, Lavi, Ma'aleh Gilboa, Meirav, Migdal Oz, Rosh Tzurim, Saad, Sde Eliyahu, Schluchot and Tirat Tzvi.

Cheap Accommodation in Tel Aviv

If you are unlucky enough to find yourself waiting a few days in Tel Aviv until you are placed you will probably need somewhere cheap to stay. Fortunately, there is a good selection of hostels in Tel-Aviv. Unfortunately, Tel Aviv hostels are a favourite target for thieves and security arrangements can be appallingly lax – e.g. a 'safe' will be a cupboard with a padlock that almost anyone could break into. You are strongly advised to ask to see the safe, if there is one, and to personally see your (hopefully few) valuables stowed in it.
Some hostels like the Gordon have been around a while and new ones appear faily regularly. Here is a selection:

The Annex: 53 Allenby Street (opposite the Carmel Market); tel 03-6201207; fax

03-6200196. Dorm beds cost NIS30 per night, and NIS 185 weekly. There is also a Travel Centre on the premises (fax 03-5275618).

Dizengoff Square Hostel: 13 Ben Ami Street; tel 03-5225184; fax 03-522 51 81; e-mail herzl@trendline.co.il website www.dizengoff.hostel com Large, central hostel with a twice weekly discotheque. Dorms NIS35, Rooftop NIS33.

48 Hayarkon Street Hostel: tel 03-5168989; fax 03-510 3113. One of the newer dormitory hostels in a converted school building. Prices include breakfast.

Gordon Inn 17 Gordon St., corner of Ben Yehuda; tel 03-5238239; fax 03-5237419; e-mail sleepin@inter.net.il Website www.PSL.CO.IL/GORDON-INN). One of Sleep in Israel Ltd.'s well-run guest houses/hostels (i.e. same management as the Gordon and No 1 hostels). 31 rooms (including dormitories). Dorm beds about NIS 70. Has lively café/bar open until 2am on the premises.

No 1 Hostel (4th Floor, 84 Ben Yehuda St, Tel-Aviv 63435; tel 03-523-7807; fax 03-5237419; e-mail sleepin@inter.net.il). Dorm beds about NIS 30.

Gordon Hostel (2 Gordon St, Tel Aviv 63458; tel 03-5229870; fax 03-5237419) corner of Ha-Yarkon St, very near the beach. There is no curfew, reception is 24-hour and there is a roof-top bar. Bus 222 from airport stops opposite. Bus 4 from the Central bus station, bus 10 from the train station. Great party atmosphere but not ideal for those who value their sleep. Four to eight-bed dorm accommodation NIS33.

The Office: 57 Allenby Street; tel 03-528 99 84 or 525 70 70. Cheap and friendly. Dorms NIS25. Rooftop NIS25. Live local bands every evening.

Hotel Josef: 15 Bograshov Steet (off Ben Yehuda Street) no longer a hostel. Rents rooms only on a long-term basis. Also operates the Annexe (see above).

Hotel Nes Ziona: 10 Nes Tziona Street (off Ben Yehuda Street); tel 03-510 60 84. Generally reckoned a quiet escape from the hurly burly. Small dorms cost $12-20 and singles from $30. Use of kitchen facilities.

Momo's Hostel: 28 Ben Yehuda Street; tel 03-5280955; fax 03-5280797. One of the oldest hostels. Dorm beds from NIS35. Internet access and e-mail for guests and non-guests (see *Telecommunications* for details.

Seaside Hostel: 20 Trumpledor Street; tel 03-6200513; fax 03-5256965. Dorm beds NIS35. Roof beds NIS30. Mainly long-termers as opposed to travellers.

Sea & Sun Hostel; (62 Ha-Yarkon St; tel/fax 517 3313; fax 517 3562. One of the youngest hostels. On the corner of Nes Tziona. Dorms cost NIS35. Has a great view of the sea. Dorm beds from NIS35.

Travellers Hostel (47 Ben Yehuda Street; 63341 Tel Aviv; tel +972 3-5232451 & 5272108; fax +972 3-5237281; e-mail travhost@inter.net.il website www.travellers-hostel.co.il Dates from 1992. Air-conditioned sleeping throughout. Dorm beds NIS36 (about US$9). Rooms from NIS140 ($35) to NIS180 ($45).

Old Jaffa Hostel: 8 Olei Zion Street, Old Jaffa; tel 03-682 23 70; fax 682 23 16; e-mail ojhostel@shani.net A bit out of the way in the atmospheric area of Old Jaffa, and attracts a hippie clientele. You can sleep on the roof for NIS22, Dorms cost NIS29 and single rooms NIS70. Use of kitchen facilities is free. expensive. Cheapest double room is about NIS120 (£20).

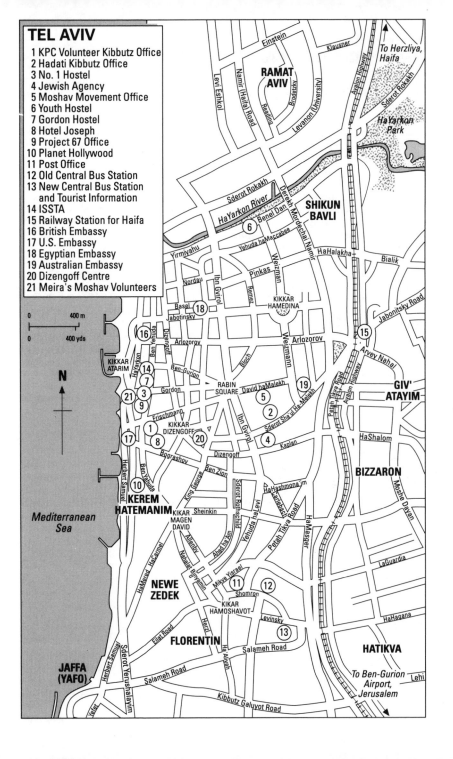

ULPAN AND OTHER KIBBUTZ PROGRAMMES

There are currently 67 kibbutzim operating Hebrew ulpan courses in conjunction with the Jewish Agency for Israel (Dept. of Information and Absorption, Jerusalem; fax +972 2 235328).

The object of these courses is to give young adults, thinking of settling in Israel or, wishing to experience life in Israel a working knowledge of Hebrew and an understanding of the Jewish way of life and history, while living and working on a kibbutz.

Course Description

Courses last $5^1/2$ months; there are 15-25 students per class; and the week is divided into 24 class hours and 33 working hours. Classwork consists of instruction in basic conversational Hebrew, simple reading of texts and newspapers, lectures on Israel and Judaism, seminars on contemporary events and educational tours. A few kibbutzim offer more advanced levels of Hebrew. For higher levels of Hebrew instruction, it is possible to study in one of the large city ulpanim.

The ulpan student works six hours a day; somewhat less than a volunteer worker, although all students are expected to take their work seriously.

Akiva Netanya (P.O. Box 6086, Netanya 42160; tel 09-8352312; fax 09-865 29 19) offers a seaside Ulpan for students from all around the world and combines studies with cultural activities. Varying costs.

Kibbutz Beerot Yitzchak (Doar Beerot Yitzchak 60905; fax +972-3-9334991) runs Ulpan twice a year beginning January or July for tourists or *Oleh* aged $17^1/2$ to 28. The cost $475 excluding flights, insurance and registration fees.

If you are particularly keen to be in Jerusalem you can enquire about the following Ulpanim:

Beit Ha-Noar Ha'Ivri: 105 Ha-Rav Herzog, Jerusalem 92622; tel 02-6789441; fax 02-678 86 42.

Moadon Ha'Oleh: 9 Alkalai Street; tel 02-563 37 18.

Accommodation

Ulpan students usually live in a part of the kibbutz set aside for them, sometimes in a complex with classrooms and study areas, although apart from study hours they live and work as an integral part of the kibbutz, sharing in all its normal activities.

Eligibility

The programme is designed mainly for Jewish students, and includes additional seminars, lectures and travel on Jewish topics. It is open to both tourists and new immigrants. Tourists pay a $300 registration fee; and new immigrants do not pay a fee. Non-Jewish students can also consider the Working Hebrew Scheme (see below).

Age limits are from $17^1/2$-35 and singles or couples without children are accepted.

Students normally receive the same material benefits as volunteers including routine and emergency medical care, emergency dental care and hospitalisation for accidents and non-chronic illness.

The kibbutz assumes no responsibility for valuables not deposited for safe keeping or for contact lenses. You are advised to insure all valuables.

Sometimes a volunteer becomes so integrated into the kibbutz that they consider becoming a permanent member. If the kibbutz accepts this idea in principle, then the first step to becoming an Israeli citizen, would be to enrol on an Ulpan course.

All of the non-religious kibbutzim are non-kosher. Observant Jews or those interested in becoming acquainted with religious life may choose to study on a religious kibbutz.

From abroad, applicants should contact the Jewish Agency representative in their country. In the United Kingdom apply to The Jewish Agency for Israel (Balfour House, 741 High Road, Finchley, London N12 OBQ; tel 020-8446 2266).

In Israel further details can be obtained from the Information and Service Center, Jewish Agency for Israel (37 King George Street, Tel Aviv; tel 03-293266).

The Israel au pair agency, Au Pair International (2 Desler Street, Bnei Brak 51507; tel 03 619 0423; fax 578 5463) can provide Ulpan addresses for those wanting to study Hebrew.

When applying in Israel, it is useful to have either a recommendation from the Jewish Agency representative in your own country or letters of introduction from Jewish leaders in your home community.

For Further Advice

Young adults interested in exploring the opportunities for an extended stay in Israel, in studying in a formal or informal setting, in volunteering, in doing an internship, travelling, or who are considering changing their status, are invited to contact the Information and Service Center in Tel Aviv (address above). The office provides personal callers with a free counselling service on a wide-range of topics, for tourists and potential immigrants alike. Written enquiries should be addressed to the Information and Service Center at the above address.

The Working Hebrew Scheme

Whereas the Kibbutz Ulpan is primarily for anyone thinking of becoming a candidate for membership of a kibbutz, there is an alternative organised by the Takam movement for those who just want to learn some Hebrew and deepen their understanding of Israel and Jewish life. Called the Working Hebrew Scheme, it lasts for three months. Studying takes place twelve hours a week in time taken out of the volunteer's working hours. The course is aimed at total beginners, even though all lessons are conducted in Hebrew. In other respects participants are treated as volunteers.

There are plans to expand this programme from the two kibbutzim participating at the time of press. At present there are 30 places for participants from around the world and they are quickly filled. Acceptance is based on suitability.

From the UK, participation in the Working Hebrew Scheme can be arranged through the Kibbutz Representatives in London (tel 020-8458 9235). The course fee is £185 in addition to the normal kibbutz registration fee, making a total of £245 for both. You can arrange a place on the Working Hebrew Scheme once you are in Israel (at the Kibbutz Program Centre), but it could take a few days to organise even if there is a place.

Other Kibbutz Programmes

From the USA, Ulpan and other kibbutz programmes can be organised through the Kibbutz Aliya Desk & Program Center in New York (Fourth Floor, 110 East 59th Street, NY 10022; tel 212 318-6130; fax 212 832-2597). As well as Ulpan (five months) the most interesting of which are the project Oren Programmes which combine the study of Hebrew, work on a kibbutz and special workshops in archaeology, fine arts, Jerusalem and environmental studies and even an active adventure and work programme called the Kibbutz Safari. Contact the above office in the first instance for the telephone number of the nearest regional kibbutz information centers of which there are ten. In the UK the Kibbutz Representatives deal with Oren.

KIBBUTZ GLOSSARY

Brikha The swimming pool used mainly in the afternoons and open usually from May to October/November.

Candidate
Candidacy to become a kibbutznik usually lasts two years. Candidates have fewer rights than kibbutzniks.

Colbo
The kibbutz shop which sells all basic necessities. Since most kibbutzim now have individual dwellings for members, colbos have become more like supermarkets. The prices should be lower than regular supermarkets because there is no VAT.

Gurrin
A group of soldiers who serve together and do part of their service in the army and part on a kibbutz. The idea is that some will want to stay and become candidates thus ensuring the future of the kibbutz.

Hader Okhel
The kibbutz dining room. At one time everyone on the kibbutz ate together in the kibbutz dining room and it was free. More and more the dining room is being turned into a commercial enterprise offering average food for less that it would cost to make it yourself. However, the food on some kibbutzim can be so awful that you end up paying a fortune in the kibbutz shop.

Kibbutznik
A member of a kibbutz. To be accepted as a member the candidate has to be voted into membership by all the other members.

Maraluz Meshek
The kibbutz secretary who is generally looked upon as the leader of the kibbutz although he or she can only act on a majority vote by other kibbutzniks. This is the problem-solving job of the kibbutz.

Mahk-Besa
The kibbutz laundry which provides everyone on the kibbutz with work clothes and a laundry and repair service. Some kibbutzim have started to charge for the laundry service.

Mazkirut
This is the office block of the kibbutz where business and administration offices are located.

Mifal
Hebrew for factory. Most kibbutzim now have one or more factories.

Miklat
The kibbutz bomb/air raid shelter. Every kibbutz has one as a precaution against an escalation of violence from hostile neighbouring countries.

Musakh
The kibbutz garage. All the kibbutz machinery and transport is maintained in the musakh. It is also the usual gathering place before work where you get your lift to the workplace (field, plantation, vineyard and so on).

Sakhir
Hebrew for salaried worker. Salaried workers are becoming more common on kibbutzim.

Taktsiv
Hebrew for allowance. This is the system for calculating the the volunteer's account at the end of each month. It shows how much earned and how much spent (and how much in debt if you have been too extravagant at the kibbutz shop).

Tivot Doar
These are the pigeon holes where mail and all written communications within the kibbutz are filed. There is always one marked 'volunteers'.

Toranut
Hebrew for duty. As a volunteer you will be expected to do one or more duties in the kibbutz. This can be anything from working in the dining room on the evening meal to milking the cows at 3am.

Useful Publications on Kibbutzim

Material helpful to the prospective volunteer to give a better insight into into the kibbutz way of life is available from the Federation of Kibbutz Movements, Department of Documentation and Information, 5 Kaplan Street, Tel Aviv. Some of the standard publications are:

Kibbutz – the Way We Live (Joel Magid)
Kibbutz Today (Moshe Kerem)
Schedmot The cultural forum of the Kibbutz Movement.Available on subscription
     from the Kibbutz Desk in New York and Takam, 10 Dubnov Street, Tel Aviv.

Although many books have been written about the sociology and psychology of the kibbutz, you may have difficulty in finding them in bookshops. However, the following titles offer an in depth guide into aspects of kibbutz life should be available, though you may have to order them:

An Alternative Lifestyle: Editor David Leichman
The Kibbutz Movement: A History, Part One: Henry Near (Oxford University Press).
Kibbutz in a Market Society: Stanley Maron (available at Yad Tabenkin, Ramat
     Efal 52960, Israel.

Moshavim and Other Work

Moshavim

Origins, Ideology & Organisation

'Moshav' literally means a seat, and so, a place that is settled. The forerunner of all moshavim is considered to be Petah Tiqwa founded in 1878. This was known as a 'moshava' and was based on the principles of equality and mutual aid. However, Petah Tiqwa has long since outgrown its origins and became a full-sized town (situated north east of Tel Aviv).

Following the founding of the kibbutz movement in 1909, moshavim were seen as an alternative to the entirely communal life and collective agriculture of the kibbutz. A breakaway group of settlers left their kibbutzim and began two moshavim, in the Jezreel Valley in 1921. Their aim was to encourage individual initiative within a co-operative. The idea spread and there are now two main groups.

Jewish immigration to Palestine from Germany before the Second World War, led to the creation of K'farim Shitufi'im; 'k'far' meaning village, 'shituf' co-operation. These settlements were based on the middle-class principle of private ownership but acted co-operatively in the matters of consumption and selling produce. There are about 50 moshavim shitufi in Israel today.

Moshavim Ovdim, ('ovdim' meaning workers), of which there are more than 325, are smallholder' settlements based upon individual initiative and profit; also mutual aid and co-operation. The land is leased from the State and an equal area is allotted to each family. Families decide individually what crops to grow, how many hours to work, and additionally how to spend their income; they can own homes, farm machinery, tractors and livestock. This kind of settlement includes co-operative marketing, and sometimes a collective crop. Most belong to the Moshav movement.

Moshavim Ovdim and Shitufi'im are the best known of Israel's 450 moshav settlements. The distinction between them and the kibbutzim is that the kibbutz is basically socialist while the moshav is a capitalist operation; also the lifestyle of members on moshavim is more private than on a kibbutz. However, now that kibbutzim are abandoning the communal dining room and separate accommodation for children, this distinction is less valid than it once was.

Increasingly moshavim are succumbing to industrialisation as part of the process of achieving a higher standard of living. Over two decades have passed since six moshavim Ovdim and Shitufi'im or collective moshavim ceded from the moshav movement, set up their own framework, and allied themselves to the kibbutz movement with whose aspirations they felt more at home. Also at that time they needed expert financial advice in the field of industry which the kibbutzim have through their organisation. The moshav movement, with its origins in agriculture was unable to provide such help, but has since co-founded a company for the industrialisation of moshavim.

The moshav movement still views the remaining collective moshavim as being affiliated to the Moshav Movement within the framework known as the 'Inter-current Commission of the Collective Moshavim'.

About 3.4% of the population live on moshavim. Each moshav elects its own council (*vaad* in Hebrew) of 15-20 members, who are responsible for economic, social and municipal affairs. From and by this council is elected the village committee which is the executive. Under the council are other committees responsible for education and culture. Each moshav has its own kindergarten, but several normally share primary and secondary schools. Cultural activities such as yoga, folk dancing etc. usually take place in the club house (moadon) and again, several settlements may share a class.

Produce

About 40% of food consumed by Israelis is produced by moshavim and 55% of all agricultural exports are produced by moshavim, some of which is exported, especially during the winter, to northern European countries including Germany and Britain. Vegetables, fruit and flowers are produced for the home market and export; some farm cattle for milk and meat. Vegetables such as tomatoes are grown in vast plastic-covered hothouses or outdoors in fields, the 'soil' of which can be desert sand, which by a seeming miracle has become fertile. The miracle is caused by drip feeding, a method of irrigation using narrow, plastic piping which has small holes on the underneath through which water, laced with nutrients is fed to the roots of the plants. The flow of irrigation and nutrients is computer controlled.

Moshav crops include red and green peppers (capiscums) and aubergines (egg-plants) grown outdoors while cucumbers are produced in hothouses. Some moshavim produce strawberries and citrus fruits in winter, and melons, planted in winter are harvested during the spring. Production of vegetables continues during the summer. Flowers produced in winter include hothouse roses and chrysanthemums. Carnations can be grown outdoors in the south. This comprises the main specialist crops but moshav farmers can and do cultivate and rear almost anything. Ostrich farming is one of the latest specialities of both moshavim and kibbutzim.

Many more moshavim are however, becoming industrial and many have one or more factories sometimes shared by two or more moshavim.

Affiliations

Before applying to be a volunteer, readers may like to know the various groups to which moshavim belong and which to some extent influence the lives of their members. The largest group to which approximately two-thirds of moshavim belong is the Moshav Movement. Lastly, there are collective moshavim some of which belong to the movement, the rest being independent.

The Moshav Movement

This was set up in the 30's in order that new settlers could be organised and advised by existing ones. At the present time the M.M. acts as a co-ordinator bringing moshavim together in joint projects and representing moshavim in government and national institutions. It is also involved in the setting up of new moshavim. The Movement comprises four separate departments: one for social, cultural and educational matters, another for advice on financial planning; a third for practical help with same from a kind of merchant bank 'Ein Hay' and a mutual assistance fund 'Kerem Hamoshavim' for mortgages, insurance, savings and securities. The fourth is for purchasing on behalf of moshavim at special rates, and creates regional centres for marketing produce, slaughtering cattle and other wholesale operations.

Other Groups

About 150 moshavim are not members but belong to smaller organisations which co-operate with the Moshav Movement. These are as follows: Hepoel Hamizrahi – politico-religious, related to a party of that name; Ha'Ihud Hahaklai – independent villages mostly organised along moshav lines often with national- ity as a cohering force; Ha'Oved Hazioni – political, connected to a party of that name; Po'Alei Agudat Israel – an extreme movement upholding religious gov- ernment of the state; Herut – political, a conservative/liberal coalition.

The Diaspora scattered the Jews throughout the world and many different languages spoken by moshavim members serve to emphasise this fact. Mem- bers of individual moshavim often have a common linguistic or national back- ground such as Russian, Yemeni (from the southern part of the Saudi-Arabian peninsula). In the 1980's there was an increase in Anglo-Saxon (English-speak- ing) moshavim which attracted South African, American and British Jews while in the 1990s the emphasis was more on Russian and eastern European immigrants.

Collective Moshavim

There are more than 20 of these which have adopted the kibbutz means of pro- duction but in common with other moshavim have the family as the basic unit for consumption.

Christian Moshavim

Although this may seem a contradiction, there are one or two non-Jewish moshavim-type villages in Israel of which Nes Ammim in northwest Galilee is one. Its members, who are mainly Dutch and German, stress that theirs is not an evangelising community and volunteers sign an agreement that they will not indulge in any missionary activity while at Nes Ammin. Further details in the section *Other Work in Israel*.

Changes

Over the last decade the moshav associations have been going through a finan- cial crisis. The many small farms that make up an individual moshavim are in many cases not efficient enough to make a profit, and they have tended to lack effectiveness in the market place. Over a period of years, many moshav farmers who have found themselves in debt have resorted to other jobs to supplement their incomes; and some have left farming altogether. A number of moshavim have become financially successful by forming large collective farms, and some moshavniks have become successful private farmers. The continuing trend how- ever is for moshav associations (which act as credit cooperatives) to disband, and without the financial management provided by these associations moshavim are changing their status to that of ordinary villages.

These changes in the moshav affect the volunteer to the extent that these days, he or she is increasingly likely to find themselves working either for a large collective farm or a private farmer.

THE MOSHAV PAID VOLUNTEER

Comparison Between Moshav and Kibbutz Volunteers

Unlike the kibbutz volunteer, a volunteer on a moshav can expect to be paid a wage (albeit a modest one) plus a bonus on completion of an agreed minimum work period (usually three months). In addition there is almost unlimited potential for overtime (at a minimal rate). Apart from the potential to earn money, the benefits of moshavim can be hard to spot. A moshav volunteer works longer hours than a kibbutz volunteer. Although the basic working week is 8 hours a day, six days a week, nearly all volunteers work longer hours; ten hours a day is more usual and for overtime payment many volunteers work more than this; 75 hours a week is not unusual and even 14 hours a day (84 hours a week) for those who really wish to save up.

Also unlike kibbutz volunteers, those on moshavim work for individual families. They have to pay for, buy and prepare their own food. Often the kitchen facilities provided are very basic and after a long day's work it can be an unwelcome chore. Volunteers can eat what is grown on the moshav free but milk, bread and eggs have to be bought. Meat is so expensive in Israel that most volunteers become involuntarily vegetarian. Chicken may be affordable if you can get to a local market and if you don't mind watching your supper slaughtered in front of you. Surprisingly perhaps, some volunteers prefer to prepare their own food as the choice is greater especially if the moshav is near a local market. Those on isolated moshavim where the moshav shop is their only source will find it limited and expensive. More than one volunteer has complained that about half her wages went on buying food this way.

Other differences between moshav and kibbutz are that officially there are no volunteer trips arranged for moshav volunteers which gives them a greater degree of independence. However, those on isolated moshavim will not be in a position to extol this advantage as the day off is Saturday and all the buses stop from Friday evening to Saturday evening so they are likely to be stuck on the moshav with little to do except to drink their way into oblivion as is sadly often the case. Life on a moshav can be very quiet compared with all the volunteer partying that goes on at kibbutzim and a moshav can seem very bleak. One unfortunate volunteer was so brought down by his surroundings as to describe his moshav, way down south, as 'a hell hole at the end of the earth.'

Although moshav wages seem a pittance by western standards, they can seem a fortune to nationals of countries such as Thailand or Korea. Hundreds of male Thais are employed on some moshavim (including Zofar and Ein Yahav) on contracts of up to two years. Volunteers from other nations whom they vastly outnumber, work alongside them. This can be a hazard for female volunteers. As one put it '..on a Friday night you had 100 drunken, sexually frustrated Thais on the loose and it wasn't very safe to walk home by yourself.'

You may not always work alongside the volunteers with whom you share accommodation. Each volunteer is usually employed by a different family, especially if it is a small moshav and you will be working on your own or with contract labourers (e.g. Thais or Palestinians), or with the farmer on his or her own plot of land. This contrasts with the kibbutz volunteer who works alongside other volunteers.

It should be pointed out that these are the negative aspects of the moshav, but unfortunately they mar the experience for many moshav volunteers. It is true that some volunteers have come away from the experience having found on balance that the good points have outweighed the bad. Apart from the work which is never particularly enjoyable, these are generally those who have worked for a largely sympathetic farmer with whom they have managed to build up a relationship that does not relate entirely to the work, and they have been well looked after by the farmer and family. The farmer may pay a small allowance for food and invite you to dine at his home one evening a week, usually on Fridays. On moshavim near the Negev on the Jordanian border or near Palestinian-ruled Gaza fellow workers are usually Palestinians and Bedouin. They are very hospitable and will invite other workers to their homes or offer them a share of their midday meal.

Moshav volunteers generally regard themselves as the hard-bitten foreign legionnaires of volunteering as opposed to the pampered Swiss Guards of the kibbutz volunteers (though of course they may be ex-kibbutz volunteers themselves). As jobs on moshavim are generally sought by the more independent and experienced traveller who is working his or her way around a large part of the globe and needs funds to move to the next place, there is likely to be a more informed travel grapevine to tap into on a moshav than amongst kibbutz volunteers, who are more likely to be on their first trip abroad. It follows that on a moshav you are more likely to meet a wider range of types and characters including desperados and social misfits as well as the more amiable broke backpackers and they will come from as wide a range of national backgrounds as the kibbutz volunteers.

One final difference for moshav volunteers is that they will normally have to supply their own work clothes but again this is a generalisation – if you are are lucky the farmer will provide at least one set and they will be laundered for you.

Moshavim generally have similar facilities open to volunteers as there are on a kibbutz. Namely, a swimming pool, sports facilities and a bar/moadon.

Pay

The moshav wages are astoundingly low; 5-8 shekels (about £1-£1.30) an hour or NIS70 per 8-hour day. Taking a ten-hour day as the average working day on a moshav the average weekly rate is about £73 or £295 per month. The rate of the shekel is subject to more fluctuation than the dollar so volunteers who have the opportunity to convert their wages, which are usually paid at the beginning of the month, usually do so. It may be advantageous to do this on the black market rather than in a bank to avoid bank commission. The volunteer grapevine can usually supply the contacts.

Volunteers who stay the whole winter season (about four months) usually receive a bonus worth from one week's up to two months' wages. There is no standard basic wage for moshavim but you may find that the various volunteer offices have managed to achieve some kind of norm from the moshavim on their books. There is however likely to be variation of pay between moshavim and the lack of dependability of moshavim farmers in paying a reasonable rate for work and a substantial end of season bonus is apt to be a source of irritation and hardship for volunteers. There are of course always exceptions and some moshavim farmers go out of their way to ensure that their volunteers are well looked after and reasonably paid; it is just that they seem to be outnumbered by the other sort.

As one volunteer summed it up 'the experience of working on a moshav can be good or bad depending on which farmer you work for.' If you find that you are not compatible with the farmer you have been allocated you can approach the volunteer organiser for a transfer to another. If you want to change moshav see *Application* or the list of moshavim below.

Time Off

One day, besides Saturday (the Sabbath) is usually allowed per month. After two months the volunteer is entitled to a trip of two to three days. The moshav may arrange the trip or give a small allowance towards it. Volunteers should expect to accompany the family on any excursions they make for shopping and sometimes sightseeing.

The Volunteer Season & Working Hours

Moshavim need volunteers all year round but the busiest time is from November to April, the main agricultural season, which is geared to winter production. Workers rise at dawn, breakfast at 8am after two hours work and resume work until lunch time at midday (normally a two-hour break but can be one hour). After lunch there are a couple more working hours in the noon-day heat until 3pm or 3.30pm. In the winter the southern part of Israel is hot enough to work in shirt sleeves by mid-morning. In the north, especially on high ground it is much colder.

Accommodation

Accommodation for a moshav volunteer can be no more than a hut/shed in the farmer's garden. More typically it will be a hut shared with fellow workers. Some huts are more modern than others. You may be lucky enough to get reasonable beds and a kitchen with something more than a basic two-burner gas stove for six people.

Location of Moshavim

Moshavim can be found anywhere in Israel, but the majority of those taking large numbers of volunteers from Thailand and Korea, etc. are in the Jordan Valley which is in the West Bank, and in the south of the country in the Negev Desert, near Palestinian-ruled Gaza, and also the Arava Valley near Eilat. Moshavim in the south tend to be rather isolated. At night the desert can be very chilly. From May onwards the sun is merciless in these arid regions and although volunteers' accommodation is air-conditioned, many volunteers find the combination of high temperatures and lack of humidity unbearable and head up north or near the coast; there are a few moshavim on the coast north of Tel-Aviv and near Kinneret (Sea of Galilee).

The Work

This includes picking dead leaves and excess shoots from hothouse cucumbers and tomatoes, also twisting strings around the growing plants, cutting flowers in hothouses and outdoors, sizing, bunching and packing them; harvesting vegetables such as cucumbers, tomatoes which are grown both in and outdoors, peppers which grow very low down and involve a lot of bending or squatting and some vineyard work. Other tasks are planting and thinning seedlings for the spring harvest and grading vegetables in packing sheds. The vegetables are usually taken to a large depot outside the moshav for final packing. You may have to spray the plants using portable equipment consisting of a backpack of liquid insecticide or fungicide and a small motor which forces the liquid as spray through a hand-held nozzle. A special breathing mask is provided for the user who sounds like a very small aircraft with engine trouble as he or she progresses along the rows of plants.

While performing less noisy tasks, a personal stereo/radio carried about your person may help to while away some of the more tedious hours, especially if it can receive the BBC World Service.

Recreation

Whereas on a kibbutz the amusement of the volunteers is to some extent a joint effort between the volunteer organiser and the volunteers, on a moshav it is usually up to the volunteers to take the initiative to entertain themselves. Regrettably this all too often take the form of extended drinking sessions, but there are usually less nihilistic options available. Many moshavim have the same sports facilities as kibbutzim, namely pitches and equipment that can also be used by the volunteers. Organising games is one possibility for entertainment. Another is to frequent the moadon (club house) where there is usually a range of options (cable television, video etc). There are usually classes organised for the moshav members covering a variety of recreational activities including Israeli folk-dancing and yoga. Volunteers can also participate in these.

APPLICATION

Volunteer Eligibility & Insurance

Prospective volunteers must be aged 18-35 and have a medical certificate attesting to their sound physical and mental health. The minimum period of work usually eight weeks. It is essential to have insurance cover against loss of baggage, accident and hospitalisation as no moshav will accept you without this. Medical insurance can be arranged with the moshav offices on arrival. The policy is similar to that arranged for kibbutz volunteers.

Where to Apply in Your Own Country (except the UK)

You can try asking private agencies (i.e. not kibbutz aliya desks) that arrange kibbutz work if they also arrange moshav places. You can first contact the Moshav Movement in Israel to see if there is an agent in your country. In Germany, Vereinigte Kibbutzbewegung (Savignystrasse 78, 60325 Frankfurt; tel 069-740151; fax 069-745860) organises kibbutz and moshav work and accepts applicants from Germany and other areas including Scandinavia and Switzerland.

Application in the United Kingdom

There are two private companies in Britain dealing with this: Project 67 and Transonic Travel who work in cooperation with the Moshav Volunteers Centre in Tel Aviv.

Project '67: 10 Hatton Garden, London EC1N 8AH; tel 020-7831 7626; fax 020-7404 5588. Project has been organising working visits to Israel for over 30 years and in that time over 50,000 clients have passed through their offices. They also have an office in Tel Aviv which is essentially a travel agent which can arrange tours in Israel and book return and onward flights. While you are in Israel they can provide additional information and advice such as how to reach the moshav you have been allocated to, allow you to leave luggage on the premises and messages for fellow travellers. Their prices include return flight London-Tel Aviv, one placement on a moshav, initial registration fee, first night at a Tel-Aviv hostel and the facilities of the Project office in Tel-Aviv (Project '67, 1st Floor, 94 Ben Yehuda Street; ground floor shop; tel 03-5230140/5230845; fax 03-5247474), from £239 inclusive price. Insurance which includes work on a moshav or kibbutz costs £45 for up to eight weeks; up to three months £60, up to six months £85 and each additional month £22.

Transonic Travel: 10 Sedley Place, London W1R IHG; tel 020-7409 3535; fax 020-7409 0030. Deals with approximately 40 moshav volunteers a month. Accepts applications from nationals of the European Union, Australia, South Africa and America. Volunteers are expected to stay not less than two months and not more than one year. A registration fee of £35 is payable in addition to the flights (prices from £200 vary according to season) and insurance costs about £45 for up to a year's cover. The first night's stay in Tel-Aviv for those arriving on a night flight is not included, but volunteers are normally met on arrival at the airport.

Application in Israel

If you are in Israel you can go straight to the Moshav Volunteers Centre in Tel Aviv (see below) or one of the other agencies there that place volunteers. If there are many applicants it may take more than a day to be placed.If you have to stay overnight in Tel Aviv there are many hostels where you can get an inexpensive dormitory bed. A list of these can be found in the *Kibbutz* section under *Application in Israel*. The IYHF Youth Hostel (36 Bnei Dan Street; tel 5441748; fax 5441030) is in the northern residential area which is not very convenient for the Moshav offices and is more expensive at NIS 43 for a dorm. There are hostels on Ben Yehuda Street which is very near the moshav offices. However, Ben Yehuda is one of the main thoroughfares and is very noisy until late at night. Another convenient place to stay is the Hotel Joseph just off Ben Yehuda and is clean and cheap with friendly staff. Take a no 4 bus from the central bus station and ask the driver to put you off at Bugrashov Street. Usually it is not necessary to book in advance.

All the moshav offices keep the same office hours: Sunday to Thursday 9am to 3pm; closed Friday and Saturday except Project '67 which is also open on Fridays to midday.

The Moshav Movement Volunteer Centre

The majority of moshav requirements for volunteers are dealt with by the Moshav Volunteer Centre (19 Leonardo da Vinci Street, Tel-Aviv 64733; tel 03-6968335; fax 03-6960139).

Private Moshav Agencies in Israel

There are usually several private moshav volunteer offices in Tel-Aviv in addition to the Moshav Movement's own recruiting centre and they have a similar procedure for placing volunteers.

Meira's Volunteers (1st Floor, 73 Ben Yehuda Street, Tel Aviv 63435; tel 03-5237369/5238073/5243811; fax 03-5241604). Open Sunday to Thursday 9.30am to 3.30pm. Bus 4 from the central bus station or 10 from the train station.

You will hear about Meira's sooner rather than later. Meira is Meira Guy who originally worked at the Moshav Movement's recruiting office and then set up on her own in 1984. She also places kibbutz volunteers. In the past some of the moshavim to which volunteer's have been sent from Meira's have been, to say the least unwelcoming, but Meira says that this is no longer the case.

Volunteers coming through Meira's can contact her office in advance with their flight details and are usually met at the airport if they are arriving at night. If the flight arrives during her office hours (see above) volunteers can go straight to her office (bus 222 from the airport and ask to get off at Mapu Street/Hayarkon corner). Meira charges NIS250 for insurance and NIS 200 handling fee (refundable at the Moshav after 2 months).

Volunteers are asked to bring three passport photographs and a driver's licence (if they have one). She quotes a standard minimum salary (NIS 1,370 plus overtime at NIS 8.5). In the past volunteers sent to the south, which is desert and much hotter than the rest of Israel, have been paid slightly higher salaries as an incentive. After two months there is a cash bonus (NIS 170). Those who stay three months get a larger cash bonus. The minimum work period is usually two months.

Project 67: 1st Floor, 94 Ben Yehuda Street; tel 03-5230140; fax 03-5230845. Although they deal mainly with kibbutzim, Project will also place moshav volunteers.

Procedure for Being Placed

This is similar whichever moshav volunteer office you go to. Just before the moshav office opens a queue will probably have formed as such offices are often run by one person and the process can be rather slow. Usually volunteers are dealt with individually but a small group of three or four friends wanting to go to the same moshav may be dealt with together. Unfortunately, British volunteers may find themselves unpopular owing to the lager lout reputation of their fellow citizens which has preceded them. One British volunteer found that when, visiting the various offices on her own she was told in no uncertain terms that kibbutzim and moshavim did not want British volunteers because of their reputation for alcohol-induced vandalism. She found a way to beat this tiresome prejudice by going to another agency accompanied by some South Africans and was placed immediately as it was assumed she was also an innocuous South African. By the time the office took down her passport details and realised the mistake it was too late to cancel her placement.

As the placement offices are normally very busy there is not a lot of time for chat, but if the moshav to which you are allocated is not listed in this chapter, you may like to ask a few questions such as how many families there are on the moshav, what languages they speak, what type of work you will be expected to do, and whereabouts on the map the moshav is. Generally speaking the Jordan Valley is not a very comfortable area to go to as it is situated in the Israeli-occupied West Bank (areas west of the Dead Sea and about as far north of it as the

Jezreel Valley) and some settlers there are particularly fanatical and heavily armed. To return to the subject of recruiting volunteers: do not be surprised if, while you are waiting to be allocated to a moshav, a marauding representative from one of the moshavim, calls in at the office to siphon off a few impatient volunteers from the back of the queue for his moshav. This is not unknown!

Advertisements for Volunteers

From time to time, individual moshavim advertise for volunteers in the *Jerusalem Post*, a daily, English-language newspaper, and on the notice boards of various hostels. The purpose of such advertisements appears to be to enlist a large number of volunteers quickly, when there is a lot of work.

Security

Moshav settlements in sensitive areas are likely to be surrounded by a steel fence, usually double, with gates securely locked at night. Soldiers are on guard round the clock, reinforced by male moshav members on a rota basis especially at night. As far as the volunteer is concerned this amounts to a curfew. Nearly all settlers are armed and when they go outside the moshav they carry a gun, or there is a pistol in the glove compartment of the car. Members have their own keys, so if you wish to visit another moshav at night, you should arrange this with them in advance.

DETAILS OF SOME MOSHAVIM (NORTH TO SOUTH)

The Moshav office in Tel Aviv has a list of about 200 moshavim which take volunteers when needs must. There is nothing to stop you applying to the moshavim direct, but unlike kibbutzim there is usually no one person responsible for volunteers as they are employed by individual families. Probably the best person to contact is the moshav secretary.

Golan Heights

The area known as the Golan Heights lies east and north east of the sea of Galilee and were seized from Syria by Israel in the 1967 war. At the time of going to press Israel's evacuation of the Golan Heights and their return to Syria looked like being part of the 'permanent settlement' begun in 1993. There are about sixteen Israeli settlements in the Golan and their inhabitants have already mobilised their resistance to handing back the Golan. However, without the return of the Golan there is unlikely to be any normalisation of Israeli relations with Syria, so the Israeli government is going to be hard pushed to please the Golan settlers. For the time being however, there are volunteers required for:

(A)**Ramot**, D.N. Ramat-Hagolan 12490; tel 06-6732130.
Ramot means height. Moshav Ramot is on a plateau between two rivers about 7kms due north of Kibbutz Ein Gev. Originally the site of Scopir, a Syrian village. Ramot moved to its current site in 1973. Comprises 2,500 acres and belongs to the Moshav Movement.
Work: field crops, cows, turkeys, vegetables, tourism (guest house and hotel), orchards. Volunteers with a licence to drive tractors are particularly welcomed. Contact the Moshav Secretary.

Galilee

The Galilee is the northwestern area of Israel. The Jordan Valley runs down from the Sea of Galilee as far south as the Dead Sea.

(B)**Kfar Hittim**, D.N. Jordan Valley 15280; tel 06-6795921/2; fax 06-6732002. The land for the moshav was originally claimed in 1905. There was an attempted settlement in 1914 and two further unsuccessful attempts in 1924 and 1934. The moshav dates its foundation (by Bulgarian settlers) from 1936. It comprises about 2,000 acres farmed by 70 families. Kfar Hittim lies in the Lower Galilee, 7kms from Tiberias. It takes a small number of volunteers (usually five or six a year) who are employed on the camping site as cleaners, maintenance persons, waiting tables in the dining room etc. The period of work lasts from April to November and volunteers who can stay the whole season are welcomed with three months being the minimum. Volunteers housing is in old buildings and facilities for preparing food are provided. During free time, volunteers can use the swimming pool in the camping area and Tiberias is easily reached, where there are all the usual facilities of a booming tourist town. The volunteer contact is Haim Cohen.

Jezreel Valley

The Jezreel Valley is south east of Haifa, between Haifa and Afula.

(C)**Ram-on**, D.N. Hevel Megido 19205; tel 06-6499857/9; fax 06-6499635.
Moshav Ram-on dates from 1960 and is named after its soldier founder. It belongs to the Moshav Movement and comprises 1,500 acres and 70 families. It is 8km due southeast of Megido (Armageddon) and 30 minutes by bus from Afula. It takes a few volunteers all year round. There is no separate accommodation for volunteers who are accommodated in their farmer's home. Few farmers are amenable to this otherwise the moshav would probably take more volunteers.
Work: agriculture, flowers, vineyards.
Facilities: there is a moshav swimming pool and volunteers are dependent on their individual farmers for trips away and outings.
   Ada Avidor is the volunteer contact.

Central Israel

(D)**Lachish**, Lachish Darom 79360; tel 07-6813361; fax 07-6816817. Used to take over a 150 volunteers but now prefers to employ Thai groups. However, does take a few individual or pairs of other volunteers occasionally. The work is mainly vineyards (table grapes) and flowers for export to Holland. In charge of volunteers: Mia.

The Negev

A geographical region which forms a rough triangle (apex downwards) between the Sinai, which belongs to Egypt, and Jordan. It extends northwards aproximately on a line from Rafah across to Arad. The lower part, i.e. apex of the triangle reaches down to Eilat on the Red Sea. In the north of the Negev lie the large towns of Be'er Sheva and Dimona, in the middle are the fantastic geological formations of the Negev craters and in the south there is little except a string of isolated moshavim along the Negev's eastern frontier (the Arava Valley) until you reach the touristic hedonism of Eilat.

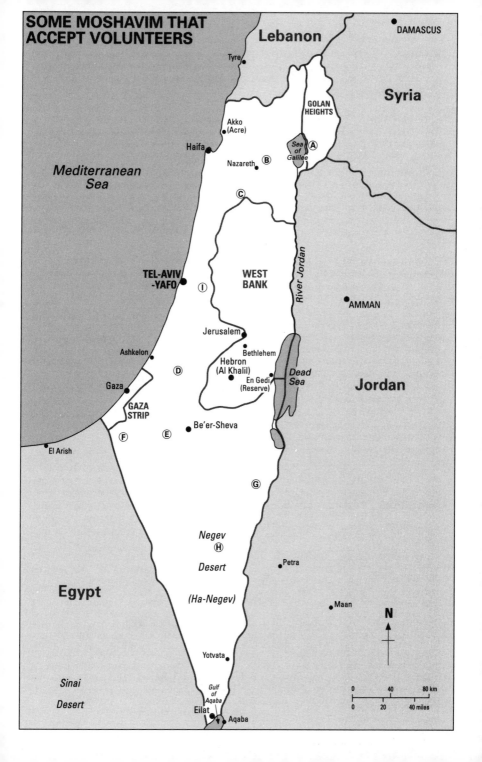

(E)**S'de Nizzan**, D.N. Ha Negev, 85470; tel +972 7-9982592 (office); fax +972 7-9985272. Situated in the upper part of the Negev, south of Gaza and Beer'sheva, which lies to the east is 45 minutes away by bus. Founded in 1973 by English-speaking Jews. Belongs to the moshav movement. Comprises 750 acres and 140 members.

Work: pineapples, flowers, hothouses, mangoes.

Volunteers: 30 at a time. Volunteer facilities include a T.V. lounge with English newspapers, films (twice a week), bar and tennis. There is also a swimming pool. A volunteer trip is arranged every two months.

Pay: according to moshav movement specifications is NIS70 per 8-hour day. Overtime possible at NIS10 per hour. Minimum stay is two months.

According to Capt. Hesh Rabinowitz in charge of volunteers, Sde Nizzan only uses volunteer workers and over 40% return for a second stint.

Apply at the moshav volunteers centre or write to the Volunteer Leader, Moshav S'de Nizzan.

(F)**Sde Avraham**, D.N. Ha-Negev 85480; tel 07-9982251; fax 07-9982165.

Founded in 1978 and has 30 members. Founded by South Americans so the main languages spoken are Spanish and Hebrew. A little English is spoken. Situated close to the border with Egypt at Rafah. Buses to Beer'sheva take about an hour and to Ofakim about 30 minutes. Work is in hot houses and fields and involves tending flowers and vegetables. Volunteer accommodation is mostly new and reasonably comfortable. The moshav has sports facilities and there is a swimming pool nearby. There are about 70 Thais working on the moshav and the basic monthly wage is NIS950 plus a bonus of about NIS150 after two months. The minimum period of work is one month and the maximum six months. Volunteers over 20 years old preferred. May take a few volunteers to work picking flowers. Contact the moshav secretary.

Arava Valley

The Arava valley is the eastern edge of the Negev and runs from the Dead Sea down to Eilat. Many moshavim in this area are some of the largest and recruit the biggest numbers of volunteers. Most of them recruit a minimum of 100 volunteers and at busy times 200 volunteers is not unknown. However, rather than relying on enough independent volunteers turning up at the right moment they arrange teams of contract labourers from Thailand who remain one or two years on the moshav. The number of places for other volunteers may therefore be quite small. The area is one of Israel's most arid. The average annual rainfall in the Arava is 1/2 inch.

Arava moshavim specialise in winter vegetables including tomatoes, capiscums, aubergines and courgettes. It may or may not be a desert myth, that one or two of these moshavim make so much money that the moshavniks (farmers) can afford to take the summer off in the Bahamas.

(G)**Id'dan**, D.N. Arava 86840; tel 07-581080/1; fax 07-581125.

Situated a few kilometres from the ancient site of Hazeva and about 8kms from the settlement of that name, Id'dan was founded in 1979 and has 40 families. The moshav has a swimming pool and basket ball yard.

Volunteers: takes 20 to 30 during November and December.

Work: Vegetables, flowers, date plantations, mango plantation.

Accommodation: old rooms; 3 to a room.

Duration of stay: one month minimum; six months maximum.

Pay: basic NIS 350 monthly. Bonus of NIS130 paid after 3 months.
The moshav is 70kms from the nearest large town (Dimona).

(H)**Paran**, D.N. Arava 86835; tel 07-581606; fax 07-581861.
100 kilometres from Eilat and 33kms south of Ein Yahav it changed from being a kibbutz to a moshav. Founded in 1971 and has 70 families.
Work: mainly vegetables and some flowers.
Volunteers: Up to 150 in the winter months.
Facilities: swimming pool, sports, bar and films.
Accommodation: Furnished rooms. Work clothes/shoes are usually provided.
Pay: approximate basic wage about £230. With overtime pay often reaches £400+. After 2 months a bonus of £28 is paid.

Tel-Aviv-Jaffo

(I)**Bnei Atarot**, D N Bnei Atarot 60991; tel 03-9711174; fax +972 3 9721076.
From the verdant surroundings and rural atmosphere it is hard to believe Bnei Atarot is a mere 20 minutes drive from the centre of Tel-Aviv. Based around buildings built by German agricultural settlers, the moshav produces sheeps' milk, peaches, plums, nectarines and grapes. Founded in 1948 there are sixty farmers and 30 to 80 volunteers depending on the season. Arab workers from the Tel-Aviv area are also employed. Facilities for volunteers include a swimming pool, a bar and the small town of Yahud is nearby. Telephone or fax and ask for Varda.

200 Moshavim Belonging to the Moshav Movement

Please note that not all the moshavim below take volunteers – a policy that changes from month to month. You may therefore have to contact a number of them before getting a positive response.

Moshav	Postal Address	Telephone
Achihod	Galil Ma'aravi 20145	04-9962425
Achisemach	D.N.Hamercaz 73105	08-9228664
Achitov	D.N.Shomron 38855	06-6258428
Alkoosh	Maaleh Yosef 25175	04-9871062
Almagor	Hevel Korazim 12340	06-6937036
Alon Hagalil	Nazareth Elite 17920	04-9865140
Amindov	Harei Yehuda 90885	02-6415130
Amirim	D.N. Carmiel 20115	06-6989571/2
Amioz	D.N. Hanegev 85435	07-9982093
Amka	D.N. Eshrot 25253	04-9969558
Amonim	Hof Ashdod 79265	08-8552130
Amouka	D.N. Tsfat 13905	06-6989389
Aniam	Ramat Hagolan 12495	06-6961266
Arbel	Galil Tachton 15285	06-6732606
Arogot	D.N. Shkemim 79420	08-8581755
Atzmon	Mishgav 20138	04-9909413
Avichil	D.N. Avichil 42910	09-8823118

Avigdor	Kiryat Malachi 70992	08-8581920
Avimin	Merom Hagalil 13850	06-6989022
Avital	D.N.Gilboa 19365	06-6597116
Azarikim	D.N. Avtach 79725	08-8583701
Azariya	D.N. Ayalon	08-9249346
Bakoah	D.N.Shimshon 99775	08-9251157
Barak	D.N. Yizrael 19375	06 6499610
Barkiya	D.N. Lakish Tsafon 79403	0-6722489
Barosh	D.N. Negev 85265	07 9924867
Balfouriya	D.N. Yizrael 19305	06-6590994
Beerotayim	D.N. Lev Hasharon 42850	09-8988032
Beer Tsofer	D.N. Arba 86830	07-6581483
Beer Tuvia	D.N. Beer Tuvia 70996	08-8583701
Ben Ami	D.N. Esheret 25240	04-9821354
Ben Shemen	D.N. Mercaz 73115	08-9229111
Bet Arif	D.N. Mercaz 73145	03-9712982
Bet Elazri	D.N. Rechovot 76803	08-9414434
Bet Ezra	D.N. Avtach 79285	08-8541001
Bet Halevi	D.N. Lev Hasharon 42870	09-8988640
Bet Hanan	D.N. Bet Hanan 60908	03-9646255
Bet Hanniya	D.N. Binyamina 30690	06-6361157/9
Bet Herut	D.N. Kfar Vitkin 40291	09-8663131
Bet Hillel	Galil Eliyon 12255	06-6951411
Bet Lechem Hagalilit	Bet Lechem Hagalilit 36915	
Bet Nkofa	D.N. Hatei Yehuda 90830	02-5342772
Bet She'arim	D.N. Bet She'arim 30046	04-9833225
Bet Shikma	D.N. Hof Askelon 79505	07-6724195
Bet Oved	D.N. Emek Shorek 76800	08-9404042
Betzaron	D.N. Katzrin 60945	08-8574158
Betzet	Hagalil Ma'Aravi 22830	04-9808082/3
Bet Yosef	Emek Bet Shean 10865	06-6584854
Bet Zayit	D.N.Harei Yehuda 90815	02-5346029
Bitcha	D.N. Negev 85415	07-9923068
Bnei Atarot	D.N. Bnei Atarot 60991	03-9711020
Bnei Dror	Hasharon Hatikon 45815	09-7961966
Bniya	D.N.Shakmim 79205	08 9437134
Borgtah	D.N. Lev Hasharon 42860	09-8988130
Chagala	D.N. Hefer 38830	06-6365131
Chagour	Hasharon Hatikon 45870	03-9388005
Chananiya	D.N. Menashe 37870	06-6350171
Chaniel	Lev Hasharon 42865	09-8988813
Chatzav	D.N. Shkamim 79842	08-8594699
Chatzba	D.N. Arava 86815	07-6581511
Cheletz	Lakish Tsafon 79310	07-6897174
Cherut	D.N. Tel Mond 40691	09-7961915
Dekel	D.N. Hanegev 85600	07-9982257
Devora	D.N.Meggido 19370	06-6499022
Dor	Hof Carmel 30820	06-6399074
Dovev	Merom Hagalil 13865	06-6989064
Eagel	D.N. Lod 71920	08-9295175
Ederet	D.N. Ha'ala 99850	02-9911252
Ederim	D.N. Gilboa 19380	06-6499183

Ehud	D.N. Negev 85450	07-6982284
Ein Ayala	Hof Carmel 30825	06-6390519
Ein Eiron	D.N. Karkur 30798	06-6377232
Ein Habashur	D.N. Negev 85465	07-9982748
Ein Vered	D.N. Tel Mond 40696	09-7961666
Ein Yahav	D.N. Arava 86820	07-6581132
Ein Yacov	Galil Ma'aravi 25135	04-9979073
Eliad	Ramat Hagolan 12570	06-6763631
Elipelet	Galil Eliyon 12330	06-6935850
Elishema	Hasharon Hatickon 45880	09-7989184
Emetz	D.N. Hefer 38870	06-6365622
Eshetaul	D.N. Shimshon 99777	02-9918456
Even Menahem	Galil Ma'Aravi 22860	04-9806171
Even Saphir	Harei Yehuda 90875	02-6412821
Gaalia	Emek Shorek 76885	08-9319289
Gadish	Hevel Megiddo 19215	06-6593523
Ganae Yochanan	Mercaz Batya 76922	08-9340410
Ganaton	D.N. Hamercaz 73110	08-9228167
Gan Haim	D.N. Kfar Saba 44910	09-7431172
Gan Sorek	D.N. Emek Soreq 76865	03-9641341
Gan Yeshiya	D.N. Hefer 38850	06-6258029
Gaolim	Hasharon Hatsfoni 42840	09-8988293
Geva Hacarmel	Hof Hacarmel 30885	04-9842030
Givat Chen	D.N. Ra'anana	09-7431122
Givat Yoav	Ramat Hagolan 72485	06-6763164
Givat Kach	D.N. Mercaz 73180	03-9721841
Givat Ya'arim	Harei Yehuda 99795	02-5342797
Givat Yoav	Ramat Hagolan 72485	06-6763164
Goren	Galil Ma'aravi 22850	04-9806154
Gilat	D.N. Hanegev	07-9923066
Giyea	Lakish Tsafon 79510	07-6722417
Hayogev	D.N. Megiddo 19232	04-9893772
Hodiya	Lakish Tsafon 79405	07-6726562
Idan	D.N. Arava	07-6581080
Kadesh Barnea	Negev Chalutza 84900	07-6533901/2
Kadron	D.N. Kadron 70975	08-8591142
Kanaff	D.N. Shomron 38855	06-6732940
Kerem Meharil	Hof Hacarmel 30840	04-9842076
Kfar Azzir	D.N. Kfar Azzir 60996	03-5356395
Kfar Achim	Lakish Tsafon 79805	08-8581744
Kfar Bilu	D.N. Rechovot 76965	08-9411740
Kfar Baruch	D.N. Kfar Baruch 30073	06-6540615
Kfar Chaim	D.N. Kfar Chaim 42945	09-8624046
Kfar Hanagid	Emek Soreq 77875	08-9437145
Kfar Hass	D.N. Tel Mond 40692	09-7961027
kfar Hittim	Galil Tachton 15280	06-6793049
Kfar Kish	D.N. Yizrael 14330	06-6767614
Kfar Mounayia	Lev Hasharon 42875	09-8988089
Kfar Melil	Hod Hasharon 45920	09-7428223
Kfar Oriyah	D.N. Shimshon 99737	02-9918250
Kfar Ruth	D.N. Mercaz 73190	08-9261014
Kfar Trueman	D.N. Mercaz 73150	03-9711115

Kfar Varberg	Kiryat Malachi 70998	08-8582140
Kfar Vitkin	D.N. Kfar Vitkin 40200	09-8666316
Kfar Yedidiya	D.N. Kfar Yedidiya 42940	09-8344566
Kfar Yehoshua	Kfar Yehoshua 30063	04-9831277
Kfar Yuval	Galil Eliyon 12215	06-6940859
Kfar Zachariya	D.N. Ha'ala 99808	02-9918593
Kfar Zaytim	Galil Tachton 13290	066796341
Kochav Michael	D.N. Sadeh Gat 79525	07-6723514
Kochel	Hevel Chorazim 12387	06-6936922
Lachish	Lachish Darom 79360	07-6813361
Lapidot	Maale Hagalil 25168	04-9872339
Liman	Galil Ma'aravi 22820	04-9824104
Livnim	D.N. Korazim 20119	06-6791373
Louzeit	D.N. Haala 99845	02-6913824
Maor	D.N. Shomron 38830	06-6372626
Mivtachim	D.N. Eshkol 85440	
Ora	Harei Yehuda 90880	02-6415444
Orot	Kiryat Malachi 70994	08-8582292
Paron	D.N. Arava 86835	07-6581320
Paami Tashaz	D.N. Hanegev 85345	07-9934701
Patish	D.N. Hanegev 85115	07-9923069
Pedaya	D.N. Ayalon 73245	08-9286457
Peduin	D.N. Negev 85108	07-9923020
Peki'in	Maaleh Hagalil 25190	04-9979991
Prazon	D.N. Yizrael 19355	06-4523053
P'tseal	Bekait Hayarden 90635	02-9941185
Ramon	D.N. Megiddo 19205	06-6499857
Ramat Zvi	D.N. Gilboa 19123	06-6331343
Ramot	Ramat Hagolan 12490	06-6732130
Ramot Meyer	Nachal Ayalon 73265	08-9410189
Ramot Naphtali	Merom Hagalil 13830	06-6940052
Ranan	D.N. Hanegev 85110	07-9923065
Rashfon	D.N. Rashfon 46915	09-9380221
Rekefet	Bet Hakerem 20179	04-9800939
Rintiya	D.N. Hamercaz 73165	03-9324938
Sadeh Itzhak	D.N. Shomron 38840	06-6365007
Sadeh Moshe	Lakish Darom 79355	07-6813530
Sadeh Nitzan	D.N. Negev 85470	07-9982592
Sadot Mica	D.N. Haalah 99810	02-9911667
Sdei Avraham	D.N. Negev 85480	07-9983351
Sdei Chamad	D.N. Hasharon 45855	09-7955367
Sdemot Devora	Galil Tachton 15240	06-6767032
Sha'ar Ephraim	Lev Hasharon 42835	09-8781701
Shachar	D.N.Sadeh Gat 79335	07-6784147
Sharona	Galil Tachton 15232	06-6767958
Shatulim	D.N. Avtach 79280	08-8640576
Shatulla	Hagalil Hma'Aravi 22865	
Shazor	Merom Hagalil 20135	04-9985325
Shefer	Bakat Bet Hakerem 20120	06-6989397
Shomra	Galil Maaravi 22855	04-9809455
Talmei Eliyahu	D.N.Hanegev 85452	07-9982292
Talmei Yichiel	Lakish Tsafon 79810	08-8582840

Talmim	Lakish Darom 79315	07-6897172
Tashur	D.N. Hanegev 85260	07-9923018
Tidhar	D.N. Hanegev 85270	07-9923018
Tel Adeshim	D.N. Yizrael 19315	06-6522693
Tel Shachar	Emek Soreq 76805	08-9340178
Tnuvot	Lev Hasharon 42830	09-8988815
Tomer	Bakat Hayarden 90680	02-9941233
Tsafririm	D.N. Ha'Ayala 99830	02-9917690
Tsalfon	D.N.Shimshon 99750	02-9913130
Tsipori	D.N. Tsipori 17910	06-6556440
Tsofit	D.N. Tsofit 44925	09-7433202
Tsroofa	Hof Hacarmel 30850	04-9842075
Tsukim	D.N. Arava 86825	07-9981366
Tsuriel	Maale Yosef 25150	04-4971557
Tsur Moshe	Lev Hasharon 42810	09-8945025
Ya'ad	Bakait Hacarmiel 20133	04-9902208
Ya'ara	Galil Ma'aravi 22840	04-9806399
Yafit	Bakat Hayarden 90685	02-9941340
Yakeini	Hof Ashkelon 79170	07-6897104
Yarchiv	Hasharon Hatikun 45860	03-9389294
Yarkona	Hod Hasharon 45915	09-7405119
Yashaa	D.N. Negev 85430	07-9982377
Yatseetz	D.N. Ayalon 73260	08-9340353
Yeinov	Lev Hasharon 42825	09-8988106
Yeinon	D.N. Shakmim 79815	08-8582285
Yeshresh	D.N. Ayalon 73275	08-9220495
Yeted	D.N. Negev 85482	07-9982555
Yordana	Emek Bet Shean 10870	06-6587032
Zarait	Galil Ma'aravi 22870	04-9807541
Zeiton	D.N. Lod 71915	08-9245242

Other Work in Israel

Overview

It is very likely that if you decide to go to Israel and spend a few weeks on a kibbutz, you will enjoy yourself so much that you will want to stay longer. It may be also that you wish to change your travel plans and go home by a different route, stopping off somewhere else to visit friends, or you may decide not to go home but just to keep moving. Whatever the reason, it is likely that you will be short of money (living at your own expense in Israel is very costly, and will want to find paid work for a while to boost your funds. If you decide a moshav (see previous chapter) is not for you, there is a variety of paid casual work in Israel if you are prepared to look for it.

A certain amount of caution is required in choosing and carrying out paid work as many employers are unscrupulous about exploiting travellers especially if they are working without a work permit. Work permits are virtually impossible to get for the kind of unskilled jobs (except kibbutzim and moshavim work) that most travellers do, so most find themselves working illegally. Fortunately the authorities generally turn a blind eye although it is wise to be discreet. However, while there is lax enforcement of the working regulations, Israeli security is very strict and it is essential to make sure your tourist visa is renewed when necessary (every three months). The cost of renewal is about NIS 50. See *Visitors' Guide to Israel* chapter for further details on renewing visas.

Before you leave the security of the kibbutz there are several things you should be aware of.

You can be sure that whatever type of job you take the work will almost certainly entail long hours, hard work and difficult conditions. An eight-hour day, six days a week is usual and in service work, shift and night duty is also likely. Secondly, casual staff are rarely secure in their job. Employers offering most of the types of work included in this chapter, take you on, at least initially, on a daily or weekly basis and there is always the possibility of exploitation (for example being dismissed half-way through a day and not being paid for that day).

It is very important that right from the start you ensure you clarify the conditions relating to your employment. One of the main points to check is whether the cost of food and accommodation is included in your wages or whether there will be a deduction for this. Also, you should find out if your employer intends to deduct taxes and if so, what they are for. Unfortunately, this can be used as an easy way to reduce your wages without the employer ever actually paying the tax to the authorities.

A fairly common practice among employers is to hold back part of your wages to ensure you stay for an agreed or minimum period. If you leave before that time, you could forfeit the held-back portion of your wages. In this case you should check with the employer what will happen to your wages in the event that you have to leave through sickness or some other event beyond your control.

Insurance

If you are expected to operate dangerous machinery or work in dangerous conditions, it may invalidate any insurance cover you have for accidents. You should find out if you are covered by your employer's policy. If you have taken out cover for working on a kibbutz or moshav, it may be possible to extend this cover but you should check with the volunteer office with which you took out the cover either in the UK, your own country or in Israel.

Sources of Jobs

Apart from the invaluable travellers' grapevine you can find out about jobs in Israel by visiting travellers hostels most of which act as unofficial job agencies. Employers telephone the hostels when they need construction workers or restaurant staff (usually dishwashers and waitresses). The Seaside Hostel in Trumpledor St in Tel-Aviv is good for the above. Waiters are less in demand than waitresses as Israel is still a pretty chauvinist country.

Hostels often have noticeboards which display temporary job vacancies: moshavim, restaurants, film companies looking for extras, bar work as well as more dubious requests ('topless models for 30 minutes work'), are just some of the ones spotted in Tel-Aviv.

In Jerusalem good sources of information include the New Swedish Hostel (29 David St, near Jaffa Gate; tel 6264124/6277855) and The Tabasco Hotel & Tea Room (8 Aqabat at-Takiya near Damascus Gate; tel 6283461), both in the Old City. It is easier however, to find jobs outside the Old City and some good sources of information in West Jerusalem are the King George Hostel (a.k.a. My Home in Jerusalem Hostel (15 King George St; tel 6232235; e-mail www.my.home.co.il), and Palestinian East Jerusalem's international Christian hostels Faisal (4 Ha-Nevi'im Street; tel 6287502) and Palm (6 Ha-Nevi'im Street; tel 6273189).

Other good sources of job adverts are the situations vacant columns of the *Jerusalem Post* (daily newspaper in English) and the notice board of the Goldsmith Building (home of the overseas students' union) just outside the campus.

Hotels and Restaurants

Eilat is not the only source of hotel and restaurant jobs in Israel. Restaurants and hotels in the large cities and the other tourist traps such as Tiberias are just as likely to prove good hunting ground for work. Dishwashing is by all accounts the worst job, as one disherwasher put it 'it's unbelievably stressful and totally humiliating.' Probably the only good thing about such jobs is that board and lodging come free. Another possibility is working in reception at a pension. For this a contributor received NIS20 a day plus free board and accommodation and described it as 'the most relaxing job I've ever had'. Runners and touts are also employed by the hotels, often on a daily basis. This tends to be a tough job as you hustle for custom at the bus station in competition with touts from rival establishments.

For those who cannot contemplate life without a burger chain in sight, three of the biggest US fast food outlets, McDonalds Corporation, Burger King, and KFC Corporation have outlets in Israel. A well-known source of temporary jobs worldwide they are likely to prove an asset to the job hungry travellers in Israel.

Work in Eilat and Other Resorts

The tourist mecca of Eilat, Israel's thriving resort on the Gulf of Aqaba, has a great abundance of casual jobs for backpackers wanting a taste of the glamour of an international playground (albeit from a grindstone vantage point). The main foreign tourist season runs from October to March which is obviously the time when jobs are most numerous. However, because so many travellers head to Eilat looking for work, it is an employer's market and they tend to take full advantage of this fact by behaving abominably towards their employees.

If you want to work in one of the resort's big hotels try to be there early in the season, or even before it, to impress your worthiness upon hotel managers. It is possible to pick up other kinds of work by the day (handing out flyers for a restaurant, selling cruise tickets), by the week (waitressing) or for several months (working in the beach cafés, on the diving and cruise boats, construction sites and as cleaners). Accommodation may be on the beach or in a berth on one of the boats, the pay will be lousy but the tips will more than make the effort worthwhile particularly for waitressing.

Men can find construction work at the Peace Café, a well-known picking up point. Recruitment starts early so you have to be there by 6am. You have to withstand the meat market atmosphere as your muscles are inspected before you are offered a day's work at the going rate of NIS 10-15 an hour. Once you are known as a good worker you may get offered a job for longer. Some describe the crowd at the Peace Café as 'rough' and it is therefore perhaps to be avoided by those of a nervous disposition.

If you have any diving qualifications there is a possibility of work at one of Eilat's many diving centres. There are jobs for women as hostesses/cooks on diving boats, cruise boats or on private yachts. There is also a possibility of crew work on private and chartered yachts and diving boats. Sometimes vacancies are posted at the marina. Otherwise, for diving jobs call door-to-door at the premises and for crew jobs ask from boat to boat. One contributor landed a job on a private boat chartered by divers, as a deck hand and hostess and as she put it 'I severely regret ever leaving it'. She went on week or month-long cruises of the Red Sea, Gulf of Suez and the Suez Canal and learned to scuba dive along the way. The downside is that working on a boat is very badly paid (if you get paid at all) and very hard work. Good workers who stay a reasonable time gradually earn the respect of their employer and get a reasonable wage and better perks.

If you sleep on the beach while working in Eilat you risk having your luggage stolen; even keeping your valuables inside your sleeping bag is no deterrent to the skilful thief who, with a razor blade, can still gain access to them and help himself. Burying things in the sand as a precaution is a non-starter as the sand in Eilat has been specially imported and in places is only a few inches deep. Underneath the sand is solid rock.

Other work possibilities in Eilat include bakeries (night shift work). There are also jobs that are nothing to do with the tourist trade of Eilat but are in the vicinity. There are several farms in the area that employ transient workers. The main season is from November (melon planting) to March/April (harvesting). These jobs pay quite well although they may entail enduring harsh and primitive conditions. Workers generally have to bring their own tents.

Most of the hazards of working in Eilat arise from the fact that hundreds of travellers are looking for work without work permits and employers can fill posts many times over and have no incentive to treat their workers at all well. You are just lucky if you find one that does. For women there is the additional hazard caused by Eilat's booming escort business fuelled by an excess of pleasure-seeking male tourists which puts pressure on any woman in Eilat. One female contributor finally admitted defeat by ensuring she had her own escort of two burly South Africans (of which there always seems to be a plentiful supply in Eilat). This apparently worked as a deterrent to possible predators.

Other Israeli resorts from north to south include Nahariya, Caesarea, Herzliya, Tel Aviv, Bat Yam and Ashkelon. There is also a Club Med village in northern Israel near the Lebanese border which made headlines in June 1995, when Hizbollah terrorists operating from Lebanon, misaimed a rocket intended for the Israeli town of Nahariya and hit the Club Med complex instead. A French cook was killed and eight others injured.

Au Pair, Nanny, Nurse

Having a live-in child-carer is something of a status symbol in Israel. At the time of writing, there are plenty of opportunities for this kind of work. However, there are some differences between being au pair in Israel and in most European countries. Au pair (which literally means 'as an equal') very likely means longer hours in Israel than elsewhere. Children tend to be given a lot of freedom in Israel and are likely to be more boisterous than many European children. Some more retiring au pairs may find this difficult to cope with. Also, keeping a kosher kitchen is one of the likely skills needed for working with a Jewish family.

It is a good idea to meet several families before deciding which you are going to be most happy with. The opportunity for doing this is better if you go through an agency (of which there is a growing number in Israel) than if you answer a family's advert personally. If you do want to respond personally to family adverts there is usually a selection in the *Jerusalem Post* but many turn out to be agencies in disguise and when you call them they say the job advertised has gone but they have others. Agents and agencies that advertise in the *Jerusalem Post* and cannot always be safely recommended. One that has received commendation is Hilma Schmoshkovitz (see below).If you answer an agency advert and know nothing previously of the agency, you will have to check them out for yourself.

There are alas, always nightmare families. One au pair was locked in the house by the family she worked for and had her passport taken away by them so that she could not leave, even if she managed to escape from the house. Her hours were 6am-11.30pm (the employer had lied about other help being kept). The final insult was when she was told that she didn't work as hard as the Mexicans they usually had. When she insisted on leaving, they hindered her then finally agreed but not before they searched her luggage at the gate for possible stolen items. The recourse for any au pair who feels their treatment is beyond reason (e.g. passport or wages withheld) is to firstly, complain to your agency if you have one, or ask the Ministry of Labour *(Sherut Ha'tasukah)* for assistance (tel 02-752405).

You are just as likely to be offered a job in a West Bank Israeli settlement as in the northern suburbs of Tel Aviv or Haifa. Salaries are pretty high (NIS600-700 monthly plus keep) but the salary is not compensation enough if the family concerned insists on treating you like a domestic. Most successful au pairings have been with families who shared much of their lives with the au pair who therefore gained a valuable insight into the Jewish way of life and found the experience very rewarding. Au pairing generally provides a comfortable base from which to experience daily life in any country. In Israel, daily life is different from many European countries in that the atmosphere is especially tense owing to the politics and the troubles involving the Israelis and the Palestinians. Some previous au pairs have found it difficult to be without a car in an isolated settlement, for instance in the West Bank, and have found that being confined in the family's home for most of the time, very tedious, even when the family themselves have been very considerate. One girl said that two months in such a situation was about all she could bear.

Israel is not among the many countries which now take male au pair applicants for granted.

Another booming industry is in private nursing care for the elderly and infirm. Shlomi Meiri (address below) arranges such jobs.

Useful Addresses

Au Pair International, 2 Desler St. Bnei Brak 51507; tel 03-619 0423; fax 03-5785463. Jobs are for 6 months to a year. Jobs are in the towns and suburbs around the country and the pay $800-$900 monthly. All staff are expected to work nine hours per day and duties include general housework and childcare. Some girls are employed as mothers helps and to have complete care of the house and children for longer hours. This is a housekeeper post and applicants must be able to prove they have had previous experience of having complete charge of running a house. NNEB nannies must be prepared to get up at night to attend to a baby. Mothers' helps, nannies, housekeepers are not normally expected to drive and will almost certainly not have the use of a car.

All staff must have taken out full health insurance cover before leaving their own country and to have have been tested for HIV and hepatitis A and B. The minimum age is 20 for mothers' helpers pairs and 30 for housekeepers. Run by Mrs. Veronica Grosbard.

Hilma Shmoshkovitz: P.O. Box 91, (Street Address – 5 Moholiver), 75100 Rishon le Zion; tel 03-9659937; fax 03-95 00 577; e-mail hilma@netvision.net.il Office also in Jerusalem. Hours: 10am-7pm Sunday to Thursday.

Langtrain International, Torquay Road, Foxrock, Dublin 18, Ireland; tel 1-289 3876; fax 1-289 2586. Langtrain International began in 1961 as Interlingua and has a limited range of placements in Israel.

Schlomi Meiri (P.O.Box 8296, Ramat-Gan 52181). This agency used to be for au pairs but is now an agency for nurses. Female nurses are preferred, as there are few requests for male nurses. The work consists of looking after elderly people in their own homes on a live-in basis.

Applicants must be qualified in nursing in a western European country or the USA, and be licensed to work in their own country. At least two years' experience is required, preferably with the elderly and handicapped. Must be in excellent health and non-smokers. The minimum contract is for a year. Age limits 22 to 30 and single. The typical salary is US$400-500 monthly, free keep and lodging. One day off is allowed per week.

Schlomi Meiri will also give free advice for jobs and travel in Israel on 052-498417 (phone within Israel) or +972 52 498417 (from outside Israel). He may be able to help with au pair jobs.

There are a few agencies in the UK that can place girls in Israel including Childcare International (020-8959 3611; e-mail office@childint. demon.co.uk), Euro Employment Centre (0161-796 8399), Homelife Employment Agency (Ty Rhosyn, Llangeitho, Tregaron, Ceredigion SY25 6TW (tel 01974-821347; e-mail homelifeag@aol.com) and Students Abroad (tel 020-8330 0777).

Working in Hostels

There are two types of hostel in Israel, the travellers' hostels which provide inexpensive accommodation, generally for young adults and have a pleasant, characterful atmosphere, and the more regulated, official youth hostels. Both types of hostel are keen to employ foreign travellers for administration/cleaning jobs in return for a small wage and bed and board. One contributor was staying at the Number One Hostel in Tel Aviv when another hostel telephoned saying they needed a receptionist. This was how she ended up working seven hours a day for two months, earning NIS1600 per month less accommodation. All meals were provided and the atmosphere very welcoming. The usual way to get such jobs is to ask at the hostels in person.

Israel has about 30 youth hostels belonging to the International Youth Hostels Federation. For a brochure containing the details of all of them contact the IHYA or IGTO in your own country or write to: The Youth Travel Bureau (I.Y.H. 1 Shezer Street, POB 6001, Jerusalem 91060; tel 02-655 84 00; fax 02-655 84 32; website www.youth-hostels.org.il). You should then contact the individual hostels direct. Board and accommodation is provided free and pocket money of about NIS150 monthly in return for six hours work a day. Normally, the minimum work period is two months.

The Youth Travel Bureau also arranges kibbutz and archaeological work.

Archaeology

You might be forgiven for thinking that the whole of Israel is one vast archaeological site. Certainly, it is one of the richest areas in the world for remains of religious and historic importance. Excavations on these sites are conducted by the Israeli Universities in conjunction with leading experts from all over the world.

Volunteers who are not archaeologists work on such digs doing the least specialised jobs. But even these have their fascination if you are lucky enough to find, or be allowed to examine tantalising fragments of human lives lived hundreds or even thousands of years ago, and help to build up a picture of them. However, you must be realistic in your expectations; the work itself will almost certainly be tedious and usually arduous. Volunteers should be over eighteen, in good health and able to work long hours in hot, dry weather as the main excavation season runs from May to September.

The work consists mainly of manual labour: digging, shovelling, hauling baskets, cleaning pottery fragments. Work normally starts early in the morning before the heat of the day and ends about lunch time. Afternoons are usually spent at leisure and during the evenings sorting, cleaning and discussion of the day's finds are carried out.

There will normally be organised trips for volunteers to other sites in the area and to local museums. Informal lectures on the history and archaeology of the site will be given by the director or other staff members.

You will be expected to pay a registration fee (usually $50-75) stay for a minimum period which can be as short as a week, but two weeks is more usual. In 1999, The Department of Classical Studies at Tel-Aviv University (e-mail fischer@ecsg.tau.ac.il) was charging $350 per week for board and lodging. Occasionally, some organisers offer basic lodging free of charge. Unfortunately self-financing yourself on a dig can be quite expensive and costs vary; the average is about US$35 per day. Most digs provide accident insurance, however, volunteers must arrange their own medical insurance. The general living conditions for digs vary considerably and you could find yourself in a hotel, a hostel, a kibbutz, or camping out under the stars.

Those with limited funds may be able to participate in a rescue excavation. These emergency salvage and rescue operations are conducted any time in the year and often need volunteers at short notice. Free food and accommodation are offered as an additional incentive.

Information on volunteering at archaeological digs in Israel is available on the internet site of the Israel Ministry of Foreign Affairs (www.israel-mfa.gov.il/archdigs.html). Adverts for volunteers sometimes appear in the Moshav and Kibbutz Volunteer centres in Tel Aviv or on hostel boards. Alternatively contact the departments, institutions and organisations listed below:

Useful Addresses

Bar Ilan University: The Martin (Szusz) Dept. of Land of Israel Studies Bar Ilan University, Ramat Gan 52900; e-mail shlosbt@mail.biu.ac.il Offers volunteers and students an opportunity to participate in several archaeological excavations including Tel es-Safi Philistine Gath (Bronze/Canaanite & Iron/Israelite) periods, Yattir (Israelite, Roman, Byzantine & early Arab), Rakit (Byzantine), Tel Harasim (Bronze/Canaanite and Iron/Israelite), and in the City of David in Jerusalem. Placements last about one month throughout the summer. Students are eligible for university credits. Accommodation is provided but volunteers need to fund their own living expenses and travel costs. For the latest information on availability contact Yigal Levin at the above address.

Centre of Nautical and Regional Archaeology (CONRAD), Kibbutz Nahsholim, Israel 30825; tel 06-6390950. CONRAD is located in the grounds of kibbutz Nahsholim on the Carmel Coast. The Centre is the homebase of the museum's maritime inspection team and the Tel Dor excavations.

Volunteers are needed at all times of year to help with a variety of projects. Field work including diving, restoration, exhibit planning, publication preparation and general maintenance of the building take place all year round. Tel Dor excavations take place during July and August and during the autumn, spring and winter; inspection diving is at its peak with underwater surveys and rescue excavations being conducted. Volunteers to act as tour guides and to assist with clerical work are always needed. Placements are for as long as the volunteer wishes, subject to visa limits (usually six months).

Volunteers must be in good health, over 18 years old and able to speak Hebrew or English. Diving volunteers must have diving licences. The volunteer is responsible for all costs including accommodation, meals and medical and accident insurance, although reduced rates for accommodation can be given.

Department of Classical Studies, Tel Aviv University: is carrying out excavations at the ancient port site of Yavneh- yam, which has several mentions in the Bible (*Book of Maccabees*). Research has been going on at Yavneh-Yam since 1972 to try to establish the nature of the conflict between the Near East civilisations and the Greek and Roman cultures. Volunteers have been helping on digs there since 1992. The next excavation camp is in 2001. Cost $700-800 inclusive of board and accommodation at youth village Ayanot, 15 minutes from the site. The camp provides training for students and enthusiasts from abroad. Two weeks minimum. Deadline for 2001 season is 31 May 2001. Cost does not include $50 non-refundable registration fee. Contact Prof. Moshe Fischer, Archaeological Project Yavneh-Yam, 69978 Ramat-Aviv; tel +972-3-6409938; fax +972-3-6409457; e-mail fischer@ post.tau.ac.il website www.tau.ac.il/~yavneyam/

Haifa University Department of Archaeology: Mount Carmel, 31905. Excavation of El Ahwat, a large fortified town dating from the 13th century BC, situated on a hilltop near the coast 12km from Caesarea. One week minimum. Cost $200 per week for food and accommodation. Apply before June to Dr Adam Zertal.

Hebrew University, Institute of Archaeology, Mount Scopus, Jerusalem 91905; tel 02-5882403; fax 02-5 2825548. Volunteers needed for the Tel Dor excavation project and museum in the grounds of Kibbutz Nasholim. July and August. Minimum two weeks. Volunteers pay their own food and accommodation costs. See also CONRAD (Centre of Nautical and Regional Archaeology) entry above.

Israel Antiquities Authority: POB 586, Jerusalem 91004 (in the Rockefeller Museum Building); tel +972-2-6204622; fax +972-2-6289066. e-mail Harriet@israntigue.org.il

Jewish National Fund, 11 Zvi Shapira Street, Tel Aviv, Israel; tel 03-2561129. Excavation of a Roman theatre 3 miles from Caesarea. Working hours 5.30am to midday, six days per week. Board and lodging about £10 per day. Minimum period of work one week. Contact Eli Shenav at the above address.

Project Oren One independent part of the Oren Kibbutz Institute's' programme is Archaeology and the Jewish Experience combining a kibbutz stay with two weeks on an archaeological dig. Further information from the Israel office of Oren (tel 04-9838739/729), or the toll free number in the USA 1-800-247-7852.

Tel Aviv University: Department of Classics, 69978 Ramat Aviv, Tel Aviv; tel 03-6409938; fax 03-6409457; volunteers needed for excavation at site of ancient port of Yavneh Yam. Two weeks in July and August in 2001. For details see Yavneh Yam (above). May have other digs at other times of year.

The Zinman Institute of Archaeology: University of Haifa, Haifa 31905; tel +972 4 8249392; fax +972-4 8249876; e-mail aronen@research.haifa.ac.il Needs volunteers for the excacavation of Tabun cave, Mount Carmel located 20km south of Haifa and 3km from the Mediterranean shore. 20 metre high accumulation of cultural layers in a complex stratigraphy. Tabun is a key site for the study of human behaviour during the Early and Middle Palaeolithic of the Levant approximately between one million and 100,000 years ago. The cave has so fare yielded Neanderthal human remains and abundant stone artifacts.

Excavation starts August 2000 under Prof. Avraham Ronen. Room and board provided in field laboratory near site. Credit points can be earned under university regulations. Minimum period is two weeks. Cost for two weeks all inclusive is US$770 and for four weeks US$1200. Further details from Michael Eisenberg, Administrator at the above addresss.

Also worth trying are the following organisations, institutes and university departments:

Albright Institute of Archaeological Research, POB 19096, Jerusalem 91190; tel +972-2-6288956; fax +972-2 626-4424; e-mail director@albright.org.il Strictly university students only, who pay fees to join an excavation during which they gain practical archaeological experience, attend courses, write exams and earn credits.

Anglo-Israel Archaeological Society, 126 Albert Street, London NW1 7NE. Provides useful information about current archaeological excavations welcoming volunteers. In many instances volunteers are required to make a payment.

Antiquities Authority, POB381, Bet She'an 10900; tel 06-585367; fax 06-585840. Minimum participation two weeks.

Ayala Travel and Tours Ltd, 13 HaZvi Street, Jerusalem 94386; tel 02-381233; fax 02-387235. Minimum participation three days.

Ben Gurion University, Department of Archaeology, POB 653, Beer-sheva 84105; tel 07-461092/3/4/5/.

British School of Archaeology in Jerusalem, POB 19283, Jerusalem 91192; tel 02-5828101 & 02-5815028; fax 02-5323844; e-mail bsaj@vms.huji.ac.il In 1999 there was no excavation work but BSAJ was offering affordable hostel accommodation close to both the old city and the Hebrew Mount Scopus Campus.

The German Institute, POB 19698, Jerusalem 91196; tel 02-284792.

Israeli Ministry of Foreign Affairs: www.israel-mfa.gov.il/archdigs.html Listing of archaeological excavations around Israel which need paying volunteers.

Shuni Excavations, Post Office Box, 111 Binyamina; tel 03-2561129.

Youth Travel Bureau, 1Shezer Street, POB 6001, Jerusalem 91060; tel 02-558400; fax 02-558432. Arranges for groups of Youth Hostel Association members to participate in archaeological expeditions for two weeks minimum period.

Useful Publications

Archaeological Fieldwork Opportunities Bulletin, Archaeological Institute of America, 656 Beacon Street, Boston, MA 02215-2006 USA; fax 617-353-6550; e-mail aiapub@bu.edu website www.archaeological.org

Biblical Archaeology Society Review, 4710 41st Street, NW Washington, DC 20016, USA; tel 202-3643300; fax 202-364-2636; e-mail bas@bib-arch.org website www.bib-arch.org Publishes the *Biblical Archaeology Review*.0

Journal of Field Archaeology, Boston University, 675 Commonwealth Avenue, Boston MA 02215,USA; tel 617-353-2357; e-mail jfa-www.bu.edu

Voluntary Work With the Palestinians

There is a a large demand for volunteer workers in diverse institutions in the Palestinian Governed Territories, which deal with education, medicine and a variety of menial but essential work. Owing to quota restrictions imposed by the Israeli government on foreign volunteers, some organisations like the Edinburgh Missionary Society have had to scale down their intake drastically. Many such projects involve caring for people in need such as handicapped children, the elderly and the sick. Non-medical/carer projects include teaching English in the Arab communities. Some projects require only that the volunteer has some commitment, others need volunteers with medical or teaching qualifications.

For teaching English in Arab communities, volunteers are needed at Arab schools in Galilee, in the Bedouin resettlement towns, Beer-Sheva and at a teacher-training college in Haifa. The Arabs in Israel learn English as their third language after Arabic and Hebrew. In Israel, a high standard of English is required in order to qualify for tertiary education and unlike the Israeli Jews they do not have a large English-speaking group in their midst. Volunteers are expected to stay six months and attend a two-week course in Teaching English as a Foreign Language prior to departure.

A range of possibilities is listed below:

British Council English Language Centre: Al-Nuzha Building, 2 Abu Obeida Street, P.O.B. 19136 East Jerusalem; tel 02-271131; fax 02-283021; Director Helen Hawari. May be able to help with contacts for teaching English to the Palestinians. Also British Council in Gaza Town: 14-706 Al-Nasra Street, Al-Rimal, P.O. Box 355; tel 07-822290; and Nablus (Harwash Building, Radidia Main Street, P.O. Box 497).

Palestinian Refugee Researchnet: www.arts.mcgill.ca/mepp/ prrn/prfront.html A Canadian website and the most comprehensive devoted to Palestinian refugees. Contains details of organisations offering voluntary work opportunities with Palestinians.

The Four Homes of Mercy: P.O. Box 19185, Old City - Jerusalem 91191; tel +972 2-6282076; fax +972 2-6274871; e-mail homes4@netvision.net.il The Four Homes of Mercy are in the Occupied West Bank: the home for elderly men and women, the home for crippled teenagers and the crippled children's home, all located in Bethany, and St Mary's Maternity Hospital is in Beit Jala. Volunteers placed at one of these homes participate in various activities dependent on their skills and field of interest such as painting, whitewashing, playing with young patients, helping them to eat at mealtimes, gardening, sewing, nursing, helping in the kitchen, teaching patients English, playing music, occupational and physio-therapy (if qualified).

Placements last from one month to two years. Previous volunteers have come from North America, Britain, The Netherlands and Sweden. English is widely spoken, but a knowledge of Arabic would be useful. Health insurance is advisable and, if bringing a car, an international driving licence. Accommodation is provided when available and for those boarding at the homes, meals are provided. Pocket money of $50 per month is given towards transportation. All other expenses must be borne by the volunteer. Applications should come preferably recommended by a well-known organisation or a church.

Friends of Birzeit University (FoBZU) 21 Collingham Road, London SW5 ONU; tel 020-7323 8414; fax 020-7835 2088; e-mail fobzu@arab-british.u-net.com Bir Zeit, one of eight Palestinian universities in the Israeli Occupied Territories and one of four in the West Bank, is 26 km north of Jerusalem. During the *Intifada* these universities were closed by the Israeli authorities. Every year BirZeit university holds international work camps which offer volunteers from Europe and North America the opportunity to experience the local situation at first hand and to contribute to improving the local conditions of life. Tasks include helping farmers with their harvest, building basic sanitation facilities in refugee camps and other community work. A wide range of visits, meetings and cultural events are also arranged. The placements last 14-15 days. Minimum age for volunteers is 18. Accommodation is provided but other expenses must be borne by the volunteer. Apply to to The Coordinator at the above address.

At the end of 1999 FoBZU launched a three-year adult literacy and family life development project aimed at women in the West Bank. The project will include using television for educational broadcasting. Setting up health clinics is also part of the project. For this and other long-term schemes, specialists in the relevant fields are needed to visit and run training schemes and act as consultants. For details of any current projects contact FoBZU.

If you are interested in studying at Birzeit, there are courses in Modern Standard Arabic, Colloquial Arabic and courses in the social sciences and arts. Language courses cost from $600. You can obtain more information from The Student Affairs Office, Birzeit University (West Bank, Palestine; tel 02-998 2000; fax 02-995 7656; e-mail pas-isp@admin.birzeit.edu www.birzeit.edu/pas). Birzeit may also be able to provide details of other organisations with programmes in the West Bank or East Jerusalem.

Gap Activity Projects; GAP House, 44 Queen's Road, Reading, Berks. RG1 4BB; tel 0118-959 4914; fax 0118-957 6634; e-mail volunteer@gap.org.uk
An educational organisation that is a registered charity, Gap specialises in projects worldwide for those between school and university. For more than two decades GAP has been sending school leavers abroad and has several programmes in Israel.

St Louis Hospital in Jerusalem is a hospice for the terminally ill just outside the walls of the Old City. Eight volunteers (four girls and 4 boys) are sent each year to help care for the 50-odd patients.

The French and Italian Hospitals in Nazareth are large general hospitals run by Catholic orders. They treat mainly the Palestinian community. Two girls are needed at each hospital.

House of Hope for the Blind and Mentally Handicapped: P.O. Box 27, Bethlehem-Hebron Road, Bethlehem, West Bank, via Israel; tel +972 2742325; fax +972 2740928; e-mail houseofhopemd@palnet.com One of the Four Houses of Mercy (see above), The House of Hope provides care for 75 handicapped people and has a waiting list of 350+. Eight to ten volunteers a year are needed for home care of the residents, and outdoors with gardening and maintenance of the grounds. A driving licence is useful and volunteers should be aged 20 to 65. Help is required year round for periods of at least six months, but longer stays are preferable. Accommodation and pocket money are provided.

For further details and an application form, contact The Director at the above address.

Interns for Peace (IFP): 475 Riverside Drive, 16th Floor, New York, New York 10115, USA; tel +001 212-870 2226; fax +001 212-870 6119. IFP, established in

Israel in 1976, was the first and remains the only programme for the purpose of training community development and peace workers in Israel, and now in the Palestinian Governed Territories of Gaza and in the West Bank. Programmes exist also in Jordan and Egypt. Over 200 voluntary peace-workers (interns) work on projects (business, athletic, cultural, educational) which involve cooperation between Palestinians and Jews. The aim is to break down the barriers of suspicion, distrust, fear and hatred between them. Volunteers often go on to become full-time professionals in co-existence work, breaking down ethnic prejudices worldwide.

Applicants must be dedicated to Israel and a peaceful Middle East, have proficiency in advanced Hebrew or Arabic, spend six months in the Middle East prior to the IFP internship, have a college education and previous work experience outside the college setting and the ability to work well with people, especially children and young adults.

Housing is provided and a stipend of $500 monthly. The minimum commitment is for a year.

Further details from the North American Executive Director at the above address.

The Jerusalem Princess Basma Hospital for Disabled Children: P.O. Box 19764, Jerusalem 91197; telephone 02-6283058; 02-6664536; fax 02-6274449. The Hospital is a non-governmental charitable organisation which cares for children up to 15 years. Non-professional volunteers may be involved in any of the following: recreational therapy, hydrotherapy and in the kindergarten classes or in maintenance (e.g. painting and gardening). About fifteen volunteers are taken on in any one year.

There is also work for professional physiotherapists, hydrotherapists and occupational therapists. At any one time there may be two or three at the centre (usually from Germany, Sweden or Britain) spending a period of practical training there as part of their course of studies. They receive pocket money of $50 per month.

Owing to traditional restrictions it is not possible for male volunteers to stay on the premises where female staff, the children and sometimes their mothers are staying. Male volunteers therefore have to make their own accommodation arrangements. Female volunteers get board and lodging on the premises.

Applications are welcome all year round and are preferred through an applicant's formal organisation (church, school, college etc.) who can provide a recommendation. Applications from individuals are also accepted with suitable references from known bodies and organisations. Preferred length of stay is for three months plus. Apply to Mrs. Betty Majaj, Director.

Medical Aid for Palestine: 33A Islington Park Road, London N1 1QB; tel 020-7226 4114; website www.map-uk.demon.co.uk

Moravian Church – Star Mountain Rehabilitation Centre: P.O. Box 199, Ramallah, West Bank, Palestine; tel +972 2 2810751; e-mail starmt@hotmail.com

The rehabilitation centre caters for 35 children aged 6-14 with mental disabilities including a boarding facility for 13 girls aged 8-14 and providing agricultural training for six young men aged 15-25 with mental disabilities in the Ramallah/Birzeit area.

Two volunteers are needed all year to help with special workshops in music, art, sports etc., support for vocational training for mentally disabled people. Volunteers work with teaching workshops run by specialists (Special Education, Severe Handicaps, CBR work, Psychology, Administration skills, Art, Music and Sports) and used as a rehabilitation method.

Volunteers should have experience and be qualified in special education/educational psychology. The ability to speak English and preferably Arabic is also desirable and a driving licence is useful. Willingness to adapt to local customs and the regime at Star Mountain needed.

Volunteers get food and lodging. For short stays, the expenses of a specialist are covered; for a long stay, a little pocket money may be possible.

Applicants should write direct to Star Mountain. Please contact Ms Sophie Körte if additional information is needed.

Oxfam-Québec: Middle East Regional Office, P.O. Box 20560, Jerusalem, Israel; tel +972-2 656 89 32; fax +972-2 656 89 33; e-mail oxfamqot@planet.edu Website www.oxfam.qc.ca
Since 1989, Oxfam-Québec has placed a handful of volunteers in the Palestinian Governed Territories (The West Bank and Gaza) each year. Volunteers work in fields such as health, disability, community development, human rights etc. The above office only accepts those of Canadian nationality. There are no particular age limits and Arabic tuition will be provided if necessary. A driving licence is useful. Normally, a commitment of 2 years is expected, but short-term stays may be possible. Accommodation and a monthly living allowance are provided. Volunteers are also insured (medical, dental and disability).

Further details from the above address.

UNIPAL: Universities Trust for Educational Exchange with Palestinians, (BCM UNIPAL, London WC1N 3XX; tel/fax 0208—299 1132). Unipal sends volunteers to the West Bank, Gaza and Lebanon for four to six weeks in the summer, teaching English to students in the refugee camps. Volunteers need to contribute about £375 and food and accommodation are provided. Applicants should be a minimum age of 20. For an application form send a 39p stamp to the above address. Some volunteers may also be needed to work with children and the handicapped.

The Canadian branch of UNIPAL is at 9 Cavendish Square, WIM 9DD, Canada.

Long and short-term placements are available. UNIPAL's Summer Programme, lasting approximately four to eight weeks, takes on about 50 volunteers annually (minimum age of 20), while the Long-term Programme is for a year, with the possibility of renewing the contract. Only about five volunteers are taken on the Long-Term Programme, and they must have at least the RSA Preliminary Certificate in TEFL and a degree. The minimum age limit is 22 years of age. Summer volunteers pay their own airfares, with food, board maintenance and insurance paid for them. In both cases, prospective volunteers must be available for interview in Britain.

UNIPAL issues a free, yearly newsletter, and through its files of ex-volunteers can bring together people interested in Palestinian issues.

Other Contacts for Work Projects in Palestine:
Al Hadaf: P.O. Box 169, Um al-Fahm 30010; tel 06-6312040; fax 06-6312915.

Al Nahdah Centre:, P.O. Box 92 Taybeh 40400; tel 02-993 3035; fax 02-993 3018.

Other Voluntary and Work/Study Programmes

The American Zionist Youth Foundation (AZYF): Israel Action Center, 110 East 59th Street, 4th Floor, New York, NY 10022; tel 212-339-6940; fax 212-755 4781. The University Student Department of the AZYF holds details of a range of programmes in Israel including volunteer work, archaeology and other work. Accredited programmes are available based in the main cities

Bridge in Britain Programme (Friends of Israel Educational Trust), POB 754525 Lyndale Avenue, London NW2 2QB; tel 020-7435 6803; fax 020-7794 0291; e-mail foiasg@foiasg.free-online.co FIET was established to promote an understanding of the geographies, histories, cultures and peoples of Israel. It sponsors a scholarship programme for 12 school leavers each year, called The Bridge in Britain Programme. Successful applicants are offered a passage to Israel and free board and lodging for five creative months in that country: spending time on a kibbutz or moshav, in community service, seminars and on tours of Israel. The trust also offers placements in Israel for young artists, farmers and horticulturalists/botanists.

Applicants must be over 18 and in good health. Scholarships are awarded to the writers of the best essays explaining their reasons for wishing to spend time in Israel.

For further details send a self-addressed envelope to Friends of Israel Educational Trust at the above address.

Computer Programmer Volunteers for Kibbutzim. A veteran volunteer of seven kibbutzim, Argentine Marcello Montagna might be able to help those going to Israel, who have a knowledge of various programmes to get work for an internet company in a kibbutz. He runs his own website for volunteers *Kibbutz Volunteers Travel Guide.* Contact him at webmaster@forum.nu or marcelo@gezernet.co.il

GAP Activity Projects (GAP) Ltd. GAP House, 44 Queen's Road, Reading, Berks RG1 4BB; tel 0118-9594914; fax 0118-957 6634; e-mail Volunteer@gap.org.uk website www.gap.org.uk
Gap Activity Projects is a global charity committed to international exchange through volunteering. About 14,000 young people from the UK took placements in 33 countries last year. In Israel, there are several possibilities: for the medically inclined there is work in a French hospital in Jerusalem, or an Arab village in a 'Home for Parents.' If your interests tend towards art and literature, you can help teach English in a teacher training college in Haifa. Other placements are in a variety of Arabic-speaking schools in and around Nazareth/Galilee with Arab-Israeli families. There is a placement in a therapeutic horse riding centre (equine experience and qualifications needed), kibbutz and conservation work. Placements last for four to six months. Board and accommodation are laid on, and in some cases pocket money is provided. Most volunteers are aged 18/19 and are between school and university. Overall costs £1,200-£1,700 depending on placement and includes registration fee (£35), Gap Fee for administration of the programme (£515), airfare (variable), Gap Insurance (from £68), Teaching skills course (only for teaching

placements). Volunteers are helped to fundraise the cost of their placement through sponsorship.

Israel Program Center: Jewish Community Centre of Greater Philadelphia, 401 S Broad Street, Philadelphia, PA 19147; tel (215) 545 1451. Keeps list and details of organisations needing volunteers in Israel.

Kishor Village: M.P. Maale Hagalil 252149; tel +972 4-958 7575; fax +972 4 9986810; e-mail Kishor@internet-zahav.net Kishor Village for people with special needs (mental disabilities) was formerly a kibbutz. The village takes Israeli and foreign (at present mostly Danes and Germans) volunteers to help in the plastics factory, kennels, goat farm, dining hall and kitchen alongside village members and staff. They help with socialising and talking with the village members.

Jewish Agency: Information & Service Center, P.O. Box 31677, Jerusalem 91030; tel 02-6232099; 6246522; fax 02-6235328. The Agency is a useful source of job opportunity information for volunteer work as well as Hebrew study and kibbutz. Note that the Agency is primarily geared to immigrant assistance and long-term visitors.

Livnot U'Lehibanot: 110 E.59th Street, 3rd Floor, New York, NY10022; tel 212-752 2390; fax 832-2597; or in Israel: 27 Ben-Zakkai, Katamon, Jerusalem 93585; tel +972-2-679 3491; fax +972-2-6793492; e-mail livpr@livnot.org.il website www.livnot.org.il *Livnot u'lehibanot* translates as 'build and be built.' This organisation runs about 20 Jewish awareness programmes in Israel a year, for young Jewish adults aged from 21 to 30. Programmes last from two weeks to three months.

Based in Tzfat and Jerusalem, Livnot takes a multi-faceted approach to learning which incorporates hiking and voluntary work, seminars on Jewish ethics, philosophy and traditions, Zionism and Jewish identity.

The voluntary work takes the form of community service such as repairing and painting the apartments of immigrants, establishing children's playgrounds and excavations of the tunnels of the Western Wall.

In addition to the regular programmes Livnot offers another opportunity for Jewish volunteers in which free accommodation is provided at the Jerusalem campus from Sundays to Thursdays, in return for about four daily hours community service work in the Jerusalem area.

Nes Ammim Village D.N. Ashrat 25225; tel 04-825522; fax 04-826872.
Nes Ammim, situated in the north-west of the Galilee region, is one of two moshav-type Christian villages in Israel. Founded in the 1960s it comprises about 100 people predominantly of Dutch and German origins. *Nes Ammim* means 'a banner for all the nations' (quoted from the book of Isaiah). The residents of Nes Ammim are 'mature, card-carrying Christians'.

Volunteers are expected to be sympathetic to the strong Christian ethos of the village and must sign a declaration that they will not undertake missionary work amongst the Jews while at Nes Ammim.

Apart from the Christian aspect, Nes Ammim functions much like any other agriculture based settlement. Its main commercial enterprises are roses grown for export, and avocados. It also has tourist facilities in the form of a guest house and youth hostel. It runs an annual work and information programme for young European students.

Volunteers essentially have to want a challenge and a chance to deepen and stretch their spiritual life. Nes Ammim demands as much as any moshav on the work front, as well as a special commitment to its aims.

Work: agricultural work; also carpentry, plumbing and maintenance skills are needed for the upkeep of the buildings; 'a fifty hour week of sweat and labour' as it is officially described in the publicity literature. Strong preference is given to those who can stay for a minimum of six months and a year is preferred. It is easier for the volunteer if they have a working knowledge of German or Dutch as these are the main languages of the village.

Volunteers apply a year in advance and must have a broad knowledge of theology. Help with practical tasks (building, construction, maintenance, horticulture, as well as adminstrative ones such as marketing. Board and lodging are provided in return for help. (Note that evangelising by Christians amongst the Jews in Israel is strongly frowned upon by the Jewish authorities).

Neve Shalom/Wahat al-Salam (Oasis of Peace)

Situated on a hilltop midway between Tel Aviv and Jerusalem, Neve Shalom/Wahat al-Salam (NSWAS) has been described as 'the Israeli village where Jews and Arabs live in peace.' NS/WAS was started in the mid-1970s by Bruno Hussar, a Dominican monk of Jewish descent, and consists of a co-operative village with unique educational institutions. The village comprises 35 families, with an equal proportion of Jews and Palestinian Arabs of Israeli citizenship.

In 1948, NSWAS started a pioneering, bilingual, binational school. Today, this includes kindergarten to sixth grade levels and has an enrolment of 260 children, who come from the village and 20 other communities in the vicinity. The NSWAS school remains the country's only comprehensive, binational, educational establishment, but has become a much-studied model for similar educational experiments.

NSWAS's main contribution to Palestinian-Jewish reconcilation is the School for Peace, which conducts Palestinian/Jewish encounter workshops and courses. Since its inception in 1979, some 25,000 young people and adults have taken part in their activities. The School for Peace, puts its wealth of experience at the disposal of other organisations dealing with conflict management and peace work, by providing professional training for facilitators in this field of work.

NSWAS welcomes volunteers (usually five to six at a time) throughout the year, for periods of six to twelve months. Volunteers perform menial tasks in the guest house, educational institutions, or outdoors. Applicants should note however that volunteers should not expect to be involved directly in educational work or peace activities. Conditions are similar to those found in kibbutzim. Volunteers work about 40 hours a week and an allowance and some perks are provided. More information, rules of the establishment and an application form can be obtained from the website www.nswas.com or by writing to the Volunteer Coordinator (Neve Shalom/Wahat al-Salam), 99761 Doar Na Shimshon, Israel; tel +972(0)2-9912222; fax +972(0)29912098; e-mail rita@nswas.com).

Through its guest house and group visits branch, NSWAS also offers interesting programmes for visiting groups. Individuals interested in paying a visit should contact the Public Relations Office (tel +972(0)2 9915621; fax +972(0)2 9911072; e-mail pr@nswas.com to make an appointment.

Project Otzma

Project Otzma is a 10 month (from mid-August to June) volunteer leadership development programme for Jewish adults aged 20-24 (college graduates preferred). Otzma provides its participants with the opportunity to live and work with Israelis on kibbutzim, youth aliyah villages, immigration absorption centres, and areas of urban renewal. OTZMA also includes an intensive educational programme including hiking trips throughout the country, and the unique experience of an Israeli adoptive family. Upon return to North America, OTZMA graduates are expected to apply their skills and knowledge to serve their local Jewish communities.

The programme costs $1850 plus flights. Further details from: Nessa Saltzman (Project Otzma, 111 Eighth Avenue, Suite 11E, New York, NY 10011; e-mail nessa.Saltzman@ujcna.org website www.projectotzma.org

Shatil

Operated by the New Israel Fund's Capacity Building Center for Social Change Organisations, Shatil places volunteers with organisations that work to safeguard democracy through the protection of the civil rights of Arabs and Jews and through promoting Jewish-Arab co-existence, fostering tolerance and promoting religious pluralism, protection of the environment and increasing accountability in government. Volunteers work alongside Israeli activists and gain insight into the complexities and challenges faced by Israeli society.

Summer camps (2-4 weeks); all other times 12 weeks or longer. Those on internships and sometimes others may get board and lodging provided. Internees with fluent Hebrew/Arabic staying six months+ will get a subsistence stipend.

Further details from Shatil, Capacity Building Center for Social Change Organisations, 9 Yad Ha-Rutzim Street, Jerusalem 91534; tel +972 2 672 3095; fax +972 2 672 30 3597; fax +972 2 6735149; e-mail volunteer@shatil.nif.org.il In the USA contact New Israel Fund (1625 K Street NW, Washington D.C., 20006; tel 202-223-3333.

Society for the Protection of Nature in Israel

This society used to employ volunteers at its field study centres, but sadly this is believed to be no longer the case. It may still be worth making enquiries. In return for bed and board and a food allowance volunteers did basic maintenance work around the Society's field study centres and occasionally participated in the centre's activities and outings. SPNI operate FSC's all over Israel and some of the activities they organise are hiking, camel, donkey and jeep tours, field-craft and survival courses, lectures and seminars.

A better bet is volunteer office work. The Director of Development, Sharon Hoffman, says that the SPNI is 'always looking for English-speaking volunteers to help with fund-raising.' As an incentive, volunteers can join in the English-speaking SPNI tours (subject to places being available) for free.

The head office of the SPNI (4 Hashfela Street, 66183; tel Aviv; tel 03-6388674; fax 03-6883940; e-mail tourism@spni.org.il website www.spni.org) where you can ask about office work volunteering and get a list of the FSCs around Israel. For outdoor jobs, you will probably stand a better chance if you contact the individual centres direct as there is no personnel department at the Tel-Aviv office.

University Studies Abroad Consortium: University of Nevada, Reno/323, Reno, Nevada 89557; tel 775-784-6569; fax 775 784 6010; e-mail usac@admin.unr.edu Website: www.scsr.nevada.edu/~usac Offers a semester or year-long Israeli and General Studies programme at Ben Gurion university, Beer Sheva. Course work may be complemented by internships, independent research, and/or volunteer work in and around the Beer Sheva area.

Volunteers for Israel: 330 W.42nd Street, 1618 New York, NY 10036; tel 212-643-4848; fax 643-4855; e-mail vol4israel@aol.com This programme places volunteers for three week stints in military support jobs at IDF army bases. Forget any Rambo amibitions as this involves only the most menial tasks including dish washing and repair work. You get a uniform for the duration, and accommodation in army barracks. Other volunteer jobs are available in hospitals, archaeological excavations and botanical gardens. Some reduced airfares are available, but there is a non-refundable registration fee of $100. Minimum age is 18 for Volunteers for Israel Program; ages 16-24 for Student Volunteers for Israel Program.

Weizman Institute of Science: P.O. Box 26, Rehovot 76100; tel +972 8 343860; fax +972 8 471667; e-mail rsmajor@weizmann.weizmann.ac.il website www.weizmann.ac.il/acadsec/kkiss—blurb.html
Research students are needed to join a research project involving the mathematical sciences, physics, chemistry, biophysics, biochemistry and biology. A small stipend is provided. Projects last for between 10 weeks and 4 months during summer. Applicants must have completed at least one year of university and have some research experience.

Application forms are available on the website and should be sent to The Academic Secretary's office by 31 December each year.

Ski Resort

Israel's only ski resort is the Mount Hermon Ski Centre in the Golan Heights (likely to revert to Syria under the peace deal) i.e. near the Lebanese border. The season is short by European and US standards running from December to the end of March at the latest. The resort recruits ski instructors and all other personnel a few weeks before the season starts through the Moshav Volunteers' Center in Tel Aviv; or you can contact the ski resort information office at Moshav Neve Ativ, DN 12010 Ramat Hagolan; 6981333. The ski station is 10km from Neve Ativ.

Career Work

There are opportunities for more career-oriented jobs in Israel. For instance, the international company Regus which provides serviced business centres worldwide has a centre in the Ramat Gan district of Tel Aviv. Staff at the centre include personal assistant, centre and sales managers and others. Graduates and those with language skills are suitable applicants. Intensive training provided.
Regus: 3, Abba Hillel Silver Street, Ramat Gan, Tel Aviv 52522 Israel; tel +972 3 754 11 11; fax +972 3 754 11 00.

Information Technology
The area along the Mediterranean Coast northwards from Tel-Aviv to Herzliya and between this area and Jerusalem has come to be recognised as Israel's Sili-

con Valley (or Wadi) in acknowledgement of the burgeoning IT industry in Israel which has developed hugely in the last decade. It is now an important phenomenon in the Israeli economy. Companies like CommTouch (e-mail services) employ hundreds of staff and are valued in millions of pounds. Other young and dynamic companies include DealTime.com (electric commerce company) with 100 staff and growing, Check Point Software (now in the world top 80 software companies). Mirabilis (an internet chat-system), so impressed AOL with its popularity (second only to household names like Yahoo! Netscape and Bill Gates's company) that it bought Mirabilis outright.

Kibbutzim Guide

Listed alphabetically

Code number indicates position on maps

FOR DETAILS OF HOW TO APPLY, SEE APPLICATION, PAGES 90-97

Due to the political situation in the Middle East, International borders have not been marked on the two maps. A few Kibbutzim are sited in occupied territory.

(22) KIBBUTZ ADAMIT
D.N. Upper Galilee 22875; tel: 04-9859100; fax 04-9806021.
Founded: 1971.
Members: 42. Volunteers: 20-30.
Responsible for volunteers: Rachel Levi/Rosa Gonzalez.
Work available: agricultural work in season, gardens, factory, kitchen/dining room, poultry, guest houses, laundry.
Working hrs.: 5 1/2 day week.
Time off: 3 days per month.
Minimum/maximum stay: 2 months up to 6 months.
Free: soap, toothpaste, toilet paper.
Accommodation: apartments with single bathroom. 2 people to a room; 4 people per apartment.
Sports/entertainments: swimming pool, basketball court, bar (twice weekly), volunteer club.
Other facilities: access to members' clubhouse with video, yoga classes, some gym equipment, library, film shows.
Nearest town: Naharia 20 minutes drive/bus ride. 3 buses daily and lifts.
Excursions: one day trip per month and a three-day trip after three months. Also nearby beach and local kibbutzim.
Main Languages: Hebrew, English, Spanish, French.
Other Information: Some distance to main road. A young, friendly kibbutz. Good location with healthy air and panoramic views. Good area for hiking and caving.
Kibbutz Movement: Ha'artzi.

(49) KIBBUTZ AFEK
Afek P.O.30042; tel: 04-9784060/9784222; fax 04-9784148.
Founded: 1947.
Members: approx 550 including children. Volunteers: 20-30.
Work available: Agriculture, factory, kitchen, laundry, children's houses, dining room, cowshed, fishponds, gardening.
Working hours: 8-hours, 6-days.

Days off: 3 extra days monthly.
Minimum/maximum stay: 6 weeks up to 9 months if visa can be obtained.
Free: 2 aerogrammes and 2 newspapers each per week.
Accommodation: wooden huts (shack), caravan, concrete houses. 2-3 to a room.
Sports/entertainments: basket/volley ball, tennis, pub, TV room.
Facilities: swimming pool.
Excursions: trips to local places of interest. Three-day trip with expert guides for groups.
Nearest town: Haifa (frequent buses).
Languages spoken: Hebrew, Yiddish, Polish, English.
Other Information: shopping mall nearby. No Ulpan courses.
Kibbutz Movement: Takam.

(54)KIBBUTZ AFIK
D.N. Ramat Hagolan 12938; tel: 06-6761211.
Founded: 1972.
Members: 100. Volunteers: 20-30 summer, 10-20 winter.
Work available: Apple orchards, avocados, factory, laundry, chickens, dairy, cotton, kitchen, dining room, tourist park.
Working hours: 8-hour day 6-day week.
Time off: 3 extra days a month.
Free: work clothes/shoes, 8 aerogrammes monthly, cleaning supplies, paper goods, laundry service.
Accommodation: 5-6 to a 3-room apartment (includes shower and toilet). Vegetarian and diet meals.
Sports/Entertainment: tennis, basketball, volleyball, soccer, softball, exercise classes, weight room, movie weekly, disco on Fridays.
Facilities: swimming pool (June-October), library, club house with TV, shop, music room.
Languages: Hebrew, English, Spanish.
Excursions: monthly day trip; and afternoon trips after work, to sights in the area.
Minimum stay: one month.

Other Information: ages 18-30. Groups and individuals. Fairly frequent bus service in the kibbutz and from main road. 45 minutes to Tiberius. Easy access to Lake Kinneret. Free entrance and bus service to our tourist site (Hammat Gader). Holidays observed. Volunteers are encouraged to join and participate at all kibbutz functions. The Golan Heights is a beautiful area for people who like the outdoors and nature hikes.

(76)KIBBUTZ AFIKIM
Jordan Valley 15148; tel: 06-6754611; fax 06-6751762.
Founded: 1927.
Members: 1500. Volunteers: 25.
Work available: banana groves, gardening, dining room, kitchen, restaurant, hostel.
Working hours: 8-hour 5-day week.
Days off, 1 weekly, plus Saturdays.
Accommodation: concrete rooms, separate toilets, 2+ people to a room. Kosher food.
Sports/Entertainments: football, tennis, weekly disco and bar daily.
Facilities: swimming pool, gymnasium, clubhouse with TV, shop selling toiletries and confectionery.
Nearest town: Tiberias.
Main languages: Hebrew, English.
Minimum stay: 2 months.
Other information: ages 18-32. Religious holidays and festivals observed. Close to bus stop and main road.
Kibbutz movement: Takam.

(157a)KIBBUTZ ALMOG
Kikar HaYarden 90665; tel 02-9945200; fax 02-9942448.
Founded: 1979.
Members: 40; Volunteers: 10-15.
Responsible for volunteers: Gazi.
Work available: date orchard, dining room, kitchen, guest house, tourist shop, gardening, cowshed.
Accommodation: fair/good. 2-3 volunteers per room with own wc, shower and air conditioning.
Free: aerogrammes.

Facilities: swimming pool, basketball court, pub. Nearby water park and Dead Sea.
Excursions: weekend every 4 months plus any additional trips together with the kibbutz.
Nearest town: Jerusalem (30 minutes).
Minimum stay: two months.
Main language: English.
Other information: no Ulpan courses.
Kibbutz Movement: Meuchad.

(61)KIBBUTZ ALONIM
Doar Alonim 30040; tel: 04-9838211.
Founded: 1935/1938.
Members: 350.
Work available: fruit trees, citrus groves, dining room, kitchen, field crops, gas station shop, poultry, factory for aluminium, ironworks, metal coating works.
Accommodation: 3 to a room. Fan in summer; heater in winter.
Free: toiletries, cleaning materials, extra fruit, cheese, cookies, tea and coffee.
Facilities: coffee house, swimming pool, tennis court, gym, library, shop.
Other Information: on the main road between Haifa and Tiberias, 45 minutes from each. 2 days holiday every month and occasional trips of 2 days in the north or 3 days in the south.
Minimum stay 2 months.
Main languages: Hebrew, English, German.
Kibbutz Movement: Takam.

(61)KIBBUTZ ALUMIM
D N HaNegev 85138; tel: 07-9949711; fax 07-9937000; e-mail www.poboxes.com/alumim
Founded: 1966.
Members: approx 150. Volunteers: 5-20.
Work available: agricultural work (including avocados, carrots and potatoes), dining room, kitchen, laundry and children's houses.
Days off: Saturday and 1 day off a month.
Free: aerogrammes.

Accommodation: Pre-cast huts, three or four to a room. Food is kosher.
Sports/Entertainments: basketball court and football ground, gym for working out, own club room with internal television channel showing films etc.
Facilities: swimming pool (summer), library, shop selling sweets, stationery, toiletries.
Main Languages: Hebrew, English.
Nearest towns: Beersheva, Ashkelon, and with a beach: Sderot.
Excursions: by arrangements with group organiser. Possibility of inclusion for individual volunteers.
Other Information: religious kibbutz whose members' lives are determined by their beliefs. Any volunteer must be committed to the observance of the Commandments, Shabbat, dress codes, synagogue attendance etc. Close to bus stop and main road. Kibbutz family can be arranged.
Kibbutz Movement: Hadati (Religious movement). Potential volunteers should applyto the Religious Kibbutz Movement offices.

(67)KIBBUTZ ALUMOT
D.N. Lower Galilee 15223; tel: 06-6653411; fax 06-6653412.
Founded: 1936/1946. Refounded: 1936.
Members: 130.
Work available: kitchen, dining room, ironing, children's houses, beach work in summer, country lodging, agriculture, cowsheds, chickens, wood workshop.
6 days per week, 8 hours per day. Three days off per month.
Accommodation: rooms for 3-4 volunteers.
Sports/Entertainments: basketball, tennis, football, pub, swimming pool, beach on the Sea of Galilee, library, club.
Main languagues: Hebrew, English, Spanish.
Other information: 20 minutes from Tiberias and 5 minutes from the Sea of Galilee; bus from Tel Aviv to Tiberias 830. Bus from Tiberias to Alumot 30,32. Bus from Haifa to Tiberias 430.
Kibbutz Movement: Takam.

(43) KIBBUTZ AMIAD
D.N. Hevel Korazim 12335; tel 06-6933550; fax 06-6933866.
Founded: 1946.
Members: 220. Volunteers: maximum of 12.
Owing to changes in the kibbutz, volunteers are no longer taken.
Kibbutz Movement: Takam.

(12) KIBBUTZ AMIR
D.N. Upper Galilee 12140; tel 06-6954442; fax 06-6954461.
Founded: 1939.
Members: 340. Volunteers: 20.
Responsible for volunteers: Lindsay Alexander & Helen Ekekrantz.
Work available: dining room, kitchen, cotton, fish ponds, apples, cows, chickens and diaper (nappy) factory, T-shirt factory.
Days off: Saturdays and 2 days a month.
Free: soap, aerogrammes, toothpaste, condoms, work clothes, tampons.
Accommodation: 2 volunteers per room. No kosher food.
Sports/Entertainments: Gymnasium, squash, football, basketball, weekly film shows, occasional dances.
Facilities: swimming pool, library, clubhouse, shop.
Main Languages: Hebrew, English, Spanish.
Excursions: 4-day trip every three months plus day trips.
Nearest town: Kiryat Shemona 7km.
Minimum stay: three months.
Other Information: festivals and religious holidays observed. Groups preferred. Ages 18-35. Close to main road and bus stop. No Ulpan for non-Jewish volunteers.
Kibbutz Movement: Hakibbutz Ha'artzi.

(84) KIBBUTZ ASHDOT YAACOV
D.N. Emek Hayarden 15155; tel 06-6756211.
Founded : 1924.
Kibbutz Movement: Takam.
No longer takes volunteers and does not envisage taking them again in the future.

(32) KIBBUTZ AYELET HASHA-HAR
Doar Ayelet HaShahar 12200; tel 06-6932111.
Other Information: owing to changes on the kibbutz volunteers are no longer needed at Ayelet Hashachar.
Kibbutz Movement: Takam.

(140) KIBBUTZ BAHAN
D.N.Hefer 38827; tel 09-8763333; 09-8763758.
Founded: 1954.
Members: 300. No Volunteers since 1989.
Agriculture work, factory work, services.
Kibbutz Movement: Takam.

(27) KIBBUTZ BAR AM
Merom Hagalil 13860; tel 06-6988111; fax 06-6987777.
Founded: 1949.
Members: 300. Volunteers: winter 35-40. summer 60-80.
Work available: packing shed, dining room, gardens, cotton, fishponds, plastics factory, apples.
Working hours: 6-hours daily; 6-day week.
Days off: 2 days off monthly
Free: three aerogrammes weekly, coffee, tea, sweets, toiletries.
Accommodation: 2 to a room in winter, 3 to a room in summer.
Sports/Entertainments: tennis, football, basketball, films,, occasional dances.
Facilities: swimming pool, small library, clubhouse, shop.
Nearest main towns: Sefad 40km; Haifa 160km.
Main Languages: Hebrew, French, English.
Excursions: 1 day-trip a month. Every 3 months 3-day trip.
Other Information: minimum stay 1 month, maximum 6 months. Ages 18-33. Individuals and groups. Possibility of kibbutz family. Near main road. No Ulpan courses.
Kibbutz Movement: Ha'artzi.

(120) KIBBUTZ BARKAI
D.N. Menashe 37860; tel 06-6387111; fax 06-6387119.
Founded: 1949.
Members: 250.
No longer takes volunteers.
Avocados, dairy, chickens, factory, services.
Nearest town: Hadera 15km. Has shopping mall and all urban facilities.
Nearest beach: 15km.
Main Languagues: Hebrew, English.
Kibbutz Movement: Ha'artzi.

(206) KIBBUTZ BEERI
D.N. Hanegev 85135; tel 07-9949111; fax 07-9949437.
Founded: 1944/1946.
Members: 380, aged 25-55.
Volunteers: winter plus/minus 40; summer plus/minus 20.
Work available: agricultural, printing, services, fruit picking.
Free: biscuits and cigarettes.
Accommodation: 2-3 to a room depending on season. Separate toilet and shower block.
Nearest town: location in Northern Negev 90km south of Tel Aviv, 45 km west of Beersheva.
Facilities: clubhouse, cable video system, weekly films, volunteers invited to all cultural events. Bus to Bethlehem for Christmas.
Kibbutz Movement: Takam.

(155) KIBBUTZ BE'EROT YITZHAK
D.N.Beerot Yitzhak 60905; tel: 03-9371972; fax 03-9334991.
Founded: 1935/1943.
Members: 200; volunteers: occasional-

ly from June 12th to July 12 or from December 12 to January 12 for one month.
Responsible for volunteers: Eli Berman/Ester Forsher.
Work available: kitchen, dining room, kindergarten teacher,children's houses, laundry, metal plating factory, garage, chickens and turkeys, farm work and orchards.
Working hours: 8-hour day, six-day week.
Days off: every Saturday and 1 day monthly.
Free: monthly budget for use in store and for mail and telephone.
Accommodation: Pre-cast huts, 3 to a room. Food strictly Kosher.
Sports/Entertainments: basketball, volleyball, tennis, swimming, weekly films.
Facilities: English and Hebrew library, volunteers' clubhouse, shop.
Main Languages: Hebrew and English.
Other Information: specialises in Ulpan courses (two a year) so there is no regular programme for volunteers. However, sometimes, the kibbutz accepts volunteers for a month in June/July, December/January. Religious holidays observed. Close to bus stop, Lod Airport, Tel Aviv. Kibbutz family arranged. Only Jewish volunteers accepted.
Ulpan: 60 students, vacancies for some couples; e-mail Ulpan oi@netvision.net.il
Kibbutz Movement: Hadati.

(111) KIBBUTZ BET ALFA
D.N. Gilboa 19140; tel: 06-6533032; fax 06-6533987
Founded: 1920/1922.
Members: 500.
Volunteers: 20-25.
Work available: citrus, tomatoes, melons, fishponds, fields, cows, poultry, fire-fighting vehicle production, kitchen, dining room, laundry, zoo, children's house, factory work etc.
Working hours: 8-hour day, 6-day week.

Days off: 3 extra days off monthly.
Free: nothing, but volunteer allowance is NIS 268 monthly.
Accommodation: built in 1980. 2-3 persons per room.
Sports/Entertainments: basketball, football, tennis.
Facilities: swimming pool, gymnasium, library, TV room, shop, clubhouse.
Languages: Hebrew, English, Spanish, German, Polish.
Excursions: full day-trip every five weeks. Hot spring (28°C all year) 2km. Nearest towns: Bet Shere (7km) is 10 minutes by bus. Afula is 30 minutes by bus.
Minimum/maximum stay: 1 month up to 6 months (because of visa limit).
Other Information: ages 18-35. No kosher food. Close to bus stop and main road. Holidays observed. Possibility of Kibbutz family. Lectures given in English. Hebrew lessons given according to demand. Application to the kibbutz by mail welcomed.
Kibbutz Movement: Takam-Artzi.

(186) KIBBUTZ BET GUVRIN
D.N. Lachish Darom 79370; tel: 07-6874210; fax 07-6874888.
Founded: 1949.
Members: 120. Volunteers: 24.
Responsible for volunteers: Tuula Golan.
Work available: fields, children's houses, laundry, dining room, cow, factory, ironing room, carpentry, kitchen, garden, tourist shop, restaurant.
Days off: 2 per month.
Free: toiletries, 2 aerogrammes, condoms.
Accommodation: wooden houses. 2 people per room. No kosher food.
Sports/Entertainments: tennis, basketball, football, disco on Fridays, videos,.
Facilities: swimming pool in summer only, library, members' clubhouse with TV and games, shops.
Main Languages: Hebrew, English,

French.
Excursions: full-day trip every second month and 3-day trip every 3 months.
Nearest town: Kiriat Gat 15km. Tel-Aviv and Jerusalem easily accessible by bus.
Minimum stay: 3 months; maximum 6 months.
Other Information: ages 18-30. Bus stop on kibbutz, some way from main road. Holidays observed. No possibility of kibbutz family. Groups and individuals. Acceptable volunteers encouraged to stay. Volunteers take part in all cultural activities. No kosher food. Compulsory, free HIV test on arrival at the kibbutz,
Kibbutz Movement: Takam.

(39) KIBBUTZ BET HA'EMEK
D.N. Ashrat 25115; tel: 04-9960511/411.
Founded: 1949.
Responsible for volunteers: David Jackson.
Work available: field work, avocados, bananas, chickens, cows, dining room, kitchens, hatchery, greenhouses, biological laboratory.
Working hours: 8-hour, 6-day week.
Days off: 3 per month.
Free: 3 aerogrammes per week.
Accommodation: 2-3 persons per room. No kosher food.
Entertainment: weekly disco, pub Wednesday and Friday nights.
Facilities: swimming pool, library, clubhouse. Shop selling all necessities.
Main Languages: Hebrew, English.
Excursions: every 3 months a 3-4 day trip.
Nearest town: Nahariya.
Minimum/maximum stay: 1 month up to 6 months (longer by application).
Other Information: ages 18-27. Close to bus stop and main road. 13kms from the sea. An AIDS test on arrival is compulsory. Groups by arrangement. Accepts volunteer applications direct, provided applicants contact the volunteer organiser prior to arrival.
Kibbutz Movement: Takam.

(106) KIBBUTZ BET-HASHITA
Doar Bet Hashita 18910; tel 06-6536535; fax 06-6536335; e-mail info@gilboa.co.il
Founded: 1928.
Members: 700.
Grapefruits, pickling and machine factories.
Facilities: swimming pool, library, shop selling all necessities, gymnasium, clubhouse, supermarket.
Main Languages: Hebrew, English, German, French.
Nearest towns: between Afula and Bet Shean in the Jezreel Valley.
Other information: close to bus stop and main road.
No longer takes volunteers.
Kibbutz Movement: Takam.

(204) KIBBUTZ BET KAMA
D.N. Hanegev 85325; tel: 07-9915111; fax 07-9918007.
Founded: 1949.
Members: 180. Volunteers: none.
Fruits (Dec-May), staples factory.
Facilities: swimming pool, small library, clubhouse, general shop.
Main Languages: Hebrew, Spanish, English.
Other Information: no longer takes volunteers.
Kibbutz Movement: Ha'artzi.

(62) KIBBUTZ BEIT KESHET
Lower Galilee 15247; tel 06-6629000; fax 06-6760111.
Founded: 1944.
Members: 145. Volunteers: 4-6.
Work available: cows, dining hall, kitchen, garden, chickens, factory, services.
Working hours: 8-hour day, 6-day week.
Days off: 3 days extra off monthly.
Accommodation: pre-cast huts. 2-3 to a room.
Facilities: swimming pool, library, shop. No bar, no video.
Nearest towns: Afula 30 minutes drive, Tiberias $1^1/2$ hours from the main road.

Main Languages: Hebrew, English, French, Spanish.
Excursions: a one-day trip monthly.
Other Information: all holidays observed.
Kibbutz Movement: Takam.

(182) KIBBUTZ BET NIR
D.N. Sadeh Gat 79560; tel: 07-6874311; fax 07-9886815.
Founded: 1957.
Members: 130. Volunteers: 15-24.
Work available: cows, orange products, factory, chickens, silver jewellery, children's house, laundry, kitchen, dining room, cotton, olives.
Free: aerogrammes, some toiletries.
Accommodation: 2-3 to a room. No kosher food.
Sports/Entertainments: handball, basketball, football, weekly film shows, videos, monthly discos (or self-organized more often).
Facilities: swimming pool, library, volunteers' pub, clubhouse. Shop.
Main Languages: Hebrew, English.
Excursions: 1 trip monthly. 3-day trip every 3 months.
Minimum stay: 1 month.
Other Information: ages 18-30. 15km from main road. Kibbutz families provided. Groups and individuals accepted. Only agricultural and national holidays. Jewellery workshop and showroom.
Kibbutz Movement: Ha'artzi.

(58) KIBBUTZ BET OREN
Beit Oren 30044; tel: 04-8397222/8397200.
Founded: 1939.
Members: 155. Volunteers: 25.
Work available: banana groves, grapefruit, cotton fields, chickens, dining room, kitchen.
Working hours: 8-hour day; 5-day week.
Days off: 2 days extra per month.
Free: subsidised cigarettes, 3 aerogrammes weekly.
Accommodation: 2 to a room. No kosher food.

Sports/Entertainments: basketball, football, volleyball, table tennis, weekly film shows and disco.
Facilities: swimming pool, shop selling all necessities, clubhouse.
Main Languages: Hebrew, English.
Minimum stay: 3 months.
Other Information: ages 18-30. Bus stop on kibbutz. Some way from main road. No kibbutz family provided. Prefer individuals. Holidays observed. Tourist Guest House, 80 rooms, restaurant, gift shop, refreshment kiosk.
Kibbutz Movement: Takam.

(70) KIBBUTZ BET-ZERA
D.N. Emek Hayarden 15135; tel: 06-6755211; fax 06-6755134.
Founded: 1927.
Members: 440. Volunteers: none.
Bananas, dates, avocados, dairy herd, poultry, blacksmith's, plastics factory.
Facilities: swimming pool, library, shop.
Main Languages: Hebrew, English, German, Yiddish, Spanish.
Other Information: stopped taking volunteers.
Kibbutz Movement: Ha'artzi.

(193) KIBBUTZ BROR CHAIL (HAYIL)
D.N. Hof Ashkelon 79195; tel: 07-6803111.
Founded: 1948.
Members: 300. Volunteers: 20.
Work available: agricultural, industrial, services.
Working hours: 6-hour day.
Days off: 2 extra days off monthly.
Free: cigarettes, aerogrammes.
Accommodation: houses. 3-4 in a room. No kosher food.
Sports/Entertainments: weekly film shows and disco.
Facilities: swimming pool, English library.
Main Languages: Hebrew, Portuguese, English.
Mininimum stay: 1 months.
Other Information: ages 18+. Bus stop

on Kibbutz, close to main road. Groups and individuals. Holidays observed.
Kibbutz Movement: Takam.

(188) KIBBUTZ CARMIA
D.N. Hof Ashkelon 79135.
Founded: 1950.
Members: 96. Volunteers: 12.
Work available: cotton fields, factory, orchards, dining room, kitchen and chicken houses.
Working hours: 6¹/2-hour day, 6-day week.
Free: 6 packs of cigarettes monthly, 3 aerogrammes weekly, coffee, tea, basic toilet necessities.
Accommodation: stone houses of four rooms some with toilets and showers. 2-3 to a room.
Sports/Entertainments: basketball, table tennis, football, volleyball, folk dancing, weekly films, self-organised disco.
Facilities: swimming pool, library, clubhouse with TV, occasional lectures. Shop selling all necessities.
Main Languagues: Hebrew, French, Spanish.
Minimum stay: 1 month.
Other Information: ages 18-32. Holidays observed. Close to bus stop. 3km from main road. Possibility of kibbutz family. Takes groups of young Israelis who are potential settlers.
Kibbutz Movement: Ha'artzi.

(4) KIBBUTZ DAFNA
D.N. Upper Galilee 12235; tel: 06-6945743; fax 06-6945750.
Founded: 1939.
Members: 410+220 children. Volunteers: 60.
Responsible for volunteers: Schlomo Zahavi.
Work available: wellington boot factory, agriculture, kitchen, laundry, dining room.
Working hours: 8-hour day, 6-day week.
Days off: 3 extra days a month.
Free: nothing, in consideration of the

present economic situation but volunteers' monthly allowance is NIS250.
Accommodation: 2-3 sharing a room with WC and shower. No kosher food.
Sports/Entertainments: tennis, basketball, film show every two weeks, volunteer-run bar, kibbutz-run nightclub with cheap beer and good music.
Facilities: swimming pool, library (few English books). Shop selling all necessaries, gymnasium, horses.
Main Languages: Hebrew, English, German, Spanish.
Nearest town: Kiryat Shmona 8km.
Excursions: 4-day trip to Eilat every three months.
Minimum stay: 2 months (volunteer loses deposit of NIS150 if leaving earlier, except in exceptional circumstances). If the volunteer stays more than two months the kibbutz pays for a renewal visa up to six months total stay.
Other Information: ages 18-40. Holidays observed. Close to bus stop and main road. Overlooked by Mt Hermon. Average summer temperature (night and day) is 25-35°C; winter 1-12°C. Groups and individuals. British volunteers welcomed; others mainly from South Africa and Scandinavia. Applicants can apply in writing direct to kibbutz. Possibility of kibbutz family.
Kibbutz Movement: Takam.

(93) KIBBUTZ DALYA (DALIA)
Dalya 19239; tel: 04-9897512; fax 04-9897566; e-mail volunteers@dalia.org.il
Founded: 1939.
Members: 450. Volunteers: 35.
Responsible for volunteers: Elizabeth Harosh.
Work available: factories, services.
Working hours: 7-hour day; 6-day week.
Days off: 3 extra days off monthly.
Free: aerogrammes, hair shampoo.
Accommodation: 2 to a room. No kosher food.
Entertainments: weekly film show.

Facilities: swimming pool, library, shops, sports hall, disco, club.
Main Language: English.
Excursions: one trip every 4-6 weeks and a 3-day trip every 3-4 months.
Nearest towns: Yaakne'am 15km, Haifa 35km.
Minimum stay: 2 months.
Other Information: ages 18-32. Visa costs NIS 65. Bus stop on kibbutz. Bus 876 from Tel Aviv. Bus 184 from Haifa. Written applications to the Kibbutz are welcomed. No Ulpan. Volunteers have to pay NIS 45 for changing their visa from tourist to volunteer status and bring with them two passport photos and $50 deposit. Drugs, alcohol and guests for the night are not permitted.
Kibbutz Movement: Ha'artzi.

(5) KIBBUTZ DAN
D.N. Upper Galilee 12245; tel: 06-6953811; fax 06-6953999.
Founded: 1939.
Members: 300. Volunteers:10-15.
Responsible for volunteers: Cliff King.
Work available: orchards, fish ponds, bees, kitchen, dining room, laundry, factory manufacturing sprinklers and plastic wall coverings.
Working hours: 9-hour day, 6-day week.
Days off, Saturdays plus 3 days monthly.
Free: toiletries, aerogrammes.
Accommodation: pre-fabs, 3 to a room with bathroom.
Sports/Entertainments: tennis (bring own racquet), weekly films and disco, rafting nearby.
Facilities: gymnasium, library, swimming pool (May to Oct), shop, clubhouse. Nearby tennis centre.
Nearest town: Kiryat Shemona 8km.
Excursions: monthly day trip; 3-day trip every 3 months, only if possible or if there are enough people.
Minimum stay: 2 months. Maximum 6 months.
Other Information: all holidays observed. Apply direct by post or tele-

phone in advance. Main holidays observed. No Ulpan.
Kibbutz Movement: Ha'artzi.

(66) KIBBUTZ DEGANIA 'A'
D.N. Emek Hayarden 15120. tel: 06-6758101.
Founded: 1910.
Members: 380. Volunteers: none.
Bananas, grapefruit, dates.
Facilities: swimming in the sea of Galilee and river Jordan, library.
Main Languages: Hebrew, English, German.
Nearest town: Tiberias, 15 minutes by bus.
Other Information: this was the first ever kibbutz in Israel, but sadly no longer takes volunteers.
Kibbutz Movement: Takam.

(69) KIBBUTZ DEGANIA 'B'
Emek Hayarden 15130; tel: 06-6755938; fax 06-6755989.
Founded: 1920.
Members: 250. Volunteers: 20-30.
Responsible for volunteers: Mrs. Bella Peters.
Work available: bananas, avocados, field crops, dates, dairy farm, gardening, dining room, kitchen, laundry, baby house, guest house.
Free: coffee, tea, sugar, fruit.
Accommodation: old, 2 to a room or 4 to a two-bedroomed flat.
Sports/Entertainments: tennis, basketball, volleyball, swimming pool, library, weekly disco, volunteers' pub, TV room with central video.
Other facilities nearby: ten minutes walk to the Sea of Galilee and the Jordan River. Beit Gabriel Cultural Centre 5 minutes by bus.
Excursions: trip every two months.
Nearest town: Tiberias, 15 minutes by bus.
Main language spoken among volunteers: English.
Minimum/maximum stay: 2 months up to 6 months.
Other Information: no Ulpan courses. Applications (even from return volun-

teers) through the Takam office in Tel-Aviv only. Recent HIV test certificate to be brought with the volunteer from abroad.
Kibbutz Movement: Takam.

(196) KIBBUTZ DOROT
D N Hof Ashkelon 79175; tel 07-9808011; fax 07-9808898.
Founded: 1941.
Members & children: 600. Volunteers: none at present.
Responsible for volunteers: Mark Bendor.
Work available: kitchen, dining room, factory, gardening, clothing store, and anywhere needed.
Working hours: 40 weekly; 6-day week.
Free: aerogrammes. For beverages etc. volunteers receive coupons.
Accommodation: 2 people to a room with shower, wc, kitchenette, fridge etc.
Sports/entertainments: football, tennis, basketball etc. , disco Friday evenings with bar, weekly films, videos nightly.
Excursions: full day trip monthly, 3-day trips every 2-3 months. Ashkelon beach is half an hour's drive.
Facilities: swimming pool, shop.
Nearest towns: Beersheva (one hour), Tel Aviv, Ashkelon & Jerusalem (1¹/₂ hours by bus).
Main languages: Hebrew, German, English.
Other information: owing to accommodation problems, the kibbutz cannot take volunteers at present. However, this may change. Mandatory HIV test on kibbutz. Volunteer allowance is NIS250 monthly and NIS50 daily on a trip. Direct applications accepted. Volunteers get one day free a week which they can accumulate to travel on their own anywhere they want. No Ulpan courses.
Kibbutz Movement: Takam.

(83) KIBBUTZ DOVRAT
D.N. Yizrael 19325; tel 06-6599407; fax 06-6597534.

Founded: 1946.
Members: 160. Volunteers: 20.
Responsible for volunteers: Dalilah Kaplan.
Work available: restaurant, kitchen, dining room, citrus groves, cows, fields, garden, laundry, children's house.
Free: beverages.
Accommodation: wooden and new stone house, 2 to a room. No kosher food.
Sports/Entertainments: football, basketball, videos, bar, discos.
Facilities: swimming pool, library, clubhouse.
Main Languages: Hebrew, Spanish, German.
Excursions: one trip every two months.
Minimum stay: 1 month.
Other information: ages 18-28. Close to bus stop and main road. Groups and individuals. Possibility of kibbutz family. No Ulpan.
Kibbutz Movement: Takam.

(208) KIBBUTZ DVIR
D.N. Hanegev 85330; tel: 07-9914211; fax 07-9918419.
Founded: 1951.
Members: 120. Volunteers: 30-40.
Work available: dining room, kitchen, cowsheds, orchards, irrigation, laundry. People with specialist skills such as electricians, mechanics, plumbers, especially welcome.
Working hours: 6 day week.
Days off: 2 extra days monthly.
Free: toiletries, cigarettes, sweets, aerogrammes, after 4 months a 10 kg parcel can be sent free, newspapers, new clothes.
Accommodation: wooden houses with toilets and showers. No kosher food.
Sports/Entertainments: basketball, football, film shows twice weekly, disco monthly.
Facilities: swimming pool, library, shop selling confectionery, wine, toiletries.
Main Languages: Hebrew, English,

some Spanish.
Excursions: 8 days over 4 months.
Minimum stay: 2 months.
Other Information: maximum 6 months' stay. Longer on kibbutz approval. If granted you are expected to work a longer week. Overall maximum stay 1 year. Ages 18-35. Holidays observed. Close to bus stop and main road. Groups and individuals.
Kibbutz Movement: Ha'artzi.

(24) KIBBUTZ EILON
Western Galilee 22485; tel 04-9858111/9858176; fax 04-9858114; e-mail keshetei@bigfoot.com
Founded: 1939.
Members: 350 + 300 children and young people. Volunteers: 10-12 approx.
Responsible for volunteers: Hanka Burstein.
Work available: mostly services, since agriculture has been a bit slow.
Working hours: 8-hour 6-day week.
Days off: Saturdays plus 1 day a month and all holidays.
Free: aerogrammes, beverages, soap, toothpaste.
Accommodation: pre-cast buildings. 2-3 people per room.
Sports/Entertainments: volleyball, basketball, weekly films, discos, library, volunteers' club with TV.
Excursions: one full-day trip per month.
Nearest town: Naharia, 20 minutes by bus.
Main languages: English, Polish.
Minimum/maximum stay: 2 months up to 3 months.
Other facilities: tennis court, swimming pool.
Other information: direct application to kibbutz accepted.
Kibbutz Movement: Ha'artzi.

(153) KIBBUTZ EINAT
Eynat 49910; tel 03-9385108.
Founded: 1952.
Members 500.
Has not had any volunteers for several years and does not envisage resuming in the near future.
Orchards, cotton, chickens, dining room, kitchen, shoe factory, biscuit factory.
Facilities: swimming pool, library, shop.
Main Languages: Hebrew, English, Yiddish.
Other Information: bus stop on kibbutz. Some way from main road. Holidays observed.
Kibbutz Movement: Takam.

(72) KIBBUTZ EIN CARMEL
Hof Hacarmel 30860; tel: 04-9844200; fax 04-9844222; phone in volunteers' club 04-9844300.
Founded: 1949.
Members: 260 members (500 including children). Volunteers: 16-24.
Work available: dining room, kitchen, children's houses, infirmary, laundry, garage, welding shop, bicycle repairs, dairy barn, chickens, pool, polystyrene factory, laundry, cotton, bananas, persimmons, citrus groves.
Working hours: 6-hour day; 6-day week.
Days off: 3 extra off monthly.
Free: workclothes & boots, aerogrammes, tampons, fruit, soft drinks, supper.
Accommodation: not smart but clean. 1 or 2 to a room.
Sports/Entertainment: basket and volleyball, tennis courts, pub (1-2 a week), TV in volunteer club, videos every evening.
Facilities: swimming pool.
Excursions: occasional organised trips, also ancient Carmel Caves 20 minutes walk, beach (Neve-Yam – 'the best beach in Israel') 20 minutes walk.
Nearest town: Haifa 20km north; 1¹/2 hours by bus.
Nearby: Carmel mountain range, canyon, horse-riding farm.
Main languages: English, Yiddish, German.
Minimum stay: 1 month but volunteers encouraged to stay as long as possible;

most stay 4 to six months.
Other Information: ages 18-35. No Ulpan but the volunteers get Hebrew lessons for their own interest. Current HIV certificate necessary but can be done on arrival free of charge at the kibbutz. Holidays observed. Possibility of kibbutz family.
Kibbutz Movement: Takam.

(80) KIBBUTZ EIN DOR
D.N. Yizreel 19335; tel: 06-6768111; fax 06-6768440.
Founded: 1948.
Members: 360. Volunteers: 25-30.
Work available: melons (summer), cotton, irrigation, flowers, agricultural experimental station, cattle, chickens, dining room, kitchen, cable factory.
Working hours: 6-hour day, 6-day week.
Days off: 2 extra monthly.
Free: toiletries, coffee, tea, sugar.
Accommodation: brick and stone houses. 2-3 to a room. No kosher food.
Sports/Entertainments: basketball, tennis, video, TV, weekly disco.
Facilities: swimming pool, library, kibbutz and volunteers' clubhouse, shop.
Main Languages: Hebrew, English, Spanish.
Minimum stay: 3 months.
Other Information: ages 18-30. Groups and individuals. 4 kms from main road, bus stop on kibbutz, buses to Afula. Possibility of kibbutz family. Holidays observed.
Ulpan: 45 students. Stone houses with rooms for 3, adjoining showers, heating, intensive study with homework. Jewish students only.
Kibbutz Movement: Ha'artzi.

(205) KIBBUTZ EIN-GEDI
D.N. Yam Hamelach 86980; tel: 07-6594657; tel/fax 07-6594902.
Founded: 1956.
Members: 275. Volunteers: 50-70.
Responsible for volunteers: Simon Spanier (tel 07-6594837).
Work available: dates, turkeys, restau-

rant, guest house, shops, gardening, kitchen, laundry, welding shop.
Working hours: 8-hour 6-day week.
Days off: 2 days off monthly plus Saturdays.
Free: fruit, aerogrammes, weekly barbecue.
Accommodation: apartments. 2-3 to a room. No kosher food.
Sports/Entertainments: tennis, football, basketball, volleyball bar, disco (once or twice weekly), movies, etc.
Facilities: swimming pool, gym, English library.
Main Languages: Hebrew, English.
Excursions: regular excursions to the many local beauty spots.
Minimum stay: 2 months.
Other Information: ages 18-32. Individuals and groups. Applications direct to kibbutz accepted. Close to bus stop and main road. Kibbutz situated in one of the most beautiful spots in Israel, the Ein Gedi Oasis. Tourist guest house. Tourist restaurant. Spa. No Ulpan. Current HIV test certificate required or test will be carried out on arrival.
Kibbutz Movement: Takam.

(53) KIBBUTZ EIN GEV
D.N. Emek Hayarden 14940; tel: 06-665 8022/3 (secretary); fax 06-665 8000.
Founded: 1937.
Members: 300. Volunteers: 45 summer, 30 winter.
Work available: banana groves, advocado groves, dining room (holiday village and kibbutz), gardening (holiday village and kibbutz), kitchen (kibbutz), fishing on lakes.
Working hours: 8-hour, 6 day week.
Days off: 3 monthly.
Free: aerogrammes.
Accommodation: 2-3 per room.
Sports/Entertainments: tennis, swimming in Lake Kinneret.
Facilities: library, music auditorium seating 2,000.
Main Languages: Hebrew, Spanish, German.

Excursions: when possible.
Minimum stay: 2 months.
Other Information: ages 22-30. Close to secondary road, buses from Tiberias. Tourist holiday village with bungalows with 2 and 4 beds, air conditioned. Lakeside beaches and lawns with swimming, boating and fishing. TV and supermarket. Individual volunteers only.
Kibbutz Movement: Takam.

(134) KIBBUTZ EIN HAHORESH
Ein Hahoresh 38980; tel: 06-6367311; fax-6366774.
Founded: 1931.
Members: 430. Volunteers: 30-35.
Work available: agricultural, factory.
Working hours: 6-hour day; 6-day week.
Free: cigarettes, stamps, tea, sugar, toiletries.
Accommodation: 2-3 to a room.
Sports/Entertainments: football, basketball, volleyball, tennis, weekly film shows and dances.
Facilities: swimming pool, shop, club.
Languages: Hebrew, English, German, Spanish, French.
Excursions: groups staying three months allowed six days of organised trips. Individual volunteers are allowed to join in.
Minimum stay: 6 weeks.
Other Information: ages 18-35. Holidays observed. Kibbutz family for long stay volunteers. Groups and individuals. Bus stop on kibbutz. 5 km main road.
Kibbutz Movement: Ha'artzi.

(44) KIBBUTZ EIN HAMIFRAZ
D.N. Asherat 25210; tel: 04-9852111.
Founded: 1938.
Members: 420. Volunteers: 35-40.
Work available: industry, agriculture, services. Practical training given on request in specialised branches, e.g., fish farming, dairy, etc.
Working hours: 6-hour, 6-day week.
Days off: 2 extra days monthly.
Free: cigarettes, stamps, other necessi-

ties subsidised.
Accommodation: rooms for 3 and some for couples. No kosher food.
Sports/Entertainments: basketball, volleyball, mini football, weekly film shows, self-organised parties and disco.
Facilities: swimming pool and nearby beach, library, shop.
Languages: Hebrew, English, German, Polish, French.
Excusions: 1-2 day trips monthly.
Minimum stay: 1 month.
Other Information: ages 18-29. Mostly individuals. Close to bus stop and main road. Possibility of kibbutz family. Holidays observed.
Ulpan: 51 students. Housed in three buildings. Some room for couples. Kitchenette, toilet and washing facilities.
Kibbutz Movement: Ha'artzi.

(123) KIBBUTZ EIN HANATZIV
D.N. Beit Shean Valley 10805; tel 06-6582911; fax 6582917; 06-6582917; 06-6582517; e-mail hanatsiv@netvision.net.il
Founded: 1946
Members: 300+300 children+100 young people.
Work available: dates, orchards, olive groves, chicken coops, milk and meat cows, plastics factory.
Nearest town: 2km south of Beit Shean.
Other information: suitable for those with orthodox Jewish background.
Kibbutz Movement: Hadati.

(101) KIBBUTZ EIN HAROD IHUD
Ein Harod 18960; tel 06-6486981; fax 06-6486563.
Founded: 1921.
Members: 320. Volunteers: 15.
Responsible for volunteers: Evi & Kenneth Hanson.
Work available: kitchen, dining room, agriculture, garden, cows, fishpond, fields, laundry.
Working hours: 6-hour 6-day week.

Days off: 3 extra days monthly.
Accommodation: stone houses. 2 to a room. No kosher food.
Sports/Entertainments: basketball, tennis, weekly film, disco, bar, videos.
Facilities: swimming pool, library.
Main Languages: Hebrew, English, Yiddish.
Excursions: 10 trips per year.
Nearest town: Afula, 13km.
Minimum stay: 8 weeks.
Other information: ages 18-35. Close to bus stop and main road. Volunteers must apply through Kibbutz Representatives abroad or in Tel-Aviv.

(98) KIBBUTZ EIN HAROD MEUHAD
Ein Harod 18965; tel:06-6485301; fax 06-6531077.
Founded: 1921.
Members: 500. Volunteers: 17-20.
Responsible for volunteers: Talma Tzabari.
Work available: field work, work in the plantations (olives, dates, grapefruit), gardening, dining room, kitchens.
Working hours: 8-hour day, 6-day week.
Days off: 3 extra days off monthly.
Free: nothing.
Accommodation: modern brick blocks. 2 to a room. No kosher food.
Sports/Entertainments: athletics, football, tennis, table tennis, bar, disco and films.
Facilities: swimming pool, library, club with TV.
Main Languages: Hebrew, English.
Excursions: monthly trips. Natural springs at Sachne, antiquities at Bet Shean.
Nearest towns: Afula and Bet Shean, 15km.
Minimum/maximum stay: 2 months; no maximum limit.
Other information: ages 18-35. The kibbutz is in a beautiful location in the Jezreel Valley, opposite mount Gilboa. Holidays observed. Close to bus stop and main road. Groups and individu-

als. Accepts non-Jewish students on Ulpan depending on the Jewish Agency.
Kibbutz Movement: Takam.

(212) KIBBUTZ EIN HASHLOSHA
D.N. Negev 85128; tel 07-9985711; fax +972-7 9985897.
Founded: 1950.
Members: 200. Volunteers: 20-30.
Work available: agricultural, factory, kitchen, dining room, dairy, kindergarten, turkeys.
Working hours: 8-hours day, 6-days a week.
Days off: 3 extra days per month.
Free: aerogrammes, tea, coffee.
Accommodation: houses. 2-3 people to a room, shared fridge, showers and WC.
Sports/Entertainments: tennis, basketball, table tennis, football, swimming pool (May to October).
Other facilities: shop/bar with twice weekly disco.
Main Languages: Hebrew, Spanish.
Excursions: 3 days every three months.
Minimum stay: 2 months.
Other Information: ages 18-32. Holidays observed. No kibbutz family provided. Groups and individuals. Groups are met at the airport.
Kibbutz Movement: Takam.

(94) KIBBUTZ EIN HASHOFET
Doar Ein Hashofet 19237; tel 04-9895151, 04-9895500, 04-9891409; fax 04-9895507.
Founded: 7 July 1937.
Members: 500. Volunters: 15-20.
Responsible for volunteers: Talmah Gonen.
Work available: *Mivrag* screws and special products factory, electric accessories factory (tends to be the occupation of most volunteers), dining room, kitchen, laundry, gardening.
Free: tea, coffee, sugar.
Accommodation: 2-person shacks.
Sports/Entertainments: tennis, football field, disco, film on Saturdays.

Facilities: swimming pool, workout room.
Nearest towns: Joqham 17km and Haifa 37km.
Main language: English.
Minimum/maximum stay: 1 month up to 6 months.
Other information: kibbutz founded by mixed Polish/American pioneers. Overlooks Jezreel Valley, about 40 minutes south of Haifa and is somewhat isolated. There are regular buses to Haifa and Tel-Aviv and the kibbutz is within walking distance of two neighbouring Kibbutzim: Daliya and Ramat Hashofet. Volunteers should apply only through the kibbutz representatives abroad or in Israel. Current HIV test certificate is essential for acceptance. Very rarely are non-Jewish volunteers accepted on kibbutz Ulpan.
Kibbutz Movement: Ha'artzi.

(124) KIBBUTZ EIN SHEMER
D.N Menashe, 37845; tel 06-6374321; fax 06-6374430.
Founded: 1927.
Members: 380.
Produces: cotton, avocados, pecan nuts, orchards, dairy produce, poultry breeding, factories – rubber and plastic goods, garage and metal workshop.
Languages: Hebrew, English, French, Spanish, Russian.
Other information: no longer accepts volunteers.
Kibbutz Movement: Ha'artzi.

(177) KIBBUTZ EIN TZURIM
D.N. Sde Gat 79510; tel 08-8588222.
Founded: 1948.
Members: 200+250 children. Volunteers: 10-15.
Work available: kitchen, dining room, laundry, children's house, turkeys, orchards, gardening, cow-sheds, turkeys, agriculture, metal workshop, garage.
Working hours: Girls: 7-hour day, 6 day week. Boys: 8-hour day 6 day week.
Days off: Saturdays plus 1 day monthly.

Accommodation: two-storey building, three to a room, toilet facilities in building. Food is kosher.
Sports/Entertainments: basketball, weekly films, almost weekly folk dancing, lectures, parties.
Facilities: swimming pool, library, shop and the Ya'akov Herzog Centre for Jewish Study.
Languages: Hebrew, English, Spanish.
Minimum stay: 1 month.
Other Information: groups and individuals, ages 18-28. Kibbutz family arranged for each volunteer. Ulpan: 45 students. Bnei Akiva Hachsharah, 30 students. Nahal Garin 30 members.
Kibbutz Movement: Hadati.

(19) KIBBUTZ EIN ZIVAN
D.N. Ramat Hagolan 12426; tel 06-6962176.
Founded: 1968.
Members: 80. Vounteers: 30.
Work available: agricultural, factory, services.
Working hours: 8-hour day, 6-day week
Days off: 4 per month.
Sports/Entertainments: basketball, football, tennis, snooker, clubhouse, disco, films twice weekly.
Facilities: swimming pool, library.
Excursions: 1-day trip every month and a 3-day trip every 3 months.
Minimum stay: 1 month.
Other Information: written applications direct to Kibbutz welcomed.
Kibbutz Movement: Takam.

(230) KIBBUTZ ELOT (near Eilat)
D.N. Hevel Elot 88805; tel: 07-6358666.
Founded: 1963.
Members: 110. Volunteers: 60.
Work available: melons, dates, grass field, packing house, mangos, cowshed. Main season April-June, Sept.-Nov.
Working hours: 6-hour day, 6-day week.
Days off: 2 extra per month.
Free: stamps, soap, aerogrammes,

toiletries.
Accommodation: stone houses. 3-4 to a room. No kosher food.
Sports/Entertainments: tennis, basketball, gymnasium. 3 km to the Red Sea with scuba and skin diving.
Facilities: swimming pool, library, clubhouse and shop. Some socialising with other kibbutzim. Very good library in nearby Eilat.
Main Languages: Hebrew, English.
Excursions: 1 day monthly. 3 days three monthly.
Minimum stay: 3 months.
Other Information: ages 18-32. Bus stop and main road nearby. Kibbutz family provided. Easy access to Red Sea beaches. Kibbutz founded on reclaimed desert. Mainly groups accepted but some individuals too.
Kibbutz Movement: Takam.

(15a) KIBBUTZ EL-ROM
D.N. Zfon Hagolan 12466; tel 06-6838291; fax 06-6982430.
Founded 1971.
Members: 130 (total population 330).
Volunteers: 25-30.
Responsible for volunteers: Moti Rosenfeld.
Work available: orchard, vineyard, avocado, field crops, dining room.
Working hours: 8-hour day; 6-day week.
Free: aerogrammes.
Accommodation: brick and concrete apartments with WC and shower; 2 rooms and 4 volunteers per apartment. No kosher food.
Sports/Amusements: regional daily free transport in summer, movie theatre, TV room, basketball, disco, tennis.
Facilities: swimming pool.
Nearest town: Kiryat Shemona 30km.
Main Languages: Hebrew, English.
Minimum/maximum stay: 6 weeks up to 6 months.
Excursions: day trip every month, 3-day trip and 3-day seminar after 3 months.
Other Information: small isolated Kib-

butz with limited facilities. Poor bus service. Highest kibbutz in Israel at 1,300m above sea level. Lies 8 miles from the Syrian border and under threat of being dismantled – the Golan Heights could be handed back to Syria as part of the Israeli peace process. Direct application welcome, and on the spot volunteers.

(192) KIBBUTZ EREZ
D.N. Hof Ashkelon 79150; tel 07-6801111.
Founded: 1949.
Members: 182. Volunteers: plus/minus 30.
Work available: agricultural, irrigation, oranges, cows, kitchen, dining room, garden.
Working hours: 8-hour day, six day week.
Days off: 6 extra days off monthly. Groups work a 6-hour day, six days a week, plus 2 extra days off monthly.
Free: 3 aerogrammes weekly.
Accommodation: 3 to a room. Each room has its own bathroom.
Sports/Entertainments: tennis, basket ball, video shows and disco on Saturday nights.
Facilities: swimming pool, well-stocked library in various languages.
Main Languages: Hebrew, English, German.
Excursions: occasional one-day trips monthly.
Minimum stay: one month.
Other Information: ages 17-34. Groups and individuals. Close to main road and bus stop. Holidays observed. Kibbutz family provided if requested.
Kibbutz Movement: Takam.

(35) KIBBUTZ EVRON
M.P.Asherat 25235; tel 04-9855311; fax 04-9855333.
Founded: 1945.
Members: 360 + 230 children +160 others (total population 750).
Volunteers: average 28.
Responsible for volunteers: Ina Tzchori.

Work available: kitchen, dining room, laundry, factory, avocados, garden, swimming pool, painting houses and rooms.

Working hours: 7-hour day, 6-day week.

Days off: one day off for every 10 days worked.

Free: aerogrammes.

Accommodation: old, 2-3 to a room.

No kosher food.

Sports/Entertainments: tennis basketball, soccer field, disco.

Facilities: reading room, coffee house, library.

Excursions: full-day trip every month; 3-day trip every three months. Sea swimming nearby.

Nearest town: Naharia, 10 minutes walk.

Languages: English, French, Spanish, German, Yiddish, Hungarian, Polish, Russian.

Minimum/maximum stay: 2 months up to six months.

Other Information: ages 18-30. Close to bus stop and trains to Tel Aviv and Haifa. Groups and individuals. Deposit of $50 or NIS 150 required from each volunteer. Mandatory HIV test on arrival at the kibbutz, free of charge. No Ulpan. Return volunteers welcomed.

Kibbutz Movement: Ha'artzi.

(147) KIBBUTZ EYAL (AYAL)
D.N. Hasharon Hatikon 45840; tel 09-7493211-4.
Founded: 1965.
Members: 140. Volunteers: 30.
Work available: optical lens factory, dairy, cotton, avocados, services.
Accommodation: new, well equipped rooms with surrounding garden.
Entertainment: weekly films, shows, video.
Nearest town: Kfar Saba, 10 minutes by bus.
Other Information: written applications welcome but not arrivals on the spot.
Kibbutz Movement: Takam.

(144) KIBBUTZ GA'ASH
Ga'ash   60950;   tel   09-9529353/521144; fax 06-6521198.
Founded: 1952.
Members: 290. Volunteers: 20-25.
Responsible for volunteers: Seppi Tirosh.
Work available: kitchen, factory, garden, grass (turf) production.
Accommodation: 2 to a room.
Sport/Entertainment: football, basketball, beach.
Excursions: monthly trip. Trips to Sinai twice a year in spring and autumn.
Nearest towns: Tel Aviv and Netanya, 20 minutes.
Languages: Spanish, English.
Minimum/maximum stay: 2 months up to six months.
Other information: no Ulpan.
Kibbutz Movement: Ha'artzi.

(34) KIBBUTZ GA'ATON
D.N. Ashrat 25130; tel: 04-9858411/12; fax 04-9858413.
Founded: 1948.
Members: 250.
Responsible for volunteers: Sara Lazar (saralazar@hotmail.com).
Work available: orchards, bananas, citrus fruits, avocados, poultry, cotton, metal work factory.
Working hours: 8-hour day and a 6-day week including split shifts (morning and evening), and night shifts.
Days off: 1 extra day each ten days worked.
Free: toiletries, postage.
Sports/Entertainment: tennis, basketball, football.
Facilities: swimming pool (June to October), library, clubhouse.
Excursions: 3-day trip every 3 months-usually to Masada, Jerusalem and the Dead Sea, and one 2-day trip during the whole stay.
Other information: situated in West Galilee about 6 miles from town of Naharia. Regular bus service to Naharia from bus stop in kibbutz. Kibbutz has a regional dance school and

artists' studios.
Kibbutz Movement: Ha'artzi.

(33) KIBBUTZ GADOT
D.N. Galil Elyon 2, 12325; tel: 06-6939111; fax 06-6939199.
Founded: 1949.
Members: 200. Volunteers: summer up to 30, winter 10.
Work available: citrus orchards, factory, services.
Working hours: 6-hour day, six day week.
Days off: 2 extra days monthly.
Free: aerogrammes.
Allowance: NIS200 monthly for the first 3 months, and NIS 50 more, for the next 3 months.
Accommodation: brick built. 2-3 to a room. No kosher food.
Sports/Entertainments; basketball, football, tennis, disco on Fridays. No volunteers' bar but there is one locally. Possible to go rafting on the Jordan river.
Facilities: swimming pool, library, shop.
Nearest town: Hatzor, 15km.
Other information: volunteers have to pay a deposit of NIS 120 on arrival and bring with them two passport photographs.
Main Languages: Hebrew, English.
Excursions: 1-day trip a month, 3-day trip every 3 months.
Minimum stay: 2 months.
Other information: ages 20-32. Ulpan arranged for non-Jewish volunteers on request.
Kibbutz Movement: Takam.

(104) KIBBUTZ GAL'ED
D.N. Hevel Megiddo 19240; tel 04-9898611/9898789.
Founded 1945.
Members 192. Volunteers: plus/minus 30.
Work available: orchards, picking pears, apples, avocados, cotton, field crops, dairy, bees, kitchen, dining room, factory producing netting and vegetable sacks.

Working hours: 6-hour day; 6-day week.
days off: 2 extra days monthly.
Free: aerogrammes.
Accommodation: wooden huts; 1-3 to a room. No kosher food.
Sports/Entertainments: weekly film shows, volleyball, tennis, lectures.
Facilities: swimming pool, library, shop, cultural centre with picture hall, study room, music room, open air theatre.
Main Languages: Hebrew, English, German.
Excursions: regular monthly trips.
Other Information: groups preferred. Possibility of kibbutz family. Ages 18-25. Buses from kibbutz to main cities.
Location: in the Ephraim hills, between Jezreel Valley and Carmel mountain range.
Kibbutz Movement: Takam.

(184) KIBBUTZ GAL'ON
D.N.Sde Gat 79555; tel: 07-6872711; fax 07-6872703; e-mail marc@galon.org.il
Founded 1946.
Members: 270. Volunteers: about 15.
Responsible for volunteers: Catherine Friedman.
Work available: dining room, kitchen, hotel, factory, children's houses or field and landscaping depending on season and length of stay.
Working hours: up to 8 hours a day, 6 day week.
Days off: 3 extra days monthly.
Free: nothing.
Accommodation: stone houses. 2 to a room. No kosher food.
Sports/Entertainments: basket and volley ball, soccer, tennis, gym, pub once a week, disco every Friday.
Facilities: library, swimming pool, shop, clubhouse with TV and table games, billiards.
Main Languages: Hebrew, English, Spanish.
Excursions: 3-day excursion every three months. Day trips at regular intervals.

Nearest town: Kiriat Gat, 15km. 50 minutes by bus from Tel-Aviv, Jerusalem and Beersheva.
Minimum stay: 1 month in summer, 2 months in winter up to 6 months.
Other information: ages 18-40. Free shuttle provides transport to main road and bus stop (6 miles away) 4 times daily. Religious holidays not observed. Groups and individuals. Applications from return volunteers welcome with advance warning (even a short one) and they are welcome to come with a friend. Others can apply a month in advance in writing. Area full of Byzantine caves. May ask you to take a free HIV test on arrival at kibbutz.
Kibbutz Movement: Ha'artzi.

(125)KIBBUTZ GAN SHMUEL
D.N. D.N. Hefer 38810; tel:06-6320320/6320938; fax 06-6320000.
Founded: 1921.
Members: 460. Volunteers: up to 20.
Work available dining room, kitchen, citrus fruit, processing factory (shift work including nights). Very little work available in agriculture.
Working hours: 8-hour day, 5-day week.
Free: short phone call/fax home on arrival. Letters up to 20 gm free, subsidised cigarettes, bread, vegetables, milk, lavatory paper. Points system for cheeses, yoghurts, fruit etc.
Allowance: small weekly sum can be used to buy subsidised items in the kibbutz shop. Extra NIS 150 if you stay more than three months.
Accommodation: 2 to a room. No kosher food.
Sports/Entertainments: weekly film shows and disco.
Facilities: year round swimming pool (heated and covered in winter), library (small collection of English books), shop, gymnasium.
Nearest town: Hadera (5 km), Caesarea (10km).
Languages: Hebrew, English, Spanish, French.
Excursions: day-trip per month.

Minimum/maximimum stay: 3 months up to 6 months.
Other Information: ages 18-32. Groups and individuals. Close to bus stop and main road. Buses direct to and from Tel Aviv. Holidays observed. HIV test mandatory and free if done on the kibbutz. Ulpan for pre-university Jewish students only.
Kibbutz Movement: Ha'artzi.

(185) KIBBUTZ GAT
D.N. Sede Gat 79565; tel: 07-6871211; fax 07-6871400.
Founded: 1942.
Members: 300.
No longer takes volunteers.
Timber factory, fruit picking, cotton, root crops, chicken incubator, dairy herd, avocados, children's house, laundry, cleaning, (dining room, showers), garage, kitchens.
Facilities: swimming pool, library, shop.
Main Language: Hebrew (and some English, German, French).
Other Information: holidays and festivals observed. Close to bus stop and main road. .
Kibbutz Movement: Ha'artzi.

(86) KIBBUTZ GAZIT
D.N. Jezreel 19340; tel 06-6768511; fax 06-6769049.
Founded: 1950
Members: 350. Volunteers: 10-30.
Work available: plastics factory, dining room, kitchen, children's house, metal shop, cows, sheep, chickens, citrus, almonds, irrigation, gardens.
Working hours: 6-hour, 6-day week
Days off: 2 extra days off monthly.
Free: basic toiletries, aerogrammes, tea, sugar, fruit.
Accommodation: wooden huts, 2 to a room.
Sports/Entertainment: basketball, soccer, weekly films, disco.
Languages: Hebrew, Spanish, English, Yiddish.
Excursions: 4-day and 2-day trips after 3 months.

Minimum stay: 1 month.
Other Information: ages 18-30. Regular buses. Holidays observed. Groups preferred. Lectures and basic Hebrew lessons given if requested.
Kibbutz Movement: Ha'artzi.

(87) KIBBUTZ GESHER
D.N. Jordan Valley 15157; tel: 06-6758610; fax 06-6753603.
Founded: 1939.
Members: 275. Volunteers: 20-25.
Responsible for volunteers: Amelia Shalem.
Work available: services, fields, orchards, dairy, factory, children's houses (occasionally).
Accommodation: good, air-conditioned. 2 to a room with communal showers, TV room and kitchen facilities.
Free: weekly aerogram and all meals.
Entertainment: films, lectures, pub on kibbutz twice weekly and weekly transport to Kibbutz Kinneret pub.
Sports Facilities: olympic-sized swimming pool, football pitch, basketball courts (floodlit).
Excursions: organized trips all over the country once every six weeks.
Nearest towns: Bet Shean, 15 minutes by bus, Tiberias, 25 minutes by bus.
Languges: English, French, German, Spanish, Russian.
Other information: individuals and couples accepted (according to room availability), and groups through recommended organisations. Allowance NIS350 per month and free entry to Kibbutz museum.
Kibbutz Movement: Takam.

(29) KIBBUTZ GESHER HAZIV
W. Galilee 22815; tel 04-9858511.
Founded: 1949.
Members: 230. Volunteers: 15-25.
Work available: kibbutz motel, fields, irrigation, factory, bananas, turkeys, avocados, dining room, kitchen, children's houses, laundry, gardening services.
Working hours: 8-hour day, 6-day

week.
Days off: 3 extra days monthly.
Accommodation: asbestos pre-fabs. 2 to a room. No kosher food.
Sports/Entertainments: basketball, tennis, football, weekly film shows, disco and bar 3 times a week, music circle.
Facilities: swimming pool, library, clubhouse with TV, gift shop in motel.
Main Languages: Hebrew, English.
Excursions: 1 day-trip monthly, 3-day trip every three months.
Minimum stay: 1 month.
Other Information: ages 18 plus. Close to bus stop and main road. Kibbutz family arranged. Individuals and groups. Holidays observed. Hotel with restaurant and gift-shop, open all year round.
Kibbutz Movement: Takam.

(97) KIBBUTZ GEVA
D.N Gilboa 18915; tel: 06-6535111; fax 06-6531445.
Founded: 1921
Members: 700. Volunteers: 35+ depending on the season.
Responsible for volunteers: Yoaf Galilie.
Work available: kitchen, laundry, chocolate factory, engineering factory (Baccara). Agricultural: almonds, dates, fish ponds.
Working hours: 6-hour day, 6-day week.
Days off: 2 extra days monthly.
Free: nothing.
Accommodation: new. 2-3 to a room. No kosher food.
Sports/Entertainments: tennis, football, basketball,volleyball, 2 bars (one exclusively for volunteers), Friday disco, videos every day.
Facilities: swimming pool, gym, library, shop.
Main Languages: Hebrew, English, Spanish.
Excursions: twice monthly (small trips). Every 3 months a big trip to Eilat. Near by at Sachne are hot springs and a Roman amphitheatre.
Nearest town: Afula (10km).

Minimum stay: 6 weeks, maximimum 6 months.
Other Information: ages 18 plus. Close to bus stop to and from Afula, and main road. Holidays observed. Groups and individuals. No Ulpan. Kibbutz Movement: Takam.

(191) KIBBUTZ GEVAR-AM
D.N. Hof Ashkelon 79130; tel: 07-6770411/07-6770400; fax 07-6770412.
Founded: 1942.
Members: 140. Volunteers: 25.
Responsible for volunteers: Schlomo P.
Work available: cows, zoo, agricultural, services, factory.
Working hours: 8-hour day; 6-day week.
Free: aerogrammes.
Accommodation: old and reconditioned blocks. 2 to a room. No kosher food.
Sports/Entertainments: basketball, football, tennis, disco, pub twice a week. Club open every night.
Facilities: swimming pool, library, shop.
Main Languages: Hebrew, English.
Excursions: One day-trip a month.
Nearest town: Ashkelon 15km (20 minutes by bus).
Minimum stay: 2 months.
Other Information: ages 18-30. Groups and individuals. Close to bus stop and main road. 1 hour from Tel Aviv by bus. Close to the beach (12km). Kibbutz Movement: Takam.

(198) KIBBUTZ GEVIM
D.N. Hof Ashkelon 79165, tel 07-6802111; fax 07-6893727/6802163.
Founded: 1947.
Members: 150. Volunteers: 5-15.
Responsible for volunteers: Gadi Tsachar, Orly Gilad.
Work available: fields, irrigation, dining room, kitchen, recorder factory, cows.
Working hours: 8-hour day, 5^1/2-day week.

Free: 3 aerogrammes weekly.
Accommodation: 2-3 to a room. No kosher food.
Sports/Entertainments: tennis, basketball, football. TV video, kibbutz video, pub and disco twice a week.
Other Facilities: swimming pool, library, clubhouse.
Nearest town: Sderot (2km). Half an hour on foot.
Main Languages: Hebrew, English, French.
Excursions: 1 day-trip every month, 3-day trip every 3-6 months.
Minimum/maximum stay: 1 month to a year.
Other Information: Ages 18-35. Groups and individuals. Holidays observed. Close to bus stop and main road.
Kibbutz Movement: Takam.

(161) KIBBUTZ GEZER
D.N. Shimshon 99786; tel: 08-9270666; fax 08-9270736.
Founded: 1945.
Members: 100. Volunteers: 15.
Responsible for volunteers: Vered Hull.
Work available: dining room, cows, fields, laundry, kitchen, vineyards, glue factory.
Working hours: 8-hour, 6-day week.
Free: 2 aerogrammes per month.
Accommodation: fair accommodation. 3 per big room, 2 in smaller rooms. Kosher food.
Sports/Entertainments: softball, soccer, basketball, tennis, folk dancing, weight lifting, films.
Facilities: swimming pool open all summer, library, clubhouse. All facilities and activities open to volunteers.
Main Languages: English, Hebrew.
Excursions: volunteer trips around the country 3 times a years.
Nearest town: Ramla (10 minutes).
Minimum stay: 2 months.
Other Information: young kibbutz with about 75% native English speakers. Volunteers given week's probation. Priority given to potential settlers. All

volunteers integrate fully into kibbutz life. Ages 20-40. Religious holidays observed.The kibbutz has no special facilities for volunteers who are nevertheless invited to join in any activity with the kibbutzniks.
Kibbutz Movement: Takam.

(156) KIBBUTZ GILGAL
D.N. Bikat Jericho 90674; tel 02-9945555; fax 02-9941205.
Founded: 1973.
Members: 80. Volunteers: 5-20.
Work available: dates, turkeys, cows, turf, dining room, grapes, mangos, fish, print-house.
Working hours: 8 hours daily.
Days off: One extra day off per month.
Free: nothing except newspapers.
Accommodation: 2-4 to a house containing two bedrooms, shower, WC and kitchen. No kosher food.
Sports/Entertainments: football, basketball, tennis, videos and pub twice a week.
Facilities: library, clubhouse with video library, swimming pool.
Nearest town: Jerusalem, 1 hour by bus.
Main Languages: Hebrew, English, Spanish.
Excursions: monthly day-trip. 3-day trip after 3 months.
Minimum stay: 5 weeks up to 6 months.
Other Information: ages 18-30, A young, new settlement. Groups and individuals. Bus connections to Jerusalem and Tiberias.
Kibbutz Movement: Takam.

(78) KIBBUTZ GINEGAR
D.N. Ginegar 30053; tel 06-6549211; fax 06-6544211
Founded: 1920/1922.
Members: 300. Volunteers 15.
Work available: field crops, dairy farm, green houses, kitchen, dining room.
Working hours: 6-hour day, 6 day week.
Days off: 3 extra days monthly.

Accommodation: 2 to a room.
Sports/Entertainments: basketball, football, swimming pool, video films, disco, pub, club house, library.
Main Languages: Hebrew, English.
Excursions: 1 day-trip every 6 weeks approximately.
Minimum stay: 1 month.
Other Information: main road close by with frequent buses. Written applications welcome, but not volunteers turning up on the spot.
Kibbutz Movement: Takam.

(48)KIBBUTZ GINOSSAR
Sea of Galilee 14980; tel 06-6798511; fax 06-6798887.
Founded: 1937.
Members: 386. Volunteers: plus/minus 36.
Work available: bananas, fishing, grapefruit, watermelons, kitchen dining room, laundry, day centre for senior citizens, greenhouse, avocados.
Working hours: $6^1/2$-hour day, 6-day week.
Days off: 2 extra days monthly.
Free: washing powder.
Accommodation: 4-person caravans and house with 2-4 persons to a room. No kosher food.
Sports/Entertainments: tennis, football, volleyball, swimming in the lake, volunteer bar and nightly disco.
Facilities: sports hall, shop, library.
Main Languages: Hebrew, English, German.
Excursions: walking routes, Tiberias.
Nearest town: Tiberias, 10 minutes by bus.
Minimum stay: 2-3 months.
Other Information. kibbutz situated on the shores of Galilee. Minimum stay 2-3 months. Ages 18-32. Holidays observed. Close to bus stop and main road.
Kibbutz Movement: Takam.

(162) KIBBUTZ GIV'AT BRENNER
Giv'at Brenner 60948; tel: 08-9443111; fax 08-9443517.

Founded: 1928.
Members: 900.
Volunteers: only Ulpan.
Work available: agricultural, factory, services.
Working hours: 7-hour day, 6-day week.
Days off: 2 extra days monthly.
Accommodation: old houses with 2-3 to a room. No kosher food.
Sports/Entertainments: football, table tennis, weekly film shows and disco.
Facilities: swimming pool, library, shop, clubhouse.
Main Languages: Hebrew, English, German.
Excursions: Depending on length of stay, day trip once a month; trips every two months.
Nearest town: Rehovot (10 minutes).
Minimum/maximum stay: 2 months up to a year.
Other Information: although this is the largest kibbutz in Israel, its volunteer requirements are adequately filled by Ulpan (for new immigrants and tourists) so to work there you need to apply for kibbutz Ulpan.
Other Information: holidays observed. Bus stop on kibbutz. Near main road.
Kibbutz Movement: Takam.

(132) KIBBUTZ GIVAT HAYIM (IHUD)
P.O Givat Hayim 38935; tel 06-6369111; 6369200; fax 06-6369611.
Founded: 1952.
Members: 850. Volunteers: 15-20.
Work available: kitchen, dining room, laundry, factory, avocados, cotton fields, gardening.
Working hours: 8-hour day, 6-day week.
Days off: 3 extra days monthly.
Free: nothing.
Accommodation: 1-3 to a room. No kosher food.
Sports/Entertainments: tennis, basketball, volleyball, football, discos, TV room.
Facilities: swimming pool, gym, library, shop.
Main Languages: Hebrew, English, German.
Excursions: 1 or 2 days every 6 weeks. Netanya beach.
Nearest town: Hadera, 15 minutes.
Minimum/maximum stay: 3 months up to six months.
Other Information: ages 20-40. groups and individuals. Kibbutz family provided. Close to bus stop and main road. Holidays observed. Two guest rooms for volunteers' relatives. U.S. $15 daily full board and entertainment. This area is very bad for asthma and hay fever sufferers. Tennis players bring your own equipment.
Kibbutz Movement: Takam.

(131) KIBBUTZ GIVAT HAYIM (MEUHAD)
Post Givat Hayim 38930; tel 06-6368111.
Founded 1932.
Members: 510. Volunteers 60-70 (winter); 30-40 (summer).
Work available: oranges, juice factory, avocados, laundry, cotton fields, cowsheds, turkeys, gardens, kitchen and child-minding.
Working hours: 7-hour day, 5-day week.
Days off: 3 extra days monthly.
Free: aerogrammes.
Accommodation: huts and rooms with 1-3 persons. No kosher food.
Sports/entertainments: tennis, squash, volleyball, football, TV room, pub & disco twice weekly.
Facilities: library, gym, swimming pool.
Main languages: Hebrew, English.
Excursions: monthly day-trip, 3-day trip every 3 months.
Minimum stay: 1 month.
Other information: ages 18-45. Groups and individuals. Hebrew lessons if requested. Bus stop on kibbutz. Main road 2km. Near the coast.

(151)   KIBBUTZ   GIVAT HASHLOSHA
Post Givat Hashlosha 49905; tel: 03-9374575.

Founded: 1925.
Members: 270. Volunteers: 20-25.
Work available: orchards, cotton,
swimming pool work, chickens, cows,
services, shoe factory.
Working hours: 6$^{1}/2$ hour day; 6 day
week.
Days off: 2 extra days monthly.
Free: stamps, coffee and sugar.
Accommodation: 2-3 to a big room.
Wooden and pre-fabricated houses. No
kosher food.
Sports/Entertainments: football, bas-
ketball, tennis, weekly films and dis-
cos, folk dancing, lectures, TV room.
Facilities: swimming pool, gym,
sauna, jacuzzi, library, clubhouse,
small supermarket.
Main Languages: Hebrew, English.
Excursions: 1-day trip every month.
Minimum stay: 6 weeks.
Other Information: ages 18-40. Prefer
individuals, couples or small groups.
On the outskirts of Tel Aviv. Close to
bus stop and main road. Holidays
observed.
Kibbutz Movement: Takam.

(105) GIVAT OZ
M.P. Hevel Megido 19225; tel 06-
6524905; fax 06-6525333.
Founded: 1949.
Members: 200. Volunteers: 20.
Responsible for volunteers: Avraham
Beni.
Work available: agriculture, services,
factory.
Accommodation: 2-3 persons to a
room.
Free: aerogrammes.
Sports/entertainments: bar, films, TV,
various sports.
Facilities: swimming pool.
Nearest town: Afula 15 km.
Main languages: Spanish, English,
German.
Minimum/maximum stay: 2 months
and up to 6 months.
Other Information: buses to and from
Afula. Ulpan for non-Jewish students.
Kibbutz Movement: Ha'artzi.

(149) KIBBUTZ GLIL-YAM
Glil-Yam 46905; tel 09-9528800; fax
09-9528983.
Founded: 1943.
Members: 180.
Other information: no longer takes
volunteers.

(17) KIBBUTZ GONEN
D.N. Upper Galilee 12130; tel: 06-
6955111/6955270; fax 06-6905503.
Founded: 1953.
Members: 110. Volunteers: 12.
Responsible for volunteers: Geoff
Falk.
Work available: fields, orchards, garden, turkeys, laundry, metal shop.
Working hours: 8-hour day, 5$^{1}/2$-day
week.
Days off: 3 extra days per month, plus
further time off for extra duties.
Accommodation: wooden cabins, 1 to
a room. Kosher food.
Sports/Entertainments: tennis, basketball and football, judo, gym, bar, every
day 2 video movies on the kibbutz
video channel, stereo in the bar, table
tennis, volleyball, disco on and near
the kibbutz.
Facilities: swimming pool, library and
shop. Nearby Cauda centre has a sport
facility including ice-skating, squash
and a sauna.
Nearest town: Kiryat Shmona, 15 minutes drive.
Minimum/maximum stay: 3 months
up to six months.
Main Languages: Hebrew, English.
Excursions: a day-trip monthly; 3-day
trip every 3 months.
Other information: individuals and
couples preferred to groups. Ages 18
plus. Involvement in all kibbutz events
(festivals, weddings, etc) is normal.
Volunteers are also encouraged to
arrange their own walks and
tractor/trailer trips in the surrounding
countryside. The kibbutz is situated on
the edge of the Golan Heights in view
of Mount Hermon, and overlooking
the Hula Valley, famous for its wildlife
and as a place for watching migrating

birds. Application can be made directly to the kibbutz, or on the spot.
Kibbutz Movement: Takam.

(228) KIBBUTZ GROFIT (North of Eilat)
D.N. Hevel Eilot 88825; tel: 07-6357777; fax 07-6357726.
Founded: 1966.
Members: 120. Volunteers: 30-40.
Responsible for volunteers: Louise Cape, Michael Hack.
Work available: agriculture including melons, dates, onions, services, gardening, building, new factory (produces nylon bags), camping village, restaurant.
Free: aerogrammes, cleaning materials for rooms.
Accommodation: old rooms in old apartments. 3-4 persons to a room.
Entertainments: volunteers' pub, club with videos supplied by the kibbutz, swimming pool, gym. Volunteers are included in all holidays and all activities on the kibbutz.
Other facilities: sports centre, discos and cinema on next kibbutz nearby.
Nearest town: Eilat (30 minutes by bus).
Main Languages: Hebrew, English.
Excursions: day-trips and longer trips twice yearly.
Minimum/maximum stay: 3 months up to 6 months.
Other Information: 4 hours by by bus from Tel Aviv. Tourist campsite owned by the kibbutz nearby. Prefers volunteers through the Kibbutz Representatives in England or the Tel-Aviv office.
Kibbutz Movement: Takam.

(75) KIBBUTZ GVAT
Doar Gvat 30050; tel: 06-6549411.
Founded: 1926.
Members: 550.
Work available: grapefruit, cotton, apples, dining room, kitchen, laundry, gardens, plastics factory.
Sports/Entertainments; swimming pool, tennis, sports hall, club house, weekly films.

Main Languages: Hebrew, English.
Excursions: 1 day trip every month.
Minimum stay: 1 month.
Other Information: ages 18-32. Close to bus stop.
Kibbutz Movement: Takam.

(221) KIBBUTZ GVULOT
D.N Haluzot 85525; tel 07-9983111.
Founded: 1943.
Members: 140. Volunteers: 30.
Work available: field crops, orchards, cows, chickens, kitchen, dining room.
Working hours: 6-hour 6-day week.
Days off: 2 extra days monthly.
Free: toiletries, stationery, postage.
Accommodation: wooden houses. Separate toilets and showers. 2-3 to a room. No kosher food.
Sports/Entertainments: basketball, badminton, football, gymnastics, Israeli cultural evenings, weekly films, monthly dances.
Facilities: swimming pool, library, clubhouse, shop.
Main Languages: Hebrew, English, Spanish.
Excursions: every 3 months a 3-day trip.
Minimum stay: a month.
Other Information: ages 18-32. Holidays observed. Close to a bus stop. Some way from main road. Possibility of kibbutz family for long-stay volunteers.
Kibbutz Movement: Ha'artzi.

(169) KIBBUTZ HAFETZ HAIM
P.O.Hafetz Chaim 76817; tel 08-8593888.
Founded: 1944.
Members: 400.
Work available: cotton, grapefruit, poultry, dairy, hotel, kitchen, dining room.
Days off: 2 extra days monthly.
Free: cigarettes, sugar, tea, fruit.
Accommodation: 2-3 in a room. Kosher food.
Sports/Entertainments: basketball, separate swimming pools for men and women, library, club house with TV

Excursions: Short trips in summer.
Other Information: ages: 17-30. Strictly orthodox kibbutz. Groups and individuals who observe the law of Torah are welcome.
Hotel: 57 rooms.
Kibbutz Movement: Poale Agudat Israel.

(7) KIBBUTZ HAGOSHRIM
Upper Galil 12225; tel: 06-6956211-2; fax 06-6956207.
Founded: 1952.
Members: 280 + 170 children under 18.
Work available: main crops are cotton and avocados. Services: kitchen, dining hall, children's houses, sewing shop, garage, welding shop etc., kibbutz hotel.
Working hours: 7 or 8 hours a day.
Days off: 3 extra days monthly.
Free: nothing. Monthly allowance of NIS 200 meant to cover the basics.
Accommodation: wooden building. 2-3 to a room. No kosher food.
Sports/Entertainments: football, athletics, volleyball, basketball, tennis, weekly films and disco.
Facilities: swimming pool, gym, library, shop, clubhouse.
Main Languages: Hebrew, English, French.
Excursions: 3-6 six days of trips during a stay of 3 months.
Minimum stay: 1 month.
Other Information: groups and individuals. Ages 18-30. All holidays observed. Close to bus stop and main road. Some possibility of kibbutz family. Hotel open all year for tourists and Israeli citizens. Kibbutz Movement: Takam.

(58a) KIBBUTZ HAHOTRIM
D.N. Hof Carmel 30870; tel: 04-8302402; fax 04-8302722.
Founded: 1952.
Members: 300.
Banana groves, citrus orchards, cows, laundry, kitchens, factory producing plastics and textiles, dining room.

Main Languages: Hebrew, English, German, Spanish.
Nearest town: Haifa, 10 minutes by bus.
Other Information: not taking volunteers at present and probably not in the future. Close to main road and bus stop.
Kibbutz Movement: Takam.

(109) KIBBUTZ HAMADIA
D.N. Beit Shean 10855; tel: 06-6589800.
Founded: 1942.
Members: 250. Volunteers: 12-18.
Work available: cattle, chicks, fish farm, services, cotton, orchards, 2 factories.
Working hours: 8-hour day, 6-day week.
Free: nothing. Some things subsidised.
Accommodation: houses, 2-3 to a room. No kosher food.
Sports/Entertainments: basketball, weekly films, self-organised, disco cultural evenings.
Facilities: swimming pool, gym, library, clubhouse, shop.
Main Languages: Hebrew, English.
Excursions: 1-day trip every 6 weeks.
Minimum stay: 1 month.
Other Information: the climate is extremely hot in summer. Ages 18-35. Groups and individuals. Close to bus stop and main road. Holidays observed. Possibility of kibbutz family. Kibbutz Movement: Takam.

(135) KIBBUTZ HAMAPIL
D.N. Hafer 38945; tel 06-6367811; fax 06-6258974; volunteer quarters (incoming tel. calls only) 06-6367820.
Founded: 1945.
Members: 250. Volunteers: 20.
Responsible for volunteers: Yoram Strul (tel 06-6367049 evenings only); e-mail strul-y@internet-zahav.net.
Work available: agriculture, gardening, dining room, factory, etc.
Working hours: 8-hour, 6-day week.
Days off: 3 extra days monthly.

Free: lots.
Accommodation: 2 to a room, 8 people to a building with two bathrooms. No kosher food.
Sports/Entertainments: volleyball, basketball, TV and disco.
Facilities: swimming pool, library, clubhouse, shop.
Main Languages: Hebrew, English.
Excursions: 2 day-trips every 6 weeks.
Minimum stay: 3 months.
Other Information: groups and individuals. Close to main road and bus stop. Deposit of US$30 and 2 passport photos needed on arrival. Volunteers can apply to the Volunteer Leader by phone (see above).
Kibbutz Movement: Ha'artzi.

(21) KIBBUTZ HANITA
Volunteer Office, D.N. Western Galilee 22885; tel/fax/answer machine 04-9859650.
Founded: 1938.
Members: 250. Volunteers: 20-28.
Responsible for volunteers: Brigitte Weidmann.
Work available: food facilities, shops, laundry, garden, children's zoo, factories, banana groves.
Accommodation: old. 1-3 persons to a room.
Sports/Entertainments: tennis, football, basketball, badminton, yoga, aerobics, dancing lessons (for groups of five or more), videos, seminars (every 2-3 months), in summer every Saturday, bus to the beach.
Working hours: 8 hours a day for five days a week.
Days off: 2 days per month.
Facilities: swimming pool, library, Hanita Museum, volunteer club and pub.
Free: nothing.
Allowance: volunteers get NIS 355 for each of the first two months and NIS 540 for each month thereafter. In addition NIS 132 per month is provided for volunteers to arrange their own excursions.
Nearest town: Nahariya, about 15 minutes by car. Kibbutz bus runs to Nahariya 6 times daily.
Main languages: Hebrew, English, French, German.
Minimum stay: one calendar month.
Other information: accepts applications direct by fax. The kibbutz asks for a cash only deposit of US$50 or NIS195 on the day of arrival. If the volunteer leaves before one month is up, the kibbutz keeps the deposit. Also if the volunteer's room is not clean on departure, volunteers pay NIS20 to cover cleaning costs. Kibbutz Movement: Takam.

(68b) KIBBUTZ HANNATON
D.N. Nazerat Illit 17960; tel 04-9864985; fax 04-9864771.
Founded: 1984.
Members: 30. Volunteers: up to 8.
Responsible for volunteers: Mazkir.
Work available: agriculture: dairy cows, citrus orchard. Tourism. Service branches: kitchen.
Accommodation: volunteer house with living room, kitchenette, 3-person bedrooms and bathroom. Kosher food.
Free: aerogrammes, rides to the bus-stop.
Sport/Entertainment: basketball court, video room, pub once a week.
Nearest town: Tivon (15 minutes), Nazareth (15 minutes). Haifa and Tiberias are both 30 minutes away by bus.
Main languages: English, Hebrew.
Minimum stay: 6 months up to 1 year maximum.
Other information: young, pioneering kibbutz in beautiful Galilee. Synagogue services on Shabbat. Only Jewish volunteers accepted. Arrangements can be made directly with the kibbutz. Associated with the Conservative Movement.
Kibbutz Movement: Takam.

(137) KIBBUTZ HA'OGEN
Haogen 42880; tel 09-8982111; fax 09-8982494.
Founded: 1948.

Members: 450. Volunteers and
Ulpanists: 10-50.
Work available: agricultural, plastics
factory, dairy, kitchens.
Working hours: 6-day week.
Days off: 2 extra days monthly.
Free: cigarettes, postage.
Accommodation: 2-3 in self-contained
flats, bathroom and kitchenette. No
kosher food.
Sports/Entertainments: volleyball,
mini-football and football field, table
tennis, weekly film shows and disco.
Facilities: swimming pool, library,
shop, clubhouse.
Main Languages: Hebrew, English.
Excursions: 1-2 day trip monthly.
Minimum stay: 1 month.
Other Information: maximum age 35.
Religious festivals observed. Direct
bus to Netanya. Close to main road.
Groups and individuals. Possibility of
kibbutz family.
Ulpan: Courses start April and Octo-
ber. Very small percentage of non-
Jewish students.
Kibbutz Movement: Ha'artzi.

(60)KIBBUTZ HA'ON
D.N. Emek Hayarden 15170; tel 06-
6656511; fax 06-6709530.
Founded: 1949.
Members: 80.
Banana groves, dates, citrus, fishponds,
ostriches, gardening and services.
Facilities: the kibbutz is on the shores
of the Sea of Galilee so lake swim-
ming available, library, shop, holiday
village.
Nearest town: Tiberias, 20 minutes by
bus.
Main Languages: Hebrew, some English.
Other information: has stopped taking
volunteers 'for economic reasons.'
Close to main road and bus stop.
Many local tourist attractions accessi-
ble.
Kibbutz Movement: Takam.

(168) KIBBUTZ HAREL
D.N. Shimshon 99740; tel 02-
9918181..

Founded: 1978.
Members: 90-110.
Work available: field crops, poultry,
sheep, almonds, avocados, orchards,
gardening, kitchen, factory.
Working hours: 8-hour day. 5-day
week.
Accommodation: good. 2-3 to a room.
Sports/Entertainments: football, vol-
leyball, seasonal clubs including yoga,
aerobics, etc., basketball, table tennis,
weekly films and dancing, craft class-
es.
Facilities: library, clubhouse, swim-
ming pool.
Main Languages: Hebrew, English,
Spanish.
Excursions: occasional outings.
Other Information: young kibbutz.
Average age of 40. 40% of members
are North American, 40% are native
born and 20% are South American.
Secular observance of Jewish holidays. Volunteers fully integrated into
kibbutz life.
Kibbutz Movement: Ha'artzi.

(55) KIBBUTZ HASOLELIM
D.N. Upper Nazareth 17905; tel 06-
6573004.
Founded: 1949.
Members: 120.
Main Languages: Hebrew, English.
Other information: stopped taking vol-
unteers after 'streamlining' their work-
force and 'doing away with
branches/production lines which relied
heavily on temporary labour.'
Kibbutz Movement: Takam.

(220) KIBBUTZ HATZERIM
D.N. Negev 85420; tel 07-6473111;
fax 07-6473684.
Founded: 1946.
Members: 250. Volunteers: 10-15.
Work available: dining room, kitchen,
garden, milking, sheds, factory.
Working hours: 8-hour day; 6-day
week.
Days off: 3 extra days monthly.
Free: everything you need.
Accommodation: 2 to a room.

Sports/Entertainments: weekly films and videos most evenings.
Facilities: swimming pool, tennis courts, gymnasium, library, shop, clubhouse.
Main Languages: Hebrew, English, Spanish.
Excursions: day-trip monthly. 3-day trip every 3 months.
Minimum stay: 1 month.
Nearest town: 8km south-west of Beer'Sheva.
Other Information: ages 18-30. Groups and individuals. Close to main road and bus stop.
Holidays observed. Kibbutz family arranged.
Kibbutz Movement: Takam.

(171) KIBBUTZ HATZOR
Lid Gedera 60970; tel 08-8579444; fax 08-8579550.
Founded: 1946.
Members: 350. Volunteers: 20-25.
Total population: 600.
Work available: citrus groves, almonds, cotton, beef cattle, turkey, dining room, kitchen.
Working hours: 6-hour day; 6-day week.
Days off: 2 extra days monthly.
Free: stationery, toiletries.
Accommodation: wooden frame buildings with plastered interiors. 2-3 to a room. No kosher food.
Sports/Entertainments: volleyball, basketball, football, monthly film, folk dancing, pub (3 nights a week).
Facilities: swimming pool, gymnasium, library with large English section. 1 clubhouse with magazines, refreshments, another for parties and gatherings, shop.
Languages: Hebrew, English, German, Spanish, French, Russian.
Excursions: 1 day-trip monthy.
Minimum stay: 2-3 months.
Other Information: ages 18-28. Mainly individuals. Holidays observed. Possibility of kibbutz family. 7 km main road. Buses 301 & 310 to Hatzor intersection where kibbutz cars pick up

each hour. Nearest bus station Gedera.
Ulpan for Jewish students only.
Kibbutz Movement: Ha'artzi.

(85) KIBBUTZ HAZOREA
Hazorea P.O. 30060; tel 04-9899709/9899700; fax 04-9899254; e-mail yitzh_li@hazorea.org.il website www.hazorea.org.il Ulpan office tel 04-9899700.
Founded: 1936.
Members: 550. Volunteers: 18-22.
Responsible for volunteers: Vivian Lay.
Work available: nursing home for elderly, Koi fish hatchery and ponds, water lilies, kitchen and dining room, caring for young calves and a milking dairy, citrus tree grafting, small animal farm and caring for young infants.
Working hours: 6-hour day, 6-day week or 8-hour day 5 day week.
Accommodation: old, 2 to a room.
Sports/Entertainments: basketball, volleyball, soccer, tennis courts, discos twice a week, lectures.
Facilities: olympic swimming pool, gym, library with access to internet use.
Main languages: Hebrew, English, German.
Nearest towns: Yokneam is 5km and Haifa is 30km west. Take any bus to Yokneam from Haifa or Tel Aviv and then bus 17 (or a 5-minute taxi ride) to Hazorea.
Minimum/maximum stay: 8 weeks up to 6 months.
Other Information: acceptable ages for volunteers is from 18 up to 30. Volunteers are accepted all year round. Hebrew Ulpan 5-month course at two levels – contact Elissa D'vir.
Kibbutz Movement: Ha'artzi.

(110) KIBBUTZ HEFTSIBA
D.N. Gilboa 19135; tel 06-6534111.
Founded: 1922.
Members: 275.
Work available: citrus groves, cows, poultry, fish ponds, field crops, factories repairing water metres and pro-

ducing plastic pipes, all services.
Sports/Entertainments: tennis, basketball, kibbutz league football, weekly discos, courses in ceramics.
Facilities: swimming pool, hot springs, Japanese gardens, archaeological site.
Other Information: in the vanguard of new developments in the kibbutz movement, e.g. the dining room is closed in the evenings; members have individual budgets.
Buses to and from Afula, Tel Aviv, Haifa. Ulpan for Jewish Bet Shan students.
Kibbutz Movement: Takam.

(47) KIBBUTZ HOKUK
D.N. Hevel Korazim 12355; tel 06-6799811.
Founded: 1947.
Members: 180. Volunteers: 20.
Work available: bananas, citrus orchards, cotton, chickens, dining room, kitchens, children's houses, light industry, mirror factory.
Working hours: 8-hour day; 6-day week.
Days off: 4 extra days monthly.
Free: toiletries, some postage.
Accommodation: houses and blocks. 2-3 to a room. No kosher food.
Sports/Entertainments: tennis, football, basketball, volleyball, weekly film shows and dance.
Facilities: swimming pool, library, clubhouse, shop.
Main Languages: Hebrew, French, Spanish, English.
Excursions: monthly day-trip locally.
Minimum stay: 1 month.
Other Information: ages 18-32. Religious holidays observed. Close to bus stop. Main road 3 1/2 miles miles. Groups and individuals accepted.
Kibbutz Movement: Takam.

(150) KIBBUTZ HORSHIM
D.N. Hacharon Hatikhon 45865; tel 03-9386211/9386330; fax 03-9386281.
Founded: 1955.
Members: 115. Volunteers: 10-16.

Work available: cotton, avocados, chicken runs, dairy, greenhouse, landscape, maintenance, dining room, laundry and other work according to season and demand.
Working hours: 6-hour day; 6-day week or or 8-hour day, 5-day week.
Days off: 2 extra days monthly.
Main Languages: Hebrew, English, French, Portuguese and Spanish.
Other Information: small kibbutz in low wooded hills, but close to Tel Aviv. Volunteers live and work as members, sharing the same entertainment facilities and trips. Ages 18-30. Preference given to single, long stay, English speaking volunteers.
Kibbutz Movement: Ha'artzi.

(28) KIBBUTZ HULATA
D.N. Upper Galilee 12110; tel 06-6933911; volunteer office: 06-6933053; fax 06-6936447.
Founded: 1936.
Members: 250. Volunteers: 15-25.
Responsible for volunteers: Yoheved Ben Ze'ev.
Work available: short kitchen and dining room duty, gardening, avocado, orchard, cowsheds, cotton fields, fish ponds.
Working hours: 8-hour day,6 day week.
Days off: 3 extra days monthly.
Free: nothing.
Accommodation: modest rooms 2-3 to a room. Shower and WC every two rooms.
Sports/Entertainments: football, basketball, volleyball, volunteer-organised discos. Clubhouse with TV and videos. At nearby Kfar Blum there are music concerts and the Metula Sport Center with ice-skating.
Facilities: swimming pool, library, well-stocked shop.
Main Languages: Hebrew, English, German.
Excursions: Saturday a day trip in the neighbourhood; day-trip once a month; every 3 months a trip to Eilat or Jerusalem for three days.

Nearest town: Kiryat Shmona 25km.
Minimum stay: 6 weeks up to maximum of 6 months.
Other Information: ages 18-35. Groups and individuals. Religious holidays observed. Close to bus stop and main road. Possibility of kibbutz family and simple Hebrew lessons. Lectures given on subjects of the volunteers' interest.
Kibbutz Movement: Takam.

(163) KIBBUTZ HULDA
D.N. Emek Sorek 76842; tel 08-9445222; fax 08-9445338.
Founded: 1930.
Members: 199.
Other information: according to the manpower co-ordinator Ruth Lipetz, Hulda has ceased its volunteer programme and is unlikely to resume taking volunteers again in the future.
Kibbutz Movement: Takam.

(31) KIBBUTZ KABRI
D.N. Ma'aleh Hagalil 25120; tel 04-9952111; fax 04-9856504.
Founded: 1949.
Members: 500. Volunteers: about 20.
Responsible for volunteers: Mette Karni.
Work available: work in the fields: bananas, avocados. Dining room, kitchen, gardening, jewellery factory, mineral water factory.
Working hours: 6-hour day, 6-day week.
Days off: 3 extra days monthly.
Free: postage.
Accommodation: rooms and caravans, 2-3 to a room. No kosher food.
Sports/Entertainments: basketball etc, disco/pub Thursday and Friday, occasional lectures.
Facilities: swimming pool (in summer), workout room, library, clubhouse, shop.
Main Languages: Hebrew, English, German.
Excursions: In summer bus to the sea every Saturday morning. Day-trips locally every 5-6 weeks, 3-day trip once every 3 months.

Nearest town: Nahariya 7km.
Minimum stay: 2 months.
Other Information: ages 18-35. Groups and individuals. Possibility of kibbutz family for long stay volunteers. Close to bus stop and main road. All holidays observed.
Kibbutz Movement: Takam.

(218) KIBBUTZ KEREM SHALOM
D.N. Hanegev 85460; tel: 07-9987555/9985211; fax 07-9985133
Founded: 1968.
Members: 70. Volunteers: 3-10.
Work available: mangoes, avocados, citrus orchards, fields (peanuts, potatoes, carrots, etc.), turkeys, dining room, kitchen, laundry, garage.
Working hours: 8-hour day; 6-day week.
Days off: 3 extra days monthly.
Free: soap, shampoo, coffee and other basic necessities.
Accommodation: 2-3 to a room. No kosher food.
Sports/Entertainments: soccer, basketball, weekly film, weekly disco.
Facilities: swimming pool, library, small shop with basic needs and refreshments.
Main Languages: Hebrew, some Spanish, French, English and German.
Other Information: small kibbutz with few volunteers. Volunteers with a real desire to understand kibbutz lifestyle have a good opportunity to integrate into the community.
Kibbutz Movement: Ha'artzi.

(227) KIBBUTZ KETURA
D.N. Hevel Eilot 88840; tel: 07-356666; fax 07-356465.
Founded: 1973.
Members 120. Volunteers: 20.
Work available: cows, kitchen, dining room, date plantation, pomello orchard, gardening, turkeys, experimental orchards, children's houses-for Hebrew-speakers only.
Free: aerogrammes, postage for letters and postcards.
Accommodation: 2-3 to a room. 1

bathroom/shower for 2 rooms. Food is kosher.
Sports/Entertainments: basketball, tennis, horse riding, weekly film, volunteers' TV and video room, pub.
Facilities: swimming pool, library, synagogue – Friday night services optional.
Nearest town: Eilat 1 1/2hours.
Excursions: all year round to the beaches of the Red Sea, Timna.
Main Languages: Hebrew, English.
Minimum stay: 1 month.
Other Information: Close to main road. Kosher kitchen, Shomer Shabbat in public places. Extremely hot summers. Religious holidays observed. Volunteers must go through the Kibbutz Volunteer office in Tel-Aviv. Volunteers accepted as candidates for membership. Ages 18-30. No Ulpan. Religious holidays observed. Close to bus stop and main road. Situated in the Arava Valley 50km north of Eilat. Kibbutz Movement: Takam.

(220) KIBBUTZ KFAR AZA
D.N. Hanegev 85142; tel 07-6809711; fax 07-6809629.
Founded: 1956.
Members: 250.
No volunteers.
Agriculture, industry services, cows, chickens.
Other Information: stopped taking volunteers. Religious holidays observed.

(11) KIBBUTZ KFAR BLUM
D.N. Upper Galilee 12150; tel 06-6948406 (volunteer office); 06-6948511 (kibbutz office); fax 06-6948555/6948666.
Founded: 1943.
Members: 350. Volunteers 30-40.
Responsible for volunteers: Itai Hameiri.
Work available: 40% of work is in the kibbutz hotel (100 rooms). Other duties are in the communal dining room, kitchen, ironing, dairy farm and garden.
Working hours: 6 1/2-hour day, 6-day

week. One Saturday monthly for 4 1/2 hours required.
Days off: 2 extra days off per month starting from the 2nd month.
Accommodation: good. 2 or 3 to a room depending on room size. Bathroom and kitchenette to every 3 rooms.
Free: aerogrammes, tampons, all cleaning materials, library.
Sports/Entertainments: tennis, soccer, basketball, horse riding (only for experienced riders), kayaking on the river (organised occasionally), TV room, bar-disco, weekly film in the kibbutz auditorium. Some events in the auditorium are free, some subsidised and some full price.
Facilities on the kibbutz: olympic swimming pool, lighted cinder running track, gymnasium, sauna.
Nearby facilities: Canado Sports Center, local pubs, Mt Hermon (only ski site in Israel) 1/2 an hour's drive.
Nearest town: Kiryat Shmona 10 minutes by bus.
Main Languages: Hebrew, English.
Minimum/maximum stay: 5 weeks up to 6 months.
Other Information: Places all year but July and August are usually booked. Mature volunteers from age 21 preferred. No Ulpan.
Kibbutz Movement: Takam.

(53a) KIBBUTZ KFAR CHARUV
D.N. Ramat Golan 12932; tel 06-6761986; fax 06-6761810.
Founded: 1973.
Members: 100. Volunteers: max: 24.
Volunteer leader: Luna Fleisch.
Work available: agriculture, metal work factory, gardens, dairy cows, services, tourism.
Working hours: 6 1/2 hour day, 6-day week.
Days off: 3 extra days monthly, plus Jewish holidays.
Free: newspapers, some postage, work clothes; allowance of NIS 380 per month and 20 unit telephone card.
Accommodation: concrete houses, 2 to

a room with toilet and shower.
Sports/Entertainments: football, basketball, discos and many interesting walks in the area of the kibbutz.
Facilities: English library, gym, swimming pool.
Languages: Hebrew, English, Spanish, French.
Nearest town: Tiberias, three-quarters of an hour by bus.
Other Information: a kibbutz with young members aged 30s to 50s. Outstanding viewpoint from the Golan Heights overlooking the Sea of Galilee. Pleasant breezes in summer; cold and windy in winter. Volunteers leave a deposit of $40 in cash with the kibbutz office on arrival. Contraceptive pills and condoms are available through the kibbutz clinic.

(183) KIBBUTZ KFAR ETZION
D.N. Harei Jerusalem 90200; tel: 02-935222; fax 02-935288.
Founded: 1967.
Members: 120.
Other Information: Kfar Etzion was the first Jewish settlement to be renewed in the West Bank after the Six-Day War in 1967. Young religious kibbutz. Does not take volunteers unless they want to be Jewish and speak Hebrew well enough. Ulpan is arranged for suitable candidates.
Kibbutz Movmeent: Hadati.

(2) KIBBUTZ KFAR GIL'ADI
D.N. Kfar Giladi 12210; tel 06-6946211; fax 06-6949267.
Founded: 1916.
Members: 430. Volunteers: 30-60.
Volunteer organiser: Jack Misraghi
Work available: orchards, fish ponds, industry, gardening, children's houses, services, hotel.
Accommodation: 1-3 to a room. No kosher food.
Sports/Entertainments: tennis, football, basketball, weekly films and volunteers' pub.
Facilities: swimming pool, library, clubhouse, shop.

Main Languagues: Hebrew, English, German, Spanish.
Excursions: 2-day-trip monthly. Groups staying 3 months or more, usually a 3-day trip.
Minimum stay: 2 months.
Other Information: ages 20-30. Groups and individuals. Places all year. Some holidays observed. Close to bus stop and main road.
Kibbutz Movement: Takam.

(112) KIBBUTZ KFAR GLICKSON
D.N. Menashe 37815; tel 06-6307444; fax 06-6307206.
Founded: 1939.
Please note: not taking volunteers 'at the moment.'
Work: avocados, oranges, cotton, cows, chickens, dining room, kitchen, dishwasher, children's houses, industry.
Working hours: 8-hour day; 6 day week.
Days off: 2 extra days monthly.
Free: credit for necessities.
Accommodation: concrete houses. 3-4 in a room. No kosher food.
Sports/Entertainments: basketball, weekly film, self-organized discos.
Facilities: swimming pool, library, shop.
Languages: Hebrew, English, Spanish, Hungarian.
Excursions: No information.
Nearest towns: Haifa 40km; Tel-Aviv 50 km.
Minimum stay: 5 weeks.
Other Information: Situated in the Upper Galilee region. Groups and singles. Ages 18-30. Bus stop in kibbutz. Religious holidays observed.
Kibbutz Movement: Takam.

(68) KIBBUTZ KFAR HACHORESH
Kfar Hachoresh 16960; tel 06-6558345; fax 06-6558527.
Founded: 1948.
Members: 250. Volunteers: 30.
Work available: bakery, kitchen, dining room, orchards, gardens.

Working hours: 8-hour day, 6-day week.
Accommodation: wooden houses. 3 persons in large rooms, with bathroom per room.
Sports/Entertainments: basketball, football, weekly film.
Facilities: swimming pool (summer), shop selling sweets, stationery, toiletries and drinks.
Main Languages: Hebrew, English, Russian.
Excursions: 1 day every month.
Minimum/maximum stay: 6 weeks up to 6 months.
Nearest towns: Nazareth 5km, Haifa 32km.
Kibbutz Movement: Takam.

(50a) KIBBUTZ KFAR HAMAC-CABI
D.N. Kfar Hamaccabi 30030; tel: 04-8441150/1.
Founded: 1936.
Members: 220.
Orchards, potatoes, factory, cotton, cows, chicken, fish ponds, dining room, kitchens.
Accommodation: camping. No kosher food.
Main Languages: Hebrew, English, German.
Other Information: at the time of press, Hamaccabi was undergoing changes and may no longer be a kibbutz. It has stopped taking volunteers. Close to bus stop and main road. Holidays observed.
Kibbutz Movement: Takam.

(40) KIBBUTZ KFAR HANASSI
Galil Elyon 1 12305; tel 06-6914901; fax 06-6914017; website www.villageinn.co.il
Founded: 1948.
Members: 320. Volunteers: 15.
Responsible for volunteers: Pat Ben Zeev (e-mail patgeoff@netvision.net.il).
Work available: gardening, services (i.e. plumbers, electricians, kitchen), factory (foundry), plant nursery, bed

and breakfast, home for the elderly.
Working hours: 8-hour day, 6-day week.
Free: nothing.
Accommodation: old and newer rooms. 2-3 persons to a room.
Sports/Entertainments: basketball, rugby in winter, badminton, tennis, football, videos, disco-pub twice weekly.
Facilities: swimming pool in summer, library, shop.
Main Languages: Hebrew, English.
Excursions: occasional day-trips. Trip to the Negev after 3 months.
Nearest towns: Tiberias and Kiryat Shmona about $1/2$ an hour and Safat.
Minimum/maximum stay: 1 month up to 6 months.
Other Information: accepts written applications direct to kibbutz. Volunteer ages 18-30. Groups and individuals.
Over 30 programme: runs special programme 'Our Way' for applicants aged 30+. This is a two-week experience for those who want to taste the kibbutz experience including working up to 4 hours a day. Costs $350 inclusive (2 meals a day); e-mail Pearlson@villagein.co.il for details.
Ulpan for non-Jewish applicants: this may be possible; write directly to the kibbutz for details.
   The kibbutz is some distance from main road and bus stop. Holidays observed. Possibility of kibbutz family. Special art programme. About 40 students.
Kibbutz Movement: Takam.

(46) KIBBUTZ KFAR MASARYK
D.N.Ashrat 25208; tel: 04-9854592; fax 04-9919353.
Founded: 1933.
Members: 700. Volunteers: 30.
Responsible for volunteers: Lea Schamir.
Work available: kitchen, dining room, cows, fields, factory.
Working hours: 6-hour day; 6 day week.

Free: aerogrammes.
Sports/Entertainments: basketball, tennis, football, weekly discos.
Facilities: swimming pool, library, clubhouse, shop.
Languages: English, Russian, Spanish, Polish, Hebrew.
Excursions: day-trip monthly, 3-day trip every 3 months.
Minimum/maximum stay: 2 months up to 6 months.
Other Information: will only accept applications through the kibbutz agency in Tel-Aviv. Do not contact the kibbutz direct. Ages 18-32. Holidays observed. Possibility of kibbutz family. Individuals and groups. No Ulpan.
Kibbutz Movement: Ha'artzi.

(174) KIBBUTZ KFAR MENACHEM
Kfar Menachem 79875; tel 08-8508404 (office); fax 08-8508411/07.
Founded: 1939.
Members: 400. Volunteers: 25-30.
Responsible for volunteers: Bert Cheney (tel 08-508685 home; e-mail cheneybert@yahoo.com
Work available: metal factory, chickens, dairy, garden, fields in season, kitchen, dining room, swimming pool in season (must be accredited lifesaver).
Working hours: 7-hour day, 6 day week.
Days off: 2 days extra off monthly.
Accommodation: blocks with showers and toilets. 2 people to a room. No kosher food.
Sports/Entertainments: basketball, handball, football, video, dancing (country and disco), pub twice a week, theatre, study and discussion groups.
Facilities: swimming pool (in summer), library, shop, clubhouse. Free: aerogrammes.
Nearest town: Rehovot 25km.
Main Languages: Hebrew, English, German.
Excursions: 3-day trip every 3rd month. Tel Aviv, Jerusalem, Beersheva, beach from Ashdod to Ashkelon.

Minimum/maximum stay: 2 months up to 6 months.
Other Information: ages 18-30. Individuals and groups. Religious holidays observed. One hour from Jerusalem and Tel Aviv. Pocket money graded: according to length of stay from NIS 310 for the first month up to NIS 720. Talks arranged if volunteers interested. 4 seminars of 3 days each per year for long-term volunteers. HIV test mandatory on arrival at kibbutz. No charge.
Kibbutz Movement: Ha'artzi.

(127) KIBBUTZ KFAR RUPPIN
D.N. Bet Shean 10850; tel: 06-589111.
Founded: 1938.
Members: 240. Volunteers: 20-25.
Work available: agricultural, services.
Working hours: 8-hour day, 5-day week.
Days off: 2 extra days monthly.
Free: postage, toiletries.
Accommodation: 2-3 to a room. No kosher food.
Sports/Entertainments: football, handball, table tennis, basketball, weekly film shows and dances.
Facilities: swimming pool, clubhouse, shop, library.
Main Languages: Hebrew, English.
Minimum stay: 1 month.
Other Information: ages 18-35. Individuals preferred. Holidays observed. Close to bus stop and main road.
Kibbutz Movement: Takam.

(9) KIBBUTZ KFAR SZOLD
D.N. Upper Galilee 12230; tel 06-947511; fax 06-6907554.
Founded: 1942.
Members: 340. Volunteers: 20.
Responsible for volunteers: David Carmi.
Work available: fields, garden, packing house, kitchen, dining room.
Working hours: 8-hour day, 6-day week.
Days off: 3 per month.
Free: nothing.

Accommodation: old houses. 2-3 to a room. No kosher food.
Sports/Entertainments: basketball, volleyball, tennis, film shows, bar, discos all over the area.
Facilities: swimming pool, library, clubhouse, shop.
Languages: Hebrew, English, Spanish, German, Portuguese.
Excursions: 1, 2 and 3-day trips depending how long the volunteer stays.
Nearest town: Kiryat Shmona.
Minimum/maximum stay: 3 weeks up to 3 months.
Other Information: Prefer groups.
Kibbutz Movement: Takam.

(63) KIBBUTZ KINNERET
D.N. Emek Hayarden 15118; tel 06-6759500.
Founded: 1913.
Members: 500. Volunteers: 40.
Inhabitants: 800.
Work available: bananas, grapefruit, vineyards, dates, cotton, mangoes, avocados, dairy unit, bees, sweet corn, dining room, kitchen, laundry, plastics factory, tourist centre.
Working hours: 6-hour day; 6-day week.
Free: daily newspapers, weekly magazine, certain beverages and some foods.
Accommodation: blocks. 3 to a room.
Sports/Entertainments: every kind of sport and water sports, large cultural centre, yearly music festival, weekly film shows, TV room, small library, private lakeside beach, live theatre, weekly disco.
Facilities: non-profit supermarket, clothes shop, watchmaker.
Main Languages: Hebrew, English, German.
Minimum stay: 1 month.
Excursions: regular 1 and 3-4 day trips.
Other Information: twice weekly a truck to Tiberias. Bus stop on kibbutz. Ages 18-30. Individuals preferred.
Kibbutz Movement: Takam.

(167) KIBBUTZ KIRIYAT ANAVIM
D N Harei Yehuda 90833; tel: 02-348621; fax 02-348720. Volunteers' Dept tel 02-348608 (day), 02-348702 (evening).
Founded: 1920.
Members: 185. Volunteers: 15-25.
Responsible for volunteers: Pip Allon.
Work available: agriculture (seasonal), dining room, kitchen, guest house, factory.
Working hours: 7-hour day, 6-day week.
Days off: 2 extra days monthly.
Free: English newspaper.
Accommodation: 1-2 per room for individuals, 2-5 sharing for groups.
No kosher food.
Sports/Entertainments: basketball, football, volunteers' club with TV, kitchen, books etc..
Facilities: swimming pool, gym, library, shop.
Main Languages: Hebrew, English, Finnish.
Excursions: 1-2 days every 3 months.
Nearest town: Jerusalem 15 minutes by bus on the Tel Aviv highway.
Minimum stay: 6 weeks.
Other Information: maximum age 32. Groups and individuals. Close to bus stop and main road. Holidays observed.
Kibbutz Movement: Takam.

(210) KIBBUTZ KISSUFIM
D.N. Hanegev 85130; tel: 07-9983811 or 9983915; for volunteers 07-9983873.
Founded: 1951.
Members: 120. Volunteers: about 15-25.
Responsible for volunteers: M Goldfarb, H Booyens, K Grosvirt.
Work available: services, orchard, field work, poultry, gardens.
Working hours: 8-hour day, 6-day week.
Days off: 3 extra days monthly.
Free: inland mail, 2 aerogrammes weekly, English newspaper, work

clothes, bedding.
Accommodation: solid rooms (once high-schoolers' rooms). 2-3 to a room, kitchen for volunteers. No kosher food.
Sports/Entertainments: football, basketball, volleyball, exercise classes, billiards, horse riding, disco, pub, TV room. The municipality offers inexpensive films, concerts etc.
Facilities: swimming pool, weights room, library, shop, boutique.
Main Languages: Hebrew, English, Spanish.
Excursions: 1 day-trip per month.
Nearest towns: Beersheva 75 minutes by bus; Tel Aviv 2 hours by bus.
Minimum/maximum stay: 2 months up to 9 months.
Other Information: ages 18-35. Religious holidays observed. Buses available throughout the day. There are no suppers in the kibbutz dining room but volunteers are provided with food to cook in their house. Volunteers are requested to bring proper work boots and a sleeping bag for trips. No Ulpan.
Kibbutz Movement: Takam.

(162a)   KIBBUTZ   KVUZAT SCHILLER
D.N. Emek Sorek 76802; tel 08-372823/4; fax 08-453120.
Founded: 1927.
Members: 220. Volunteers: 45.
Responsible for volunteers: Pablo Frydlender (e-mail Roeea3@hotmail.com).
Work available: orchards and citrus groves, services.
Free: allowance and credit in shop.
Days off: 2 extra days a month.
Accommodation: houses. 3 to a room. No kosher food.
Sports/Entertainments: basketball, handball, volley ball, football, tennis, pub/disco.
Facilities: swimming pool, library, clubhouse, shop.
Languages: Hebrew, English, Spanish.
Excursions: Saturday trip once every 2 months. Every 6 weeks a trip after work hours.

Minimum stay: 6 weeks.
Nearest town: Tel Aviv, 25 minutes by bus.
Other Information: volunteers can write to the kibbutz in the first instance to check vacancies and the kibbutz will then arrange registration with the kibbutz office in Tel-Aviv. Ages 18-34. Individuals and groups. Religious holidays observed. Close to bus stop and main road. Kibbutz Movement: Takam.

(169a)KIBBUTZ KVUTZAT YAVNE
M.P. Yavneh 79233; tel 08-8548311; fax 08-85478311.
Founded: 1941.
Members: 350 (total population 850).
Volunteers: 5-20.
Work available: poultry, fieldcrops, kitchen, dining room, children's houses, laundry.
Working hours: 7-8 hour day; 6-day week.
Accommodation: 2-3 to a room. Food is kosher.
Facilities: Judaica library, general library, swimming pool, shop.
Languages: Hebrew, English.
Other Information: Jewish atmosphere. Volunteers are only accepted if recommended by the religious kibbutz (Hadati)offices in Tel Aviv, or as Ulpan graduates from the Kibbutz Ulpan. Short stays and only when appropriate housing exists. Ulpan lasts for 5 months.
Kibbutz Movement: Hadati.

(211)KIBBUTZ LAHAV
D.N. Negev 85335; tel 07-913211; fax 07-910380.
Founded: 1952.
Members: 200. Volunteers: 20-30.
Responsible for volunteers: Yuval Rattner.
Work available: kitchen, garden, turkeys, plastics factory, restaurant, meat factory.
Free: nothing.
Accommodation: wooden huts. 2 to a room. No kosher food.

Sports/Entertainments: football, tennis, basketball, disco-pub, videos.
Facilities: swimming pool, library, clubhouse.
Main Languages: Hebrew, English, German.
Excursions: trips every 3 months for volunteers staying at least 3 months.
Shopping in Beersheva.
Nearest towns: Beersheva (30 minutes by bus); Tel-Aviv (90 minutes).
Minimum/maximum stay: 2 months up to 6 months..
Other Information: ages 17-40. Groups and individuals. Holidays celebrated. 11 km main road and bus stop. Possibility of kibbutz family. No Ulpan.
Kibbutz Movement: Ha'artzi.

(52) KIBBUTZ LAVI
D.N. Lower Galilee 15267; tel 06-799211; fax 06-899299,
Founded: 1949.
Members: 200. Volunteers: organised groups only.
Kibbutz secretary: Uzzi Amiram.
Work available: girls work in the kitchen, dining room, laundry repair room, children's houses and hotel.
Boys: farm work, cows, poultry, garage, metal workshop, carpentry factory specialising in synagogue furniture and the hotel for Israeli and international visitors.
Working hours: 8-hour day (boys $8^{1/2}$ hours). 6-day week.
Days off: Saturdays and 1 extra day per month.
Accommodation: 3-4 to a room.
Sports/Entertainments: basketball, tennis, weekly film show, visits to shows and concerts. Courses in a variety of subjects, mainly in Hebrew.
Facilities: swimming pool, library, shop selling sweets, stationery, toiletries.
Main Languages: Hebrew, English.
Excursions: half-day trip monthly.
Minimum stay: 6 weeks.
Other Information: the kibbutz lies in the eastern Lower Galilee, overlooking the Kinneret (Galilee) valley. Ortho-

dox Jewish religious observance mandatory. Forms part of a lower Galilee religious bloc with Kibbutz Beit Rimon. Close to bus stop and main road. Kibbutz family can be arranged.
Kibbutz Movement: Hadati (religious movement).

(8a) KIBBUTZ LEHAVOT HABASHAN
Upper Galilee 12125; tel 06-6952111; fax 06-6952232.
Founded: 1945.
Members: 260. Volunteers: 12.
Responsible for volunteers: Ava Gabai.
Work available: agriculture, kitchen, dining room, industrial.
Free: aerogrammes.
Accommodation: old. 2-3 to a room. No kosher food.
Sports/Entertainments: football, basketball tennis, pub-disco (twice weekly), video channel, lectures in the Youth Club.
Facilities: swimming pool (June to September), library, shop. Nearby is a sports centre.
Languages: Hebrew, English, German, Spanish.
Excursions: trips once a month on Saturday; after 3 months a 3-day trip.
Possibility of rafting and visiting nature reserves in the vicinity.
Nearest town: Kiryat Shmona (12km).
Minimum/maximum stay: 2 months up to 6 months.
Other Information: situated in the far north of Israel, 3 hours by car from Tel-Aviv. Very scenic part of Israel. Very hot in summer, winters cold and wet. Ages 18-32. Close to bus stop and main road. No Ulpan.
Kibbutz Movement: Ha'artzi.

(133) KIBBUTZ LAHAVOT HAVIVA
D.N. Emeq Hefer 38835; tel 06-368611-10; fax 06-368650.
Founded: 1949.
Members: 160.

Facilities: swimming pool, library, shop, clubhouse.
Languages: Hebrew, English, German, Spanish.
Other Information: close to bus stop. Some holidays observed. No longer takes volunteers because of 'financial difficulties.'
Kibbutz Movement: H'artzi.

(38)   KIBBUTZ   LOCHAMEI HAGETA'OT
D.N. Asherat 25220; tel 04-858711
Founded: 1949.
Members: 270. Volunteers: 30.
Work available: avocados, factory, grapefruit, cows, chickens, field work, dining room, kitchen, laundry, fish ponds.
Working hours: 6-hour day, 6-day week.
Days off: 3 days monthly plus Saturdays.
Accommodation: 3 to a room. No kosher food.
Sports/Entertainments: weekly films, football, occasional shows, basketball, tennis.
Facilities: swimming pool, library, shop.
Main Languages: Hebrew, English.
Excursions: Once every 3 months, for 3 days.
Minimum stay: 1 month.
Other Information: maximum age 32. Individuals or groups. Close to bus stop, main road and sea.
Tourism: famous holocaust museum, admittance free.
Kibbutz Movement: Takam.

(138) KIBBUTZ MA'ABAROT
D.N. Ma'abarot 40230; tel 09-8982566 (work); fax 09-8946726; e-mail sandy—kl@maabarot.org.il
website www.maabarot.org.il
Founded: 1933.
Members: 500. Volunteers: 10-30.
Responsible for volunteers: Sandy Kleinhouse.
Work available: 5 large factories producing pet and calf food, powder formula infant food and pharmaceutical products. Other work includes dining room, kitchen, gardens, folding laundry and occasionally fruit picking and dairy cows.
Free: basic necessities.
Accommodation: new, pre-fab houses near Kibbutz member housing so proper conduct regarding noise level is essential. Two people to a room. No kosher food.
Sports/entertainments: basketball, tennis.
Facilities: swimming pool (May to October), library, clubhouse with refreshments.
Main Languages: Hebrew, English.
Excursions: 1 day-trip monthly. Netanya beach very near.
Nearest town: Netanya (10km, 15 minutes by bus or taxi).
Minimum stay: 6 weeks.
Other information: ages 18-26. Mainly individuals. Evidence of recent HIV test essential. Religious holidays observed. Close to bus stop and main road. Bus 26 goes to Maabarot from Natanya. Volunteers should contact Sandy Kleinhouse, Volunteer Organiser at the kibbutz; they don't have to go through the volunteer office. Two week's before arrival, prospective volunteers should confirm their date of arrival, flight details and arrival time. No Ulpan.
Kibbutz Movement: Ha'artzi.

(64) KIBBUTZ MA'AGAN
M.P. Jordan Valley 15160; tel 06-753703); fax 06-753707.
Founded: 1951.
Members: 192 (total population 400). Volunteers: 25-30.
Responsible for volunteers: Shimi Shitrit.
Work available: bananas, kitchen, dates, dining room, laundry, ostriches, cowsheds, mangos, avocados, watermelons, camp site, chickens.
Working hours: 7-hour day, 6-day week.
Free: coffee, tea, sugar.

Accommodation: pre-fab buildings. 3 per room. Air- conditioned. Kitchen facilities, kettle and fridge each. No kosher food.
Sports/Entertainments: basketball, football, swimming in Lake Kinneret, films and discos.
Facilities: library, clubhouse, shop.
Main Languages: Hebrew, English.
Excursions: trip every 3 months. Possiblities in the vicinity include the Jordan River, Tiberias, hot springs, water park.
Nearest town: Tiberias (12km).
Minimum/maximum stay: 2 months, no maximum.
Other Information: ages 18-32. Groups and individuals. Situated on the shore of the Sea of Galilee (5 minutes walk to the beach). Close to main road and bus stop. Holidays observed. No Ulpan.
Tourism: Lake-side camping ground. Self-contained bungalows and caravans, some air-conditioned. Kiosk for light meals, TV area, refrigerators, supermarket.
Kibbutz Movement: Takam.

(103)KIBBUTZ MA'AGAN MICHAEL
D.N. Menashe, 37805; tel: 06-6394111.
Founded: 1949.
Members 560.
Work available: factory, orchards, banana plantations, dining room.
Working hours: 6-hour day, 6-day week.
Free: allowance for most necessities.
Accommodation: pre-fab. huts. 2-3 to a room. No kosher food.
Sports/Entertainments: twice weekly film shows, weekly dances.
Facilities: library, clubhouse.
Main Languages: Hebrew, English.
Excursions: by arrangement with group organisers.
Minimum stay: 3 months.
Other Information: ages 20-30. Groups only.
Ulpan: 70 pupils. Opportunity for non-

Jewish people. Courses last 5 months and start January and July.
Kibbutz Movement: Takam.

(121) KIBBUTZ MA'ALE GILBOA
D.N. Gilboa 19145; tel 06-6539511; fax 06-6585895.
Founded: 1968 and again 1974.
Members: 50.
Responsible for volunteers: Eyal Ben Zvi.
Work available: fields, cows, fish ponds, gardening, kitchen, tourism.
Working hours: 8-hour day; 6-day week.
Days off: 1 day extra monthly.
Free: nothing.
Accommodation: new houses near the kibbutz for enlarging the community (see 'Other information' below). Food is kosher.
Entertainment: basketball, hikes, dances.
Facilities: library, swimming pool (non-mixed men and women) clubhouse with TV and table games, shop, classes in Judaism.
Nearest towns: Beit She'an, Afula and Haifa are from 20 to 45 minutes away.
Main Languages: Hebrew, English.
Minimum stay: longer term volunteers (see note below).
Other Information: This kibbutz takes only religious Jewish volunteers and prefers families doing Aliya (i.e. who will stay a long time; they do not have to be kibbutz members). At the time of press no volunteers were needed but this is likely to change. Religious holidays and festivals observed. Remote location on the Gilboa mountain range. Surrounded by rich agricultural land. Superb views. Comfortable climate throughout the summer. The kibbutz also has facilities for tourists.
Kibbutz Movement: Hadati.

(166) KIBBUTZ MA'ALE HACHAMISH
D.N. Harai Yehuda 90835; tel 02-5347350; fax 02-5347353.
Founded: 1938.

Members: 200.
Work available: agriculture, factory, hotel, services.
Other information: lies off the highway between Tel-Aviv and Jerusalem.
Kibbutz Movement: Takam.

(126) KIBBUTZ MAANIT
D.N. Menashe 37855; tel 06-6375111; fax 06-6376367.
Founded: 1942.
Members: 330. Volunteers: 25.
Work available: banana groves, avocados, gardening, egg store, chickens, cows, dining room, kitchen, field crops.
Working hours: 8-hour day, 5-day week, plus six hours on Fridays.
Days off: 3 extra days monthly.
Free: food, tea, coffee.
Accommodation: stone houses. 2 to a room. No kosher food.
Sports/Entertainments: football, volleyball, TV room, disco on kibbutz and on nearby kibbutzim, walks in local surroundings organised according to wishes.
Facilities: swimming pool (May-October), library, clubhouse, Shops for general supplies, food, clothes.
Languages: Hebrew, English, German, Yiddish.
Excursions: a day-trip every month.
Nearest town: Hedera (15 minutes by bus).
Minimum/maximum stay: 2 months up to 6 months.
Other Information: ages 18-30. Individuals all year. Possibility of kibbutz family. Close to bus stop and main road. Some holidays observed. Written applications welcomed. No Ulpan on the kibbutz but can help to organise elsewhere.
Kibbutz Movement: Ha'artzi.

(3) KIBBUTZ MA'AYIN BARUCH
D.N.Upper Galilee 12220; tel 06-6964611.
Founded: 1947.
Members: 160. Volunteers: 15-45.
Work available: apple orchards, avocados, cotton fields, cows, chickens, gardens, kitchen, dining room, children's houses, factory.
Working hours: 6-hour day, 6-day week.
Free: aerogrammes per month.
Accommodation: concrete building. 2-4 in a room. No kosher food.
Entertainments: basketball, tennis, regular film shows, volunteers' club with facilities for discos and parties.
Facilities: swimming pool, library, shop.
Main Languages: Hebrew, English.
Excursions: day-trip monthly; 3-day trip every 3 months.
Minimum stay: 1 month.
Other Information: ages 18 plus. Individuals and groups. Religious holidays observed. Possibility of kibbutz family. Close to bus stop and main roads.
Kibbutz Movement: Takam.

(99) KIBBUTZ MA'AYAN TSVI
D.N. 30805 Hof Hacarmel; tel 06-6395111; 06-6395350.
Founded: 1938.
Members: 450. Volunteers: 10-15; occasionally 20.
Responsible for volunteers: Dalia Segal.
Work available: orchards, fishponds, optics industry, kitchen, dining room.
Working hours: 7 or 8 hour day, 6-day week.
Days off: 2 extra days monthly.
Accommodation: renovated building. 2-3 to a room. No kosher food.
Sports/Entertainments: large gymnasium, basketball, volleyball, very new films, discos.
Facilities: swimming pool, library, clubhouse with TV and periodicals from all over the world.
Languages: Hebrew, English, German, some French.
Excursions: No information available.
Nearest towns: Zichron-Ya'acav (5-10 minutes), Hadera (20 minutes), Haifa (40 minutes).
Other Information: groups and individuals. ages 18-30. Holidays

observed. Possibility of kibbutz family. Close to bus stop and main road. Ulpan for Jewish students only. Kibbutz Movement: Takam.

(37) KIBBUTZ MACHANAYIM
D.N. Hevel Korazim 12315; tel 06-6933711; fax 06-6934410.
Founded: 1952.
Members: 200. Volunteers: 10-40 depending on the season.
Responsible for volunteers: Amanda Hickman-Gideoni.
Work available: orchards, factory, garden, dining room, kitchen.
Working hours: 6-hour day, 6-day week or 8-hour 5-day week.
Free: postage, toiletries, coffee and tea.
Accommodation: old rooms. 1-3 per room; 1 shower for every 2 room. No kosher food.
Sports/Entertainments: basketball, tennis, football, films broadcast every night on the internal cable channel.
Facilities: swimming pool, library, shop selling wines, beer, confectionery, toiletries.
Main Languages: Hebrew, English.
Excursions: 3-day trip after 3 months. The Sea of Galilee is 30 minutes by bus and Mount Hermon ski resort 1 hour.
Nearest town: Hazor, 2 minutes by bus, but volunteers usually walk (30 minutes).
Minimum/maximum stay: 3 months, up to 6 months.
Other Information: ages 18-35. Groups and individuals. Holidays observed. Close to main road and bus stop. Welcomes returns from previous volunteers who can write direct to the kibbutz. Mandatory HIV test on arrival at the kibbutz. No charge.
Kibbutz Movement: Takam.

(136) KIBBUTZ MAGAL
D.N. Hefer 38845; tel 06-367111.
Founded: 1953.
Members: 175.
Work available: cotton, avocados,

bananas, drip-irrigation systems factory, dining room, kitchen.
Working hours: 6-hour day; 6-day week.
Days off: 2 extra days monthly.
Free: allowance per month of tea, coffee, sugar.
Accommodation: 4 to a room. No kosher food.
Sports/Entertainments: basketball, tennis, volleyball, film shows, video.
Facilities: swimming pool, clubhouse.
Main Languages: Hebrew, English, Spanish.
Excursions: short trips once a month, longer trips every 2 months. Individual volunteers are encouraged to make their own trips.
Other Information: ages 18-35.
Possibility of kibbutz family.
Kibbutz Movement: Takam.

(216) KIBBUTZ MAGEN
D N Negev 85465; tel 07-6983085.
Founded: 1949.
Members: 200. Volunteers: 25 approx.
Responsible for volunteers: Nati Avraham.
Work available: kitchen, plastic factory, dairy, dishwashing, fields & irrigation, garden, laundry.
Working hours: 6¹/2hour day, 6-day week.
Free: aerogrammes, food, drinks, condoms, toiletries.
Days off: 2 extra days monthly.
Accommodation: 2 per room. Modest but comfortable. No kosher food.
Sports/Entertainments: tennis, weekly films, disco, pub.
Facilities: swimming pool.
Nearest towns: Beersheva (45km).
Minimum stay: 2 months up to 6 months maximum.
Other Information: ages 18-35. Beautiful but fairly isolated surroundings. Volunteers are integrated with the kibbutzniks. Good bus connections with Beersheva (1 hour) and Tel Aviv (2 hours) by bus.
Kibbutz Movement: Ha'artzi.

(18) KIBBUTZ MALKIA
D.N. Galil Elyon 13845; tel: 06-6946711; fax 06-6945 436; e-mail byahad@israsrv.net.il   website www.israsrv/net.il/malkia
Founded: 1949.
Members: 180. Volunteers: none (since 1991)
Mainly agricultural.
Facilities: swimming pool, library, shop.
Main Languages: Hebrew, English.
Other Information: includes B'yahad Seminar Centre for Educational Tourism.
Kibbutz Movement: Takam.

(118) KIBBUTZ MA'OZ CHAIM
D.N. Emek Beit Shean 10845; tel 06-6589565; fax 06-6580840.
Founded: 1937.
Members: 300. Volunteers: 12-14.
Responsible for volunteers: Judith Eshel.
Work available: dining room, kitchen garden, dates, mango, fields, fish ponds.
Working hours: 7-hour day; 6-day week.
Days off: 3 per month, Shabbat and holidays.
Free: aerogrammes, tampons.
Meals: breakfast and lunch only provided in the kibbutz dining room. Volunteers prepare their own supper (see below). No breakfast on Shabbat.
Accommodation: old but reasonably good. Rooms are air-conditioned. 2 people to a room. No kosher food.
Sports/Entertainments: basketball, tennis, football, films in nearby cinema, pub twice weekly.
Facilities: swimming pool, gym, volunteers' clubroom with TV, fridge, cooking and baking facilities. Volunteers buy food for their supper in the kibbutz shop and cook it themselves.
Main Languages: Hebrew, English.
Excursions: trips organised when possible including to nearby Sahne (waterfalls and clear pools used for swimming since Roman times).

Nearest town: Beit Shean (5km).
Minimum/maximum stay: 2 months up to 6 months (sometimes 9 months).
Other Information: ages 18 plus. Accepts individuals referred only by the main kibbutz office in Tel-Aviv or overseas kibbutz desks, or private contact with Judith Eshel through friends, word-of-mouth etc.. Close to bus stop. Mandatory HIV test on arrival at the kibbutz. No charge. Volunteers must have insurance that is represented in Israel.
Kibbutz Movement: Takam.

(224)   KIBBUTZ   MASH'AVEI SADE
(South of Beer Sheba)
D.N. Halutza 85510; tel 07-565111.
Founded: 1949.
Work available: agriculture, factory, services.
Kibbutz Movement: Takam.

(67a) KIBBUTZ MASSADA
Emek Hayarden 15140; tel 06-6758211; www.inter.net.il/givat/massada.htm
Founded: 1937.
Members: 280. Volunteers: 40-60.
Work available: bananas, avocados, dates, olives, dairy, chickens, irrigation, cotton, factory, dining room, kitchen.
Working hours: 6-8 hour day, 6-day week.
Days off: one day off for every 5 days worked.
Free: aerogrammes, coffee, tea, sugar, cookies, fruit. Allowance for shop. Clothing allowance after 4 months.
Accommodation: 2-3 to a room. No kosher food.
Sports/Entertainments: tennis, football, basketball, weekly film.
Facilities: swimming pool, library, shop, bar.
Main Languages: Hebrew, English.
Excursions: 1 trip every 3 months; if no trip a $25 allowance.
Kibbutz Movement: Takam.

(152) KIBBUTZ/MOSHAV MAS-SU'A
D.N. Bikat Hayarden; tel 02-922299.
Founded: 1973.
Members: 50. Volunteers: 30.
Work available: Sept/May – agricultural. Each volunteer works for one member and takes all meals with family. Opportunities for responsbility and to learn new skills.
Working hours: 7-hour day.
Days off: 6 days monthly.
Free: coffee, tea.
Accommodation: room with small kitchen. 3 to a room. No kosher food.
Sports/Entertainments: basketball, inter kibbutz moshav parties. Jordan valley special entertainments. Weekly film shows and dances.
Facilities: library, clubhouse, shop.
Languages: Hebrew, English, French.
Excursions: occasional visits to different parts of the country.
Minimum stay: 1 month.
Other Information: individuals and groups. Ages 18-35. Close to the bus stop and main road.
Kibbutz Movement: Oved Hatsioni.

(25) KIBBUTZ MATZUVA
Western Galilee 22835; tel 04-858000.
Founded: 1940
Members: 270. Volunteers: 10-25.
Work available: orange groves, banana, avocado, mango plantations, services, textile factory
Working hours: 8-hour day, 6-day week.
Free: nothing except work clothes.
Accommodation: stone houses, 2 to a room. No kosher food.
Sports/Entertainments: regular video film shows, dances, pub.
Facilities: swimming pool, tennis, library, clubhouse, mini-market.
Languages: Hebrew, English, German, Dutch, Spanish.
Excursions: day-trips monthly; 3-day trip around Israel every 3 months.
Nearest town: Nahariya (15 minutes by bus).

Minimum stay: 8 weeks.
Other Information: ages 19-25. Individuals and groups. Possibility of kibbutz family for long stay volunteers, some Hebrew tuition on request. Close to main road and bus stop. Religious holidays observed. Applications through Takam office. Mandatory HIV test on arrival at the kibbutz. Free of charge.
Kibbutz Movement: Takam.

(199) KIBBUTZ MEFALSIM
D.N. Hof Ashkelon 79160; tel 07-9804111; 9804228.
Founded: 1949.
Members: 200. Volunteers 15-33.
Work available: chickens, kitchen, gardens, fields, cows, hatchery, orchards, furniture factory.
Working hours: 8-hour day, 6-day week.
Days off: 3 extra days off monthly.
Free: postage.
Accommodation: pre-fab. houses. 3 to a room. No kosher food.
Sports/Entertainments: football, basketball, films, weekly dances.
Facilities: swimming pool, library, clubhouse, shop.
Languages: Hebrew, Spanish.
Excursions: 3-day trip after 3 months.
Minimum stay: 1 month.
Other Information: ages 18-33. Groups and individuals. Not all holidays observed. Possibility of kibbutz family. Close to bus stop and main road.
Kibbutz Movement: Takam.

(96) KIBBUTZ MEGIDDO
D.N. Hevel Megiddo 19230; tel 06-6525757; 06-6525799; e-mail bbmegido@internet.il
Founded: 1949
Members: 200. Volunteers: 20 approx.
Responsible for volunteers: Malka Ben-Yakar.
Work available: agriculture, services (kitchen, children), industry (jewellery and plastics factories).
Working hours: 8-hour day, 6-day week.

Days off: 2 extra days monthly.
Free: aerogrammes.
Accommodation: 1-room apartments.
3 people per room. No kosher food.
Sports/Entertainments: basketball, football, tennis, twice weekly films, discos, concert visits. Kibbutz organised visits by singers and musical groups, occasional lectures and slide shows in English.
Facilities: swimming pool, volunteers' library, TV room clubhouse with table games, Small shop selling alcoholic drinks, confectionery, toiletries, gifts, beer.
Languages: Hebrew, English, Spanish.
Excursions: 3-day trips for groups by arrangement.
Nearest town: Afula (10km).
Minimum/maximum stay: 3 months up to 1 year maximum.
Other Information: ages 18-30. Groups and individuals. No direct applications. Bus stop on kibbutz 3km from main road. Small, friendly, hospitable kibbutz. Ulpan candidates accepted only through the Jewish Agency.
Kibbutz Movement: Ha'artzi.

(8) KIBBUTZ MENARA
D.N. Upper Galilee 12165; tel 06-6946111.
Members: 150
Work available: gardening, irrigation work, fruit picking (apples, avocados), rooms for tourist accommodation, glass factory (ampoules, small bottles, mostly packing) metalwork (for experienced metalworkers), chickens, dining room, kitchen.
Working hours: 8-hour day, 6-day week.
Days off: 2 extra days monthly.
Free: stamps, tea, coffee, toiletries.
Accommodation: brick buildings. 1-2 people to a room. No kosher food.
Sports/Entertainments: basketball, weekly film shows, visits to regional centre for concerts and plays.
Facilities: swimming pool, library, clubhouse, shop.
Languages: Hebrew, English, German, Spanish, French.
Excursions: 1 day-trip monthly for short stay. 2-3 days after longer stay.
Minimum stay: 1 month.
Other Information: ages 18 plus. Groups and individuals. Although close to Lebanese border it is safe and well protected. Regular buses. No main road. Cold wet winters. Work clothes provided.
Kibbutz Movement: Takam.

(191) KIBBUTZ MERHAVIA
Afula 19100. tel 06-6598611; fax 06-6523254.
Founded: 1929.
Members: 400. Volunteers: 35.
Responsible for volunteers: Micha Ben-David.
Work available: dairy, poultry, gardens, factory, dining room, kitchen, occasionally children's houses.
Working hours: 8-hour day, 6-day week.
Days off: 3 extra days monthly.
Accommodation: 2-3 to a room. No kosher food.
Sports/Entertainments: basketball, volleyball, tennis, table tennis, films, discos.
Facilities: swimming pool, library, shop. Cinema and shopping centre near the kibbutz.
Languages: English and main European languages.
Excursions: day-trip monthly; 2-3 day trip every 3 months.
Nearest town: Afula is a 15 minute walk. Kibbutz also provides transport to and from Afula.
Minimum/maximum stay: 6 weeks up to 3 months.
Other Information: ages: 18-32. Individuals and couples only. Close to main road and bus stop. Accepts direct applications from volunteers but they must be insured through the Ha'artzi office in Tel-Aviv or provide their own insurance that has representation is Israel. Mandatory HIV test on arrival at the kibbutz. No Ulpan.
Kibbutz Movement: Ha'artzi.

(15) KIBBUTZ MEROM GOLAN
D N Tzfon Ramat Hagolan 12905; tel 06-690111; fax 06-690236.
Founded: 1969.
Members: about 160. Volunteers: 15 (summer); 10 (winter).
Responsible for volunteers: Jeremiah Levine.
Work available: apple orchards. Also some work in guest house and restaurant, gardening and field crops.
Accommodation: typical kibbutz flats, fairly old but decent, 3 people per flat.
Free: nothing.
Facilities: swimming pool, gymnasium, billiards room, pub, restaurant, video library.
Excursions: day-trips about once a month. 3-day trip after 3 months.
Nearest towns: Qatzrin (20 minutes), Kiryat Schmona (35 minutes).
Minimum/maximum stay: 2 months up to legal limit possible.
Other information: rather isolated, but volunteers are treated warmly and in a personalised way and get more contact with Israeli culture than volunteers on many kibbutzim. Most volunteers settle in happily and tend to stay for 6 months or longer.
Kibbutz Movement: Takam.

(116) KIBBUTZ MESILOT
D.N. Gilboa 19155; tel 06-6580211; fax 06-6580300.
Founded: 1938.
Members: 340. Volunteers: 24.
Responsible for volunteers: Jackie.
Work available: garden, zoo, fields, olives, dates, greenhouse, factory (steel cables), fishponds, garage, peeling, cooking, dining room.
Accommodation: big rooms for 3 people, smaller ones for 2 persons. Air-conditioned.
Free: nothing.
Sports/Entertainments: films, concerts, theatrical presentations, lectures, swimming, discos.
Nearest towns: Afula and Beit Shean.
Languages: English, Hebrew, Portuguese, Swedish.

Other Information: buses every hour to Afula and Beit Shean. Volunteers' allowance NIS 200 monthly. No Ulpan.
Kibbutz Movement: Ha'artzi.

(128) KIBBUTZ METZER
D.N. Hefer 38820; tel 06-6387711; fax 06-6387815.
Founded: 1952.
Members: 160. Volunteers: 20.
Work available: picking, avocados, apricots, bananas, grapefruit, oranges, plastics and hat factories, dining room, kitchen, laundry, children's houses.
Working hours: 6-hour day; 6-day week.
Days off: 2 extra days monthly.
Free: aerogrammes, basic toiletries.
Accommodation: pre-fab. buildings with accessible showers and toilets. 2-3 to a room. No kosher food.
Sports/Entertainments: basketball, football table tennis. Very active social life with many young members. Weekly films, monthly dances, tennis.
Facilities: swimming pool, library, shop.
Languages: Hebrew, English, Spanish.
Excursions: 6 days of trips over a 6-month period.
Minimum stay: 1 month.
Other Information: ages 18 plus. Groups and individuals. Holidays observed.
Kibbutz Movement: Ha'artzi.

(57) KIBBUTZ MEVO HAMA
D.N. Ramat Hagolan 12934; tel 06-6764511; fax 06-6764519.
Founded: 1967.
Members: 180+. Volunteers: 15+.
Responsible for volunteers: Harry Poler.
Work available: mangos, avocados, melons (greenhouse), chickens, gardening, laundry, dining room, kitchens, field crops, electronics, factory (plastics), tourism complex.
Working hours: 6-8 hour day, 6-day week.
Days off: 3 extra days monthly.

Free: aerogrammes, fruit, toiletries.
Accommodation: comfortable, 2-3 to a room. No kosher food.
Sports/Entertainments: snooker, basketball, tennis, pub (twice weekly), videos, films, clubhouse entertaining.
Facilities: swimming pool, library, gym.
Languages: Hebrew, English.
Excursions: Tiberias and the Sea of Galilee are nearby.
Nearest town: Tiberias (45 minutes by bus).
Minimum/maximum stay: 2 months, no maximum.
Other Information: ages 18-30. Individuals only. Close to bus stop. Some way from main road. Possibility of kibbutz family.
Tourist Complex: hot sulphur bathing springs, archaeological site, observation point for seasonal migration of Europe's starlings. No Ulpan at present.
Kibbutz Movement: Takam.

(1) KIBBUTZ MISGAV AM
D.N. Upper Galilee 12155; tel: 06-6953199 (volunteers); 06-6953111 (office); fax 06-6953145.
Founded: 1945
Members: 117. Volunteers: 25-40.
Responsible for volunteers: Dalia Bennun.
Work available: orchards, cotton fields, fishponds, kitchen, dining room, gardens, textile factory.
Working hours: 6-hour day, 6-day week.
Days off: 2 extra days monthly.
Free: aerogrammes, coffee, tea, washing powder, light bulbs.
Accommodation: small apartments with WC and shower each. 2-3 volunteers per apartment. No kosher food.
Sport: basketball.
Facilities: heated indoor swimming pool, clubhouse with TV, refreshments and table games, shop, kibbutz pub.
Languages: mainly Hebrew, English and some Dutch, French and Afrikaans.

Excursions: 3 day-trips in 6 months.
Nearest town: Kiriat Shmona (11km).
Minimum/maximum stay: 1 month up to 6 months.
Other Information: ages 18-30. Groups and individuals. Most northerly kibbutz in Israel, situated 840m up in the Nafali mountains. Is also a permanent station for the army.
Small, fairly poor kibbutz. Bus stop on kibbutz. 10km from main road. Bank, post office, bars, cinema in nearest town Kiriat Shmona. No Ulpan.
Kibbutz Movement: Takam.

(165)   KIBBUTZ   MISHMAR DAVID
Nahal Eylon 73250; 08-444705/7.
Founded: 1949.
Members: 70
Work available: vineyards cotton, chickens, services, printshop, metal workshop, carpentry, garage, cows, gardening.
Free: stamps, good advice.
Accommodation: stone houses 3-4 to a room. No kosher food.
Sports/Entertainments: weekly films, occasional dances, football, basketball.
Facilities: library, shop, club, swimming pool.
Main Languages: Hebrew, English.
Other Information: not taking volunteers at present.
Kibbutz Movement: Takam.

(90) KIBBUTZ MISHMAR HA'E-MEK
Doar Mishmar Ha'emek 19236; tel 04-9896111; fax 04-9896888.
Founded: 1922.
Members: 500. Ulpan: 20.
Work available: agriculture, factory, services.
Working hours: 4-hour day; 6-day week.
Days off: 1 extra day monthly.
Free: coffee, tea, sugar, all cleaning materials.
Accommodation: comfortable. 3 to a room and rooms for married couples. No kosher food.

Sports/Entertainments: basketball, tennis, weekly film shows, regular dances.
Facilities: swimming pool, library, clubhouse, shop.
Main Languages: Hebrew, English.
Excursions: day-trip monthly.
Minimum stay: 4½ months.
Other information: ages: 18-35. Groups and individuals. Kibbutz family arranged. Holidays observed.
Ulpan: 45 students 2 courses yearly. Young singles and couples without children, some non-Jewish students accepted.
Kibbutz Movement: Ha'artzi.

(213) KIBBUTZ MISHMAR HANEGEV
Doar Na Hanegev 85315. tel: 07-9911218; fax 07-9919116; e-mail alloun@mishmarhanegev.org.il
Founded: 1946.
Members: 330. No volunteers accepted.
Work available to Ulpan students: chicken houses, milking, kitchen, dining-room, children's houses. There is also factory work (polystyrene products).
The Ulpan: 50 students housed in prefabricated buildings. Two people to a room.
Sports/Entertainments: films, concerts, theatre, basketball, music.
Facilities: swimming pool, shooting range, sports hall.
Nearest town: northwest of Beersheva.
Other Information: non-religious kibbutz. Public transport bus no. 371 from Tel Aviv; bus no. 445 from Jerusalem.
Kibbutz Movement: Takam.

(139) KIBBUTZ MISHMAR HASHARON
Doar Mishmar Hasharon 40270 ; tel: 09-8983111; fax 09-8983357.
Founded: 1924 by Jews from Russia.
Members: 540. Ulpan volunteers only.
Work available: sub-tropical orchards, citrus fruits, poultry, fish ponds, cot-

ton, turkeys, plant nursery, kitchen, dining room.
Working hours: 3 days work and 3 days study per week.
Sports/Entertainments: basketball, football, swimming pool, cable TV station, pub.
Nearest towns: between Netanya and Hadera.
Other Information: this kibbutz specialises in Ulpan within a framework of Hebrew classes for immigrants and foreign students. There is regular public transportation. The kibbutz is 7km from the beach.
Ulpan: 50 students, 4½-month course. Some non-Jewish students. Contact Elie Barak, Human Resources manager.
Kibbutz Movement: Takam.

(114) KIBBUTZ MISHMAROT
D.N. Menashe 87430; tel 06-374611.
Founded: 1933
Members: 150. Volunteers: 30-40.
Work: picking fruit, gardening, field work, chickens, dining room, kitchen.
Working hours: 6-hour day; 6-day week.
Days off: 2 extra days monthly.
Free: cigarettes, aerogrammes.
Accommodation: 2-3 to a room. No kosher food.
Sports/Entertainments: basketball, tennis, football, volleyball, weekly films.
Facilities: swimming pool, library, clubhouse with T.V., lectures, dancing, shop.
Main Languages: Hebrew, English.
Excursions: trip every 2 months with an official guide.
Minimum stay: 1 month.
Other Information: ages 17-30. Mainly individuals. Possibility of kibbutz family. All holidays obsrved. Close to bus stop and main road.
Kibbutz Movement: Takam.

(189) KIBBUTZ MITZPE SHALEM
D N Dead Sea, 86983. tel 02-9945111; fax 02-9944110; e-mail metzoke@internet-zahav_net.

Founded: 1977
Members: 80.
Responsible for volunteers: Oren Klieorman.
Work available: gardens, turkeys, dates, dining room, greenhouses. Occasional work at Metzoke Dragot tourist village.
Working hours: 8-hour day, 6-day week.
Days off: Saturdays plus 3 extra days monthly.
Accommodation: apartments. 2-3 to a room.
Free: aerogrammes, toiletries.
Sports/Entertainments: football, weekly film, concerts, pub.
Facilities: swimming pool, library, gym, shop.
Excursions: trip every 3 months. Some rapelling and touring in the Judean desert.
Main languages: Hebrew, English.
Other information: situated on the shore of the Dead Sea and 15 minutes from Ein Gedi Spa. Jerusalem 1 hour by bus. Tourism village Metzoke Dragot and school for rapelling and touring in the Judean desert. Discounts available for volunteers at the Ahava Cosmetic factory shop selling mineral rich, Dead Sea products.
Kibbutz Movement: Takam.

(82) KIBBUTZ MIZRA
D.N. Afula 19312; tel 06-6429198; fax 06-6528554.
Founded: 1923.
Members: 430. Volunteers: 25-30.
Work available: dining room, kitchen, restaurant, high tech factory, laundry, gardening.
Working hours: 7-hour day, 6-day week.
Days off: 3 extra days monthly.
Free: aerogrammes, postcards, coffee, tea.
Accommodation: 2-3 to a room.
Sports/Entertainments: basketball, tennis, football, lectures, concerts, and self-organised parties.
Facilities: video TV channel, large library, shops, swimming pool.
Main Languages: English, Portuguese, Spanish.
Excursions: day-trips once a month. Participation in national programmes and seminars.
Minimum stay: 3 months.
Other Information: not all holidays observed. Close to bus stop and main road. In Jezreel Valley with direct bus connections to Haifa, Tel Aviv and Jerusalem. Prefer ages 18-32. Individuals only. Mandatory HIV test; current certificate to be shown on arrival at the kibbutz.
Kibbutz Movement: Ha'artzi.

(160) KIBBUTZ NAAN
Naan 76829; tel: 08-9442836; fax 08-9442207.
Founded: 1930.
Members: 850. volunteers: about 60.
Work: services, dairy, gardens, hospital, children's houses, factories, agriculture, dairy, factories.
Working hours: 6-hour day; 6-day week.
Days off: 2 extra days monthly.
Accommodation: concrete pre-fab. 2 to a room. No kosher food.
Sports/Entertainments: rugby, football, netball, volleyball, tennis, twice weekly films, weekly dancing.
Facilities: swimming pool, library, shop.
Main Languages: Hebrew, English.
Excursions: day-trip per month, 3-day trip every 3 months.
Minimum stay: 3 months.
Nearest towns: centrally located; between Ramleh and Rehovot.
Ulpan: 64 students, possibility for some non-Jewish students. Courses last 5+ months.
Other Information: ages 18-32. Close to bus stop with good service. Possibility of kibbutz family. Kibbutz Movement: Takam.

(157) KIBBUTZ NA'ARAN
D.N. Hevel Jericho 90672; tel: 02-9946333; fax 02-9946343.

Founded: 1975.
Population: 50.
Responsible for volunteers: Eti Dublin.
Work available: agricultural, gardening, cooking, dining-room.
Accommodation: 1-room apartments for 1 person each.
Facilities that can be used by volunteers: swimming pool (May to September).
Excursions: none organised for volunteers. Can join members on trips.
Languages: Hebrew, English.
Nearest town: Jerusalem (1 hour drive).
Minimum stay: according to visa validation otherwise no limits.
Other information: very small kibbutz only employs one or two volunteers at a time and sometimes none at all. Desert location. Dry summer 30°C-45°C. Wet winter 5°C-15°C. All conditions as members.
Kibbutz Movement: Takam.

(164) KIBBUTZ NACHSHON
D.N. Shimshon 99760; tel: 08-9278611; 08-9278700 (volunteers' houses); fax 08-9213241.
Founded: 1950.
Members: 200. Volunteers: about 30.
Work available: agricultural, factory, services.
Free: basic needs and certain dairy products and vegetables.
Accommodation: 3 to a room. No kosher food.
Sports/Entertainments: basketball, soccer, tennis (no tennis rackets), TV, video.
Facilities: library, two shops, one for accessories, confectionery and ice-cream, the other a food mini-market.
Main Languages: Hebrew, English.
Excursions: volunteer trip every three months. Minimum stay : 1 month.
Other Information: ages: 18-32. Older or younger on a special request basis.
Buses to Jerusalem leave only in the morning from the bus-stop at the kibbutz gate; the rest of the day they leave from a junction 4 km from Nachshon. Buses to Tel-Aviv leave from a junction 5 km from the kibbutz on the other side of the road from the Jerusalem junction. Religious holidays observed.
Kibbutz Movement: Ha'artzi.

(88) KIBBUTZ NACHSHOLIM
D.N. Hof Hacarmel 30815; tel 06-6395426; fax 06-6397613.
Founded: 1948.
Members: 250 (total population 400).
Volunteers: 20-24.
Responsible for volunteers: Rina Zimran.
Work: bananas, avocados, guesthouse, kitchens, cowsheds, fishponds.
Free: aerogrammes, soap, toothpaste, shampoo, tampax, condoms.
Accommodation: 4 to a caravan. No kosher food.
Sports/Entertainments: basketball, bar, clubhouse with TV, sea swimming, beach games and activities, tennis, archaeology, bar-disco every Friday.
Facilities: shop.
Main Languages: Hebrew, English.
Excursions: trip every six weeks.
Nearest towns: Haifa (20 minutes), Hadera (1½ hours) by bus.
Minimum/maximum stay: 2 months; no maximum as far as the kibbutz is concerned but visa problems arise for stays of more than six months.
Other Information: ages 18-30. Must have own medical insurance. Direct applications from return volunteers welcome. Groups and individuals. Possibility of kibbutz family. Close to bus stop and main road. All holidays observed. Located on the Mediterranean with private beach. Mandatory HIV test on arrival at the kibbutz. No charge. No Ulpan.
Tourism: beach-side guest house open all year round.
Kibbutz Movement: Takam.

(154) KIBBUTZ NACHISHONIM
D.N. Hamerkaz 73190; tel: 03-9386513; fax 03-9386484.

Founded: 1949.
Members: 150. Volunteers: 15-20.
Responsible for volunteers: Irene Henzi & Sara Goor.
Work: kitchen, dining, room, cows, chickens, park, garden, oranges, avocados, baby-house.
Working hours: 8-hour, six-day week.
Days off: 4 extra days per month.
Free: nothing.
Accommodation: old stone buildings, 2-3 to a room.
Sports/Entertainments: tennis, football, basketball, folk dancing, horse riding, amusement park, pub, video, disco.
Facilities: swimming pool, weights room, clubhouse, library.
Nearest towns: Peta-Tiqwa (20 minutes; six buses daily), Tel-Aviv (45 minutes; buses every 10 minutes from Peta Tiqwa.
Main Languages: Hebrew, English, French, Spanish and some German.
Excursions: trips every 6 months.
Minimum/maximum stay: 2 months up to a maximum of 6 months.
Other Information: 20 minutes from Ben Gurion airport. Good connections to nearby cities. Girls especially welcome.
Kibbutz Movement: Ha'artzi.

(201) KIBBUTZ NAHAL OZ
D.N. Negev 85145; tel 07-805200; fax 07-805201.
Founded: 1953.
Members: 500. Volunteers: 15.
Responsible for volunteers: Chaya Ovnat & Guy Hershkovitz.
Work available: field, dining room, laundry, factory, chicken coops, turkeys etc.
Working hours: 7-8 hours a day. 6-day week.
Accommodation: just like the other kibbutz members. 2 to a room.
Free: aerogrammes, items of personal hygiene, cleaning materials.
Sports/Entertainments: basketball, football, tennis, dances, diving club, bicycles, disco-bar.

Facilities: swimming pool, clubhouse, English Library.
Main Languages: Hebrew, English.
Excursions: trip every 3 months.
Nearest town: 15 minutes drive.
Minimum stay: 1 month up to 6 months maximum. Longer on special request.
Other Information: ages: 17-30. Buses to and from Tel Aviv. No Ulpan.
Kibbutz Movement: Takam.

(14)   KIBBUTZ   NA'OT
MORDECHAI
Galil Elyon M.P. 12120; tel 06-948111; fax 06-944515.
Founded: 1946.
Members: 400. Volunteers: 10-25.
Responsible for volunteers: Ravit Ben Dor.
Work: packing house, cotton, sanitation, dining room, turkeys – these are the main ones.
Free: lavatory paper, light bulbs.
Accommodation: wooden houses with a bathroom and kitchen for each room; 2 to a small room, 3-4 people in the larger rooms.
No kosher food.
Sports/Entertainments: tennis, football, basketball, weekly films, discos most Fridays.
Facilities: swimming pool, library, shop, sports centre.
Main Languages: Hebrew, German, Spanish.
Excursions: at present no volunteer trips owing to a cash shortage.
Nearest town: Kiryat Shmona (15 minutes by car).
Minimum/maximum stay: 2 months up to 6 months maximum.
Other Information: ages 18-30. 3km from the main road. Accepts volunteer applications in writing direct to the volunteer organiser. Medical insurance is compulsory; can be arranged at Takam office in Tel-Aviv. The kibbutz pays the cost of changing the visitor visa to a working visa but not for extensions of the working visa. Mandatory HIV test on arrival at the

kibbutz. No charge. Buses to and from kibbutz daily.
Religious holidays observed. No Ulpan.
Kibbutz Movement: Takam.

(180) KIBBUTZ NEGBA
D.N. Zafon 79408; tel 07-744711.
Founded: 1939.
Members: 340. Volunteers: 25.
Work available: plastics and clothing factories, agriculture, services and tourism.
Working hours: 6-hour day; 6-day week.
Days off: 3 extra days monthly.
Free: all basic requirements.
Accommodation: stone buildings. 3 to a room. No kosher food.
Sports/Entertainments: sports stadium, football, basketball, tennis, table tennis, horse riding, pub & disco weekly.
Facilities: swimming pool, multi-lingual library, shop.
Main Languages: Hebrew, English, (22 different nationalities).
Excursions: regular excursions by agreement.
Minimum stay: 2 months.
Other Information: Opportunity to work paid extra hours on Saturdays. Groups and individuals. Ages: 18-30. 4km from main road and bus stop. Participation in kibbutz choir and band encouraged. Mandatory HIV test on arrival at the kibbutz. No charge.
Kibbutz Movement: H'artzi.

(178) KIBBUTZ NETIV HALAMED-HEY
D.N. Emek Haeyla 99855; tel 02-9900212; fax 02-9900600.
Founded: 1949.
Members: 220.
Agriculture, orchards, peaches, avocados, cotton wheat, cows, chickens, garage, fruit packing and sorting, metalwork, factory, kitchens, dining room, gardening.
Facilities: library, clubhouse, shop, swimming pool.
Main Languages: Hebrew, English.

Other Information: no longer takes volunteers.
Kibbutz Movement: Takam.

(159) KIBBUTZ NETZER SIRENI
Beer Ya'acov 70395; tel 08-9278122/100; fax 08-9241459; e-mail bell@netzer.org.il; website www.netzer.org.il
Founded: 1948.
Members: 300. Volunteers 15-20.
Responsible for volunteers: Ruti Bell.
Work available: dining room, kitchen, mini-market, laundry, greenhouses, cows, children's house.
Accommodation: old houses. 3 rooms per house, 2-3 per room.
Sports/Entertainments: basketball, table-tennis, football, cable TV, occasional films, pub and disco twice a week.
Facilities: library, theatre, swimming pool.
Main Languages: Hebrew, English, German.
Nearest town: Rishon la Tzion (bus every 20 minutes 6am-10pm).
Minimum/maximum stay: 2 months, up to 6 months.
Other Information: train every half hour to Tel Aviv. Close to beach (rides to and from available). Direct applications to the Kibbutz welcomed also from individuals and groups.
Kibbutz Movement: Takam.

(117) KIBBUTZ NEVE EYTAN
D.N. Beit Shean 10840. tel 06-6583511.
Founded: 1938.
Members 200.
Work available: agriculture, factory, services.
Working hours: 8-hour day; 5-day week.
Days off: 2 extra days monthly.
Free: cigarettes, postage, refreshments.
Accommodation: 2 to a room.
Entertainments: weekly films, occasional dances.
Facilities: swimming pool, library, clubhouse, shop.

Main Languages: Hebrew, English.
Excursions: Regular monthly excursions.
Minimum stay: 1 month.
Other Information: individuals preferred. Ages 18-30. Opportunity for kibbutz family. Close to bus stop and main road. All holidays observed.
Kibbutz Movement: Takam.

(95) KIBBUTZ NEVE UR
D.N. Bet Shean 10875; tel 06-538411; fax 06-6538202; e-mail sinbadito@yahoo.co.uk
Founded: 1948.
Members: 160. Volunteers: 10-15.
Responsible for volunteers: Ian Greenwood.
Work available: dates, dairy, factory, laundry, kitchen, dining room, fishponds, orchards.
Working hours: $7^1/_2$-8 hour day; 6-day week.
Days off: 3 extra days monthly.
Free: aerogrammes.
Accommodation: old but well-kept. 2-4 volunteers in a room. No kosher food.
Sports/Entertainments: tennis, basketball, disco, bar, cultural evenings, table games.
Facilities: swimming pool, library, shop.
Main Languages: Hebrew, English.
Excursions: day-trip monthly.
Nearest towns: Tiberias and Bet Shean.
Minimum stay: 2 months.
Other Information: ages 18-30. Groups and individuals. Possibility of kibbutz family for long stay volunteers. Close to bus stop and main road. All holidays observed. Non-Jewish people accepted on Ulpan.
Kibbutz Movement: Takam.

(71) KIBBUTZ NEVE YAM
D.N. Hof Hacarmel 30885; tel 04-844844.
Founded: 1939.
Members: 100. Volunteers: 25.
Work available: kitchen, dining room,

garden, laundry, children's houses cotton fields, plastics factory, camping site, poultry, water park.
Free: 3 aerogrammes weekly, plus a weekly allowance.
Accommodation: 2-3 to a room. No kosher food.
Sports/Entertainments: basketball, sea swimming, football, weekly film shows.
Facilities: swimming pool, library, clubhouse, shop.
Main Languages: Hebrew, English, German.
Excursions: monthly.
Minimum stay: 1 month.
Other Information: ages 18-32. Prefer individuals. Close to main road and train station in Atlit. Bus stop on kibbutz. Festivals observed. Only takes volunteers through the kibbutz agency.
Tourism: Camping grounds, beach and water park.
Kibbutz Movement: Takam.

(195) KIBBUTZ NIR AM
D.N. Hof Ashkelon 79155; tel 07-809911; 07-809014 (volunteers); fax 07-809131.
Founded: 1943.
Members: 270. Volunteers: 20 approx.
Work available: cutlery factory, cows, chickens, wheat, services, gardens.
Working hours: 8-hour day; 6-day week.
Free: 3 aerogrammes weekly.
Accommodation: 2-3 in a room.
Sports/Entertainments: football, tennis, basketball, disco, TV room.
Facilities: swimming pool (summer only), coffee shop, library.
Nearest town: Sederot (1km) has cinema and supermarket.
Minimum stay: 1 month.
Languages: Hebrew, English, Spanish, French, Russian.
Other Information: members originate from Eastern Europe, Argentina and France.
Kibbutz Movement: Takam.

(115) KIBBUTZ NIR DAVID
D.N. Gilboa 19150; tel 06-6488059/6488055; fax 06-6488521.
Founded: 1936.
Members: 700. Volunteers: 20-30.
Work available: kitchen, dining-room, fishponds, zoo, garden, shop, health house, turkeys, fields.
Working hours: 8-hour day; 6-day week.
Days off: 3 extra days monthly.
Free: vegetables and some dairy products, sugar, coffee, tea, fruit.
Accommodation: shared house; 3 per bed-room, kitchen, TV room, dining room, showers. No kosher food.
Sports/Entertainments: basketball, football, occasional movies, discos twice weekly on the kibbutz and once weekly at a neighbouring kibbutz with transport provided.
Facilities: Sachne National Park (natural spring) for swimming, library, shop selling confectionery, stationery, wine.
Languages: Hebrew, English, Yiddish, Polish, German.
Excursions: a day-trip for a 1-month stay or a 2-day trip for a 2-3 month stay. Individual volunteers are encouraged to make their own excursions.
Nearest town: Bet Shean (2km), Afula.
Minimum/maximum stay: 6 weeks up to 9 months maximum.
Other Information: ages 18-35. Close to bus stop and main road. Holidays observed.
Tourism: nearby restaurant, shop, public gardens, swimming area and entertainments; museum of Mediterranean art; archaeology.
On Kibbutz: Lectures in English with slides and model of the historic 'stockade and watchtower.' Nir David was the first settlement built this way.
Kibbutz Movement: Ha'artzi.

(148) KIBBUTZ NIR ELIAHU
Hasharon M.P. 45485; tel 09-927111.
Founded: 1951.
Members: 280. Volunteers: up to 12.
Work available: kitchen, dining room, factory, laundry. Dairy work for long-term volunteers.
Accommodation: 4 to a room.
Free: nothing.
Sports/Entertainments: basketball, tennis, pub.
Facilities: swimming pool, clubhouse, library.
Languages: English, German, Spanish, French.
Excursions: trip after 2-month stay.
Minimum/maximum stay: 6 weeks up to 9 months.
Nearby towns: kibbutz bus service to Kfar Saba (6km). Tel Aviv (30-minute bus ride).
Other Information: ages 17-30. Many returnees. No Ulpan.
Kibbutz Movement: Ichud.

(214) KIBBUTZ NIRIM
D.N. Hanagev 85125; tel: 07-985511; fax 07-985055.
Founded: 1946.
Members: 200. Volunteers: 12-14.
Work: kitchen, dining room, chicken houses, dairy, avocados, fields, irrigation, gardening, greenhouses.
Working hours: 6-hour day; 6-day week.
Days off: 2 extra days monthly.
Free: aerogrammes, tea, coffee, toiletries.
Accommodation: 1 to a room, showers and WC every 2 people. No kosher food.
Sports/Entertainments: basketball, football, films, discos.
Facilities: swimming pool, library, clubhouse with bar, table games, shop.
Main Languages: Hebrew, English, Spanish.
Excursions: 2-day trip every month.
Minimum stay: 1 month. No maximum.
Nearest towns: Ofakim (25km); Beersheva (50km).
Other Information: ages 18 plus. Groups and individuals. Bus stop on kibbutz, close to main road. All holidays observed. Only volunteers with working knowledge of English accept-

ed. No Ulpan.
Kibbutz Movement: Ha'artzi.

(215)KIBBUTZ NIR OZ
D.N. Negev 85122; tel 07-9983611;
fax 07-9983525.
Founded: 1949.
Members: 280. Volunteers: 30.
Work: field work, chicken houses, cattle, orchards, kitchen, dining room, laundry, children's houses.
Working hours: 7-hour day; 6-day week.
Days off: 3 extra days monthly.
Free: cigarettes, telephone tokens, coffee, tea, sugar, biscuits.
Accommodation: wooden houses. 1-2 a room. No kosher food.
Sports/Entertainments: weekly films, monthly dances, music, disco.
Facilities: swimming pool, library, clubhouse, shop.
Main Languages: Hebrew, English, French.
Excursions: day-trip monthly; 3-day trip every 3 months.
Minimum stay: 2 months.
Other Information: ages 18-32. Groups and individuals. Possibility of kibbutz family. Close to bus stop and main road. All holidays observed.
Kibbutz Movement: Ha'artzi.

(219) KIBBUTZ NIR YITZHAK
D.N. Ha Negev M.P. 85455; tel 07-9983411; fax 07-9983525.
Founded: 1949.
Members: 280. Volunteers: 15-20.
Work available: kitchen, dining room, children and baby houses, gardens, chickens, cows, field and laundry.
Working hours: 8-hour day, 6-day week.
Free: toiletries, writing paper, aerogrammes, a T-shirt and a certificate when you leave. Small amount of monthly pocket money.
Accommodation: concrete cabins comprising 2 rooms plus bathroom and kitchen; 2 people per room.
Sports/Entertainments: tennis courts, videos/films 2-3 times a week, disco

once or twice weekly, basket ball.
Facilities: swimming pool, gym, clubhouse, library, small zoo, general store and dairy store.
Main Languages: Hebrew, Spanish, English.
Excursions: 3-day trip every 2-3 months.
Minimum/maximum stay: 6 weeks up to a maximum of 6 months.
Nearest towns: Beer'sheva 1½ hours by bus from the kibbutz.
Other Information: situated on the edge of the Negev. Regular buses leave from the kibbutz and just outside it for Beer'Sheva and Tel Aviv. Ages 18-32. Groups and individuals. Applications through Ha'artzi office in Tel-Aviv. No Ulpan.
Kibbutz Movement: Ha'artzi.

(176) KIBBUTZ NITZANIM
Evtach M.P. 79290; tel 07-721011.
Founded: 1943.
Members: 220.
Work: chair factory, oranges, beach, kitchens, dining room.
Working hours: 6-hour day; 6-day week.
Accommodation: houses. 2-3 in a room.
Sports/Entertainments: basketball, tennis, swimming pool, sea sports.
Kibbutz Movement: Takam.

(194) KIBBUTZ OR HANER
D.N. Hof Ashkelon 79190; tel 07-802511/802611; 07-898300 (volunteers).
Founded: 1957.
Members: 390. Volunteers: 15.
Work: services, agricultural, factory, garden, poultry, dairy, café campus (at the college next to Sederot).
Working hours: depending on the work; 6-day week.
Days off: 1 extra day monthly.
Free: toiletries, aerogrammes, sugar, tea, coffee, sometimes fruit and cake, haircuts, cinema once a week.
Accommodation: brick houses. Single rooms for couples available. Own

shower and toilet. 2-3 to a room. No kosher food.
Sports/Entertainments: basketball, tennis, football, TV and a local video channel twice a day. The pub is not open every week but there is the possibility of going to other kibbutzim with the younger kibbutz members.
Facilities: swimming pool, library, clubhouse, supermarket, workout machines in Sderot.
Main Languages: Hebrew, English, Spanish.
Nearest town: Sederot (10km).
Minimum stay: 1 month.
Other Information: pre-arranged groups are accepted all year round. Possibility of kibbutz family for groups. Close to bus-stop and main road. Return volunteers can apply direct to the kibbutz. Mandatory HIV test on arrival at the kibbutz. No charge. Ages: 18-32. No Ulpan courses.
Kibbutz Movement: Takam.

(158) KIBBUTZ PALMACHIM
D.N. Emek Sorek 76890; tel 03-9681133; fax 03-9678229.
Founded: 1949.
Members: members: 200. Volunteers: 20.
Work available: spancrete factory, orchard, kitchen, dining room, garden.
Working hours: 8-hour day, 6-day week.
Days off: 3 extra days monthly.
Free: aerogrammes.
Accommodation: new and old. 2 to a room. No kosher food.
Sports/Entertainments: tennis, pub, television and video. Monthly disco.
Facilities: library, clubhouse, shop selling confectionery, alcoholic drinks, toiletries.
Main Languages: Hebrew, English.
Excursions: a day-trip monthly.
Nearest towns: Rishon Lezion (10 minutes' drive); also very near Tel-Aviv.
Minimum/maximum stay: 3 months up to 9 months.

Other Information: ages 18-33. Groups and individuals. Bus stop on kibbutz. 9 km main road. Near beach. All holidays observed. Possibility of kibbutz family. Has Ulpan.
Kibbutz Movement: Takam.

(170) KIBBUTZ (PALMACH) TSUBA
D.N. Harei Yehuda 90870; tel 02-347711; fax 02-347955.
Members: 240 (total population 600).
Volunteers: 20-30.
Work available: zoo animals, kitchen, dining room, garden, poultry, dairy, orchards, garage, carpentry, windscreen factory, cotton fields, laundry, cows/milking.
Working hours: 6-hour day; 6-day week.
Days off: Saturdays and 2 extra days monthly.
Free: soap, tea, coffee, sugar, toilet paper, working clothes and shoes. Small allowance of NIS260 a month also provided.
Accommodation: concrete buildings. 3 to a room equipped with bath/showers and kitchenette. No kosher food.
Sports/Entertainments: basketball, football, volleyball,tennis, TV/films, disco etc.
Facilities: swimming pool, zoo, library, shop.
Main Languages: Hebrew, English.
Excursions: day-trip monthly, but nearly every trip that the kibbutz organises, the volunteers can join. Trip to Jerusalem to the Yad Vashem (Holocaust museum) and free card for Israel Museum. 3-day trip every 3 months.
Nearest city: Jerusalem is only 20 minutes away.
Minimum/maximum stay: 2 months up to a year.
Other Information: kibbutz volunteers interested in having a kibbutz family should ask. The Ulpan is for Jewish people but volunteers who stay a long time can apply. Mandatory HIV test on arrival at the kibbutz. No charge; or,

own doctor's certificate dated not more than 2 weeks prior to arrival. Groups and individuals. Ages 18-30. Religious holidays and festivals observed. Regular buses to and from Jerusalem. Written applications welcomed, but on-the-spot volunteers not accepted.
Kibbutz Movement: Takam.

(42)KIBBUTZ PAROD
D.N. Bikat Beit Hakerem 20110; tel 06-6989271.
Founded: 1949.
Members: 200.
Main Languages: Hebrew, English, Spanish, Hungarian.
Other information: Parod stopped taking volunteers some years ago, but may possibly take them again in the future.
Kibbutz Movement: Takam.

(73) KIBBUTZ RAMAT DAVID
Ramat David P.O. 30093; tel 06-6549901 (volunteer leader); 06-6549002 (main office); fax 06-6440611.
Founded: 1926.
Members: 300. Volunteers: 10-20.
Work: kitchen, dining room, garden, fields, dishes, children's house, pub work (day-time only), cowshed.
Working hours: 8-hour day; 6-day week.
Days off: Saturdays and 3 extra days monthly.
Free: aerogrammes.
Accommodation: 1 main building, 2 to a room. Separate kitchen/lounge.
Sports/Entertainments: football, volleyball, basketball, tennis, table tennis, colour TV and newspapers (*Jerusalem Post*), 2 pubs (one for young and the other for older people), one of which opens 4 nights a week with drinking and dancing in a large area. Volunteer night for all the volunteers in the area is held once a month.
Facilities: swimming pool (May to October).
Nearest towns: Afula (20 minutes),

Haifa (30 minutes). Buses every 20 minutes. Also easy access to Nazareth.
Minimum stay: 3 months.
Other Information: groups and individuals. ages 18-30. Holidays and festivals observed. Volunteers get half-price drinks in the kibbutz pub. Applicants only through the volunteer offices. Mandatory HIV test on arrival at the kibbutz. No charge.
Kibbutz Movement: Takam.

(146)   KIBBUTZ   RAMAT HAKOVESH
Ramat Hakovesh P.O. 44930; tel 09-458555.
Founded: 1932.
Members: 600. Volunteers: 30-35.
Work available: orchards, potatoes, cotton fields, avocados, peanuts, cows, chickens, dining room, kitchen, factory, gardens, laundry.
Working hours: 8-hour day; 6-day week.
Days off: 2 extra days monthly.
Free: tea, sugar, cigarettes, toiletries, allowances for other necessities.
Accommodation: 2 to a room. No kosher food.
Sports/Entertainments: basketball, volleyball, tennis, weekly film and disco.
Facilities: swimming pool, library, shop. volunteers' coffee club, gymnasium.
Languages: Hebrew, English, Yiddish, French, Spanish, Russian, German, Dutch, Italian, Polish.
Excursions: day-trip monthly.
Minimum stay: 6 weeks.
Other Information: ages 18-32. Groups and individuals. All holidays observed. Close to bus stop and main road. Buses to and from Tel Aviv.
Kibbutz Movement: Takam.

(89) KIBBUTZ RAMAT-HASHOFET
Doar Ramat Hashofet 19238; tel 04-9898111; fax 04-9898134.
Founded: 1941.
Members: 750. Volunteers 15-35.
Work: cows, avocados, wood factory, plastics factory, dining room, kitchen,

laundry, children's houses, guest house.

Working hours: 6-hour day; 6-day week.

Days off: 2 extra days monthly.

Free: aerogrammes, coupons for Marcolet (kibbutz shop).

Accommodation: apartments – 2 to a room. No kosher food.

Sports/Entertainments: ball games, cultural centre, weekly films, videos, discos.

Facilities: swimming pool, library, shop.

Main Languages: Hebrew, English, Spanish.

Excursions: day-trip once a month, plus small trips and activities.

Nearest town: Yokneam (15km).

Minimum/maximum stay: 2 months up to 6 months.

Other Information: ages 18-31. Groups and individuals. Religious holidays observed. Close to bus stop and main road.

Ulpan 65 students (Jewish only).

Kibbutz Movement: Ha'artzi.

(175) KIBBUTZ RAMAT RAHAL D N Stafon Yehuda 90900; tel 02-702888.

Founded: 1926.

Members: 135.

Work available: laundry, dining room, kitchen.

Free: tea, coffee and work clothes.

Accommodation: 3 to a room. No kosher food.

Sports/Entertainments: weekly films, discos, tennis, football, basketball, lectures.

Facilities: swimming pool, weightroom, cafeteria.

Languages: Hebrew, English, German, Yiddish.

Excursions: regular trips of 1-3 days duration.

Minimum stay: 1 month.

Other Information: ages 19-32. groups and individuals. All holidays observed. Close to main road and bus stop. Frequent buses to and from Jerusalem.

Tourism: Country Club with heated, olympic size pool, 3 tennis courts, handball field, shop, overlooking Bethlehem. Guest-houses and restaurant, self-service and à la carte. Bungalows and camping with ablutions block. Summer only.

Kibbutz Movement: Takam.

(51) KIBBUTZ RAMAT YOHANAN Kfar Hamacabbi P.O. 30035; tel 04-8459222; fax 04-8459705.

Founded: 1932.

Members: 360.

Location and nearest town: Zvulun Valley, east of Kiryat Ata and about 20km from Haifa.

Other Information: Kibbutz Ramat Yonohan runs a Hebrew Ulpan twice a year. Most recently, the majority of candidates for this have been Olim Hadashim (new immigrants) from the former Soviet Union. Anyone interested in Ulpan can contact Rachel Yoffe, (e-mail ulpan@ry.org.il).

Kibbutz Movement: Takam.

(92) KIBBUTZ RAMOT MENASHE D.N. Hevel Megiddo 19245; tel 04-9895711 or 04-9895042; fax 04-9895727.

Founded: 1948.

Members: 350. Total Population: 700.

Volunteers: 30.

Volunteer Leader: Gabi Yoel.

Work Available: agriculture, factory, services, gardening, kitchen etc.

Sports/Entertainments: tennis, football, basketball, discos.

Facilities: swimming pool (summer), big commercial pub.

Languages: Hebrew, Spanish, English.

Other Information: archaeological Museum on kibbutz. Not planning to give up having volunteers.

Kibbutz Movement: Ha'artzi.

(107) KIBBUTZ REGAVIM Doar Na Menashe 37820; tel 06-307711.

Founded: 1949.

Members: 160. Volunteers: 40.
Work: agriculture, factory, services.
Working hours: 6-hour day; 6-day week.
Days off: 2 extra days monthly
Free: cigarettes, aerogrammes, basic necessities.
Accommodation: stone houses. 3 to a room. No kosher food.
Sports/Entertainments: basketball, tennis, 2 films weekly, weekly disco.
Facilities: swimming pool, clubhouse, shop.
Main Languages: Hebrew, French.
Excursions: trips after 3 months.
Minimum stay: 1 month.
Other Information: ages 18-30. Groups and individuals. Holidays observed.
Ulpan: 42 students, Jewish only. Courses at 2 levels.
Kibbutz Movement: Takam.

(209) KIBBUTZ RE'IM
D.N. Negev 85132; tel 07-940200/1; fax 07-940497.
Founded: 1949.
Members: 150. Volunteers: 25-30.
Work: kitchen, laundry, factory, fields, chicken house and cowshed.
Free: nothing.
Accommodation: block buildings. 2-3 to a room. No kosher food.
Sports/Entertainments: basketball, tennis, football, twice weekly disco.
Facilities: swimming pool, library, shop, gym.
Main Languages: Hebrew, English and French.
Excursions: no information.
Nearest towns: Beersheva (60km).
Minimum/maximum stay: 2 months; up to 6 months.
Other Information: ages 18 plus. Groups and individuals. 10 km from main road. 120km from Tel Aviv. Some holidays observed.
Mandatory HIV test on arrival at the kibbutz. No Ulpan. Return volunteers can contact the kibbutz direct.
Kibbutz Movement: Takam.

KIBBUTZ RESHAFIM
D.N. Habeka 10905; tel 06-583111; fax 06-583120.
Founded: 1948.
Members: 280. Volunteers: 25-30.
Work: cotton fields, dairy, field crops, citrus orchards, mangoes, avocados, orchards, dates, plastics factory dining room, kitchen, laundry, children.
Working hours: 6-hour day; 6-day week.
Days off: 2 extra days monthly.
Accommodation: houses, 2-3 to a room. No kosher food.
Sports/Entertainments: basketball, volleyball, soccer, cable TV (films), disco.
Facilities: swimming pool, library with English, French, Spanish and German books available, shop selling confectionery.
Main Languages: Hebrew, English, Spanish.
Excursions: day-trip once a month, longer trips every 3 months.
Nearest town: Beit Shean 3km (5 buses daily).
Minimum stay: 1 month.
Other Information: holidays observed.
Tourism: nearby restaurant, National Park with natural springs.
Kibbutz Movement: Ha'artzi.

(172) KIBBUTZ REVADIM
D.N. Shikmim 79820; tel 08-8588700; fax 08-8588626.
Founded: 1948.
Members: 120. Volunteers: 10.
Volunteer Organiser: Angel Kohan, e-mail anhel-c@revadim.org.il
Work available: cotton fields, cows, turkeys, kitchen, dining room, jewellery factory.
Working hours: 6-8 hour day, 6 day week.
Days off: 2-3 extra days per month.
Free: aerogrammes, fruit, tea, coffee, toiletries.
Accommodation: 2 to a room with adjoining bathroom. No kosher food.
Sports/Entertainment: basketball, tennis, football, films, videos, disco.

Facilities: swimming pool, shop.
Excursions: monthly trip.
Languages: Hebrew, Spanish, some English.
Nearest town: Rehovot (20 minutes).
Minimum stay: 3 months.
Other Information: ages 18-32. Groups or singles. Very close to bus stops for Tel Aviv, Jerusalem and Beer'sheva. Adoption by kibbutz family possible. Lectures provided. Historic site with archaeological collection and tourist cafeteria.
Kibbutz Ha'artzi.

(223) KIBBUTZ REVIVIM
(South of Beer Sheba)
D.N. Halutza 85515; tel 07-6562511; fax 07-6562240.
Founded: 1943.
Members: 350. Volunteers: a few.
Volunteer Organiser: Gaby Kave (tel +972 7 6562403 8pm-10pm only, or e-mail gkave@ramat-negev.org.il).
Work: no outdoors work; factory, kitchen and laundry only available.
Working hours: 6-hour day; 6-day week.
Days off: 2 extra days monthly.
Free: coffee, tea, sugar and cleaning materials.
Accommodation: 3 to a room. No kosher food.
Sports/Entertainments: basketball, tennis, football. etc.
Facilities: swimming pool, library, clubhouse, shops, library.
Main Languages: Hebrew, English.
Excursions: none because too few volunteers.
Nearest town: about 35km south of Beersheva (30 minutes by bus).
Minimum/maximum stay: 1 month up to six months.
Other Information: ages 18-50. People over age 32 should contact Kibbutz directly to get more information. Individuals preferred. All holidays observed. Close to bus stop and main road.
Ulpan: Jewish students only.
Kibbutz Movement: Takam.

(20) KIBBUTZ ROSH HANIKRA
D.N. Western Galilee 22825; tel 04-9857111 (main office); fax 04-9824333.
Founded: 1948.
Members: 300. Volunteers: 15-30.
Work available: bananas, orchards, greenhouses, restaurants, cable-car, kitchen, dining room, swimming pool in season, dairy, turkeys.
Working hours: 8-hour day; 6-day week.
Free: aerogrammes, visa.
Accommodation: 3 to a room with own toilet and shower. No kosher food. No facilities for couples.
Sports/Entertainments: basketball, football, daily videos, TV in volunteers' club room.
Facilities: swimming pool, gym (down the road from the kibbutz), weight room, bar, shop. Beach is 10 minutes' walk from the kibbutz.
Main Languages: Hebrew, English.
Excursions: day trip once a month, 2-day trip every 3 months.
Nearest town: Nahariya (10km).
Minimum stay: seven weeks.
Other Information: ages 18-30. Individuals and groups if arranged in advance. Close to bus stop and main road. Some holidays observed.
Tourism: Tourist restaurant and gift shop next to famous sea caves and grottos.
Kibbutz Movement: Takam.

(179) KIBBUTZ ROSH TZURIM
M.P. North Judah 91999; tel 02-935411; fax 02-935411.
Members: 190.
Produces: water filter devices and motor vehicle light factories, field crops, dairy, turkeys, orchards.
Facilities: library, gym, shop, swimming pool.
Languages: Hebrew, English, Spanish.
Other Information: no longer takes volunteers. All religious holidays observed. Bus stop on kibbutz and main road. Close to Jerusalem, buses hourly.

Part of the Etzion bloc of kibbutzim which run combined enterprises. New type of kibbutz philosophy aimed at increasing the freedom of the individual kibbutz member while retaining the character of a kibbutz.
Kibbutz movement: Hadati.

(197) KIBBUTZ RUHAMA
D.N. Hof Ashkelon 79180; tel 07-807111; fax 07-807773 (not for volunteer use).
Founded: 1944.
Members: 575. Volunteers: 20.
Work: kitchen, dining room, children, factory, garden, irrigation.
Working hours: 8-hour day, 5-day week or, 6-hour day, 6-day week.
Days off: 3 extra days monthly.
Free: aerogrammes and shared daily English-language newspapers, cleaning materials.
Accommodation: stone-built blocks for 8 persons; 2 to a room. Showers and toilets in block. No kosher food.
Sports/Entertainments: various volunteer organised sports, twice weekly bar, disco with bar on Fridays, volunteer room with TV, weekly film nearby (pay for entrance).
Facilities: swimming pool (May to October), weight room, library, shop, amphitheatre, cinema hall.
Languages: Hebrew, English, French, Italian.
Excursions: day-trip every month. 3-day trip every 3 months depending on long-termers. Summer trips to the beach with organised transport.
Minimum stay: 2 months.
Nearest town: Sderot (12km).
Other Information: ages 20-35. Individuals preferred but groups generally accepted. 11km from main road. Buses from Tel Aviv arrive on the main road 8 times daily. Mandatory HIV test on arrival at the kibbutz (no charge). Ex-volunteers can apply direct to the kibbutz, but all applications have to go through the central office in Tel-Aviv. Volunteers who stay 6 months have the opportunity to go to a 2-day seminar.

Ulpan: 45 students (Jewish only).
Kibbutz Movement: Ha'artzi.

(202) KIBBUTZ SA'AD
D.N. Hagenev 85140; tel 07-6800111; fax 07-6800434.
Founded: 1947.
Members: 350. Volunteers: 25 max.
Volunteer Organiser: Leah Karo.
Work available: carrots, orchards, dairy cows, chickens, kitchen, dining room.
Working hours: 8-hour day; 6-day week.
Days off: 1 extra day monthly.
Accommodation: pre-fab. huts. 3-4 to a room. Food is kosher
Sports/Entertainments: table tennis, mini-football.
Facilities: swimming pool, library with books in English and Torah collection, shop, gym.
Languages: Hebrew, English, Spanish, German.
Excursions: If numbers justify.
Other Information: Orthodox Jewish volunteers preferred. Non-Jewish volunteers accepted only in exceptional cases and are expected to conform. Groups and individuals. Ages 18-30. Situated near Gaza city in the plains of the northwest Negev.
Kibbutz Movement: Hadati.

(30) KIBBUTZ SA'AR
D.N. Western Galilee 22805; tel 04-9856711; fax 04-9856698.
Founded: 1948.
Members: 180. Volunteers: 20.
Volunteer leader: Rami Alpern (e-mail ramial@yahoo.com)
Work available: citrus groves, field crops, avocados, poultry, dairy, gardening, factory (water valves), kitchen, dining room.
Working hours: 7-hour day; 6-day week.
Days off: 2 extra days monthly.
Free: toiletries, food, aerogrammes.
Accommodation: cabins. 3 to a room. No kosher food.
Sports/Entertainments: beach volley-

ball, football, basketball, films, cable TV, discos.
Facilities: swimming pool, volunteers' clubhouse, shop, beach 10 minutes.
Main Languages: Hebrew, English, Spanish.
Excursions: day-trip every 45 days; 3-day trip every 3 months.
Minimum/maximum stay: 2 months up to six months.
Nearest towns: 10 minutes from Nahariya.
Other Information: applications must be sent to the kibbutz office in Tel-Aviv. Ages 18-30. The kibbutz office reserves the right to ask volunteers to leave the kibbutz if they ignore the general rules of the kibbutz. Close to bus stop and main road.
Kibbutz Movement: Ha'artzi

(229c)KIBBUTZ SAMAR
D.N. Hevel Eilot 88815; tel 07-6356711; fax 07-6356758; (e-mail samar-office@samar.ardom.co.il).
Founded: 1976.
Population: 180 (includes 80 children); Volunteers: 6-10, sometimes none.
Volunteer organiser: Shelly Ashkenazi (samar-turf@tamar.ardcom.co.il).Work available: dates (organic), animal fodder, dairy herd, tropical fish, desert tourism.
Accommodation: 2 to a room, but depending on the number of volunteers at one time.
Free: aerogrammes, cigarettes, beverages etc.
Sports/Entertainment: basketball, disco every fortnight at regional centre, weekly film, bar.
Facilities: swimming pool (May to October).
Nearest town: Eilat (30 minutes by bus).
Main languages: Hebrew , English.
Minimum/maximum stay: 2 months; no maximum within legal limits.
Important information: Samar is run along anarchist lines. There is no kibbutz committee to organise where kib-butzniks work and when, as it is believed that that the members can manage to impose their own self-discipline and dialogue. Everything is allowed and nothing is locked and money is given to the members on demand relying on individual will to restrain spending. A very special type of volunteer is required who is able to set his or her own parameters. It is not suitable for people who need to be told what to do and when. It should be pointed out that any volunteers wishing to take advantage of Samar will not last long as they will alienate members. Samar is small, friendly, isolated and a close community. Samar is not suitable for those looking for a good time and easy work; the work is not easy. Volunteers who are not put off by this description should apply (preferably) through the kibbutz movement offices where they should ask to be placed at Samar; this saves Samar paperwork and bureaucracy. However, the offices do not usually send volunteers to Samar as there are no facilities for groups. Samar is used to volunteers applying direct to the kibbutz. Shelly Ashkenazi points out with all due modesty, that volunteers tend to enjoy themselves at Samar. Volunteers are needed mainly in January and for the May vegetable harvest season. Other times are possible but these are the seasons when volunteers are needed the most.

(79) KIBBUTZ SARID
Sarid 30099; fax 06-6507220; e-mail chiel@sarid.org.il
Founded: 1926.
Members: 400.
Work available: orchards, oranges, avocados, dairy herd, operating farm machines, metal and garage workshop, poultry, factory producing abrasive stones. Dining room work on rotation of 3-4 weeks, kitchen.
Volunteer organiser: Eva Chiel.
Working hours: 6-hour day; 6-day week.

Days off: Saturday and 2 days monthly.
Free: stamps, toothpaste, soap, shaving cream, shampoo, cotton wool, etc.
Accommodation: concrete houses. 2-3 to a room. Possibility of single room for longer stay.
Sports/Entertainments: films, volleyball, basketball, tennis, all kibbutz festivities, disco.
Other Facilities: swimming pool, gymnasium, kibbutz, clubhouse, volunteers' rest-room, T.V., shop.
Main Languages: Hebrew, English, German.
Excursions: day-trip by bus monthly. Day-trips to the beach occasionally.
Nearest towns: Afula (15 minutes); Haifa (45 minutes).
Minimum/maximum stay: 1 month up to 6 months.
Other Information: ages 18-40. All holidays observed. Bus stop on main road at kibbutz gates. Adoption by kibbutz family possible. Medical insurance arranged by kibbutz. Written application direct to the Kibbutz welcomed. No Ulpan. Dog breeders and handlers especially welcome on the kibbutz. Mandatory HIV test on arrival at the kibbutz. No charge.
Kibbutz Movement: Ha'artzi.

(26) KIBBUTZ SASA
D.N. Merom Hagalil 13870; tel 06-988700; fax 06-988702.
Founded: 1948.
Members: 160. Volunteers: 32.
Work available: dining room, kitchen, garden, laundry, children's house, avocados.
Working hours: 8-hour day; 6-day week.
Free: aerogrammes.
Accommodation: 3 to a room.
Sports/Entertainments: most sports, weekly films, discos etc.
Facilities: swimming pool.
Languages: Hebrew, English, French, Italian, Russian.
Excursions: quarterly 3-day trips to Eilat, Judean Desert, Golan etc; Saturday hikes.
Nearest towns: Zfat, Haifa.
Minimum/maximum stay: 2 months up to 6 months.
Other Information: ages 20-27. Groups and individuals. Bus stop on kibbutz. 10km to main road. Individual direct application welcomed.
Kibbutz Movement: Ha'artzi.

(225) KIBBUTZ SDE BOKER
(South of Beer Sheba)
Ramat Hanegev 84993; tel 07-6560111 (office until 13.30); fax 07-6560119.
Founded: 1952.
Members: 160. Volunteers: 30-40 (summer); 20-25 (winter).
Work available: service (kitchen, dining room, laundry), gardening, agriculture (orchards, fields, chicken houses), sellotape factory, restaurant, tourist shop.
Volunteer organiser: Tamar Weinberg.
Working hours: 8-hour day; 6-day week.
Days off: 3 extra days monthly.
Free: 3 aerogrammes weekly.
Accommodation: small houses. 3 people to a room with toilet, shower and kitchenette. No kosher food.
Sports/Entertainments: basketball, soccer, weekly films, discos, tennis.
Facilities: swimming pool, library, clubhouse, shop, clothing shop. Nearby facilities include Campus Ben Gurion (4km).
Languages: Hebrew, English, Spanish, some French and German.
Excursions: 3-day trip after 3 months.
Nearest town: Beer'sheva (50 km).
Minimum/maximum stay: 1 month up to 6 months.
Other Information: ages 18-35. Groups and individuals. Some holidays observed. Bus stop on kibbutz. Home of Ben Gurion. The kibbutz is very strict with excessive drinking cases. HIV test can be done on arrival at the kibbutz unless the volunteer brings their own certificate dated shortly before arrival. No charge.

Tourism: Ben Gurion's hut, open to the public, nearby gift-shop and restaurant.
Kibbutz Movement: Takam.

(129) KIBBUTZ SDE ELIYAHU
D.N. Emek Bet Shean 10810; tel 06-6580525; fax 06-6580909; e-mail mazkir@selyahu.org.il; website www.seliyahu.org.il
Founded: 1939.
Members: 250. Volunteers: 10-20.
Work available: agriculture, spice factory, children, kitchen, dining room, biological plant etc.
Working hours: 8-hour day; 6-day week.
Days off: 1 extra day monthly.
Monthly allowance of NIS250 monthly is paid.
Accommodation: 2-4 to a room. Kosher food.
Sports/Entertainments: weekly films, many sports, regional movie channel on TV.
Facilities: swimming pool, large, library, clubhouse, lectures. Ulpan private instruction in Jewish studies.
Languages: Hebrew, English, French, Italian, Spanish, German.
Excursions: occasional trips.
Nearest towns: Bet Shean (7km), Afula (25km), Tel Aviv (120km), Haifa (75km).
Other Information: suitable for individuals or groups with a Jewish religious background after recommendation from Hadati Movement office or Shaliach. Volunteers must respect religious rules and dress codes including no shorts for women. Ages 17-32. Religious holidays observed. Regular buses from Bet Shean.
Kibbutz Movement: Hadati.

(108) KIBBUTZ SDE NAHUM
D.N. Gilboa 19160; tel 06-582611/811.
Founded: 1937. Members: 160. Volunteers: 25 in winter, 30 in summer.
Work available: kitchen, dining room, dish washing, laundry, clothes store,

children's house, orchards, field work, cotton, chicken houses, fish ponds, electrical workshop, plastics factory.
Working hours: 6-hour day; 6-day week.
Days off: 2 extra days monthly.
Free: weekly aerogrammes.
Accommodation: rooms with private toilets and shower. 1-2 to a room. No kosher food.
Sports/Entertainments: basketball, football, weekly films, occasional lectures and discos.
Facilities: swimming pool, library, clubhouse shop.
Main Languages: Hebrew, English.
Excursions: monthly day-trip.
Minimum stay: 2 months.
Other Information: ages 20-30. Mainly individuals. Holidays observed. Close to bus stop and main road.
Kibbutz Movement: Takam.

(10) SDE NEHEMIA
M.P. Upper Galilee 12145; tel 06-6946911; 06-945100 (volunteer office); fax 06-6951444.
Founded: 1941.
Members: 220 (total population 500+).
Volunteers: plus/minus 30.
Work available: citrus orchards, cotton fields, gardening, kitchen, dining room, sewing room, children's houses.
Working hours: 7-hour day, 6-day week.
Volunteer leader: Dov Gerschman.
Days off: 2 extra days monthly.
Free: nothing.
Accommodation: 2-3 to a room. No kosher food.
Sports/Entertainments: basketball, tennis, football, films weekly, discos, videos etc.
Facilities: swimming pool, library, clubhouse, supermarket.
Languages: Hebrew, Dutch, English, German, Spanish.
Excursions: 1/2-day trip monthly. 3-day trip every 3 months.
Nearest town: Kiryat Shmona (8km).
Minimum stay: 2 months. Maximum: 6 months.

Other Information: ages 18-34. Groups and individuals. Close to bus stop and main road. No Ulpan.
Kibbutz Movement: Takam.

(181) KIBBUTZ SDE YOAV
D N. Lacish Darom 79351; tel 06-721211; fax 07-6721115.
Founded: 1966.
Members: 120. Volunteers: 8-10.
Work available: guest houses, cattle, dining room, laundry, kitchen.
Volunteer leader: Abir-Orgil.
Working hours: 6-hour day; 6-day week.
Days off: Saturdays plus 3 extra days monthly.
Accommodation: pre-fab. houses, 2 to a room. No kosher food.
Sports/Entertainments: basketball, tennis, films.
Facilities: nearby swimming pool.
Languages: Hebrew, English, Spanish, French, German.
Minimum stay: 3 months.
Other Information: ages 17-32.
Kibbutz Movement: Ha'artzi.

(113) KIBBUTZ SDOT YAM
D.N. Hefer 38805; tel 06-6364289 (volunteer office); fax 06-6361659.
Founded: 1940.
Members: 300. Volunteers: 25-30.
Work available: kitchen, dining room, clothes store, factory, carpentry, dairy, zoo, mini-market, children's houses.
Working hours: 7-hour day, 6-day week.
Days off: 2 extra days monthly.
Free: aerogrammes, phonecard.
Accommodation: 2 to a room. No kosher food.
Sports/Entertainments: basketball, tennis, pub with disco, TV room.
Facilities: beach and sea swimming, fitness room, antiquities museum, library.
Main Languages: Hebrew, English, German, French.
Excursions: 2-day trip every 2 months.
Nearest town: Hadera (20 minutes by bus).

Minimum/maximum stay: 2 months up to 6 months.
Other Information: prefer long stay individuals only. Ages 18-32. Some holidays observed. Bus stop on kibbutz. 4km main road.
Kibbutz Movement: Takam.

(59) KIBBUTZ SHA'AR HA'A-MAKIM
D.N. Sha'ar Ha'amakim 30097; tel 04-9839300/9839391; fax 04-839546.
Founded: 1935.
Members: 400.
Work available: first 2-3 weeks kitchens, then poultry, cows, gardens, factory, children's houses.
Working hours: 6-hour day; 6-day week.
Days off: 2 extra days monthly. Other hours sometimes by arrangement.
Free: 3 aerogrammes weekly, toiletries, pocket money.
Accommodation: 2-4 to a room. Hot water and showers inside rooms.
Sports/Entertainments: weekly films.
Facilities: swimming pool, gymnasium, library, clubhouse, shop.
Main Languages: Hebrew, English, German French.
Excursions: monthly day-trip.
Minimum stay: 1 month.
Other Information: ages 18-40. Written applications and on-the-spot volunteers welcome. Close to Haifa and Nazareth.
Kibbutz Movement: Ha'artzi.

(77) KIBBUTZ SHA'AR HAGOLAN
D.N. Jordan Valley 15145; tel 06-757211; fax 06-757390.
Founded: 1937.
Members: 720.
Plastics factory, bananas, grapefruit, avocados, grapes, fish ponds, chickens, cows, dining room, kitchen, laundry.
Facilities: swimming pool, library, shop.
Main Languages: Hebrew, English.
Other information: Bus stop on kibbutz. $1/2$km from main road. At the

time of going to the press, this kibbutz was not accepting volunteers.
Kibbutz Movement: Ha'artzi.

(13) KIBBUTZ SHAMIR
D.N. Upper Galilee 12135; tel 06-6947292; fax 06-6951302.
Founded: 1944.
Members: 600. Volunteers: 20-25.
Work available: garden, orchards, cotton fields, services (kitchen, laundry, dining room), factory (laboratory).
Working hours: 6-hour day; 6-day week.
Days off: 2 extra days monthly.
Free: aerogrammes and telephone cards.
Accommodation: old with 1-2 to a room. No kosher food.
Sports/Entertainments: basketball, volleyball, football, games organised and self-organised, cultural evenings, films and discos.
Facilities: swimming pool, library, volunteers, tea house, club and bar; clothes and shoe shop.
Main Languages: Hebrew, English, Russian, Spanish.
Excursions: short trip every month. 2 long trips a year.
Minimum/maximum stay: 1 month up to 6 months.
Nearest town: Kiriat Shmona 13km.
Other Information: ages 18-35. Groups and individuals. Bus stop on kibbutz. 12 km main road. All holidays observed. Good kibbutznik-volunteer relationship. From time to time, Hebrew classes are arranged for volunteers. Free entry to kibbutz gallery and museum. No Ulpan.
Kibbutz Movement: Ha'artzi.

(145) KIBBUTZ SHFA'IM
Doar Shefayim 60900; tel 09-523459.
Founded: 1935.
Members: 400. Volunteers: 20-30.
Work available: cotton, peanuts, citrus groves, avocados, poultry, dairy products, plastics factory, guest-house, swimming pool, childrens houses, services.

Working hours: 8-hour day; 6-day week.
Days off: 3 extra days monthly.
Free: cigarettes, aerogrammes, drinks.
Accommodation: 2-3 to a room. No kosher food.
Sports/Entertainments: weekly films and dances, basketball, volleyball.
Facilities: swimming pool, library, shop, clubhouse, cultural auditorium, sportshall.
Main Language: Hebrew.
Minimum stay: 6 weeks.
Other Information: ages 18-30. Individuals and groups. Applications by post/telephone direct to the kibbutz welcomed. Possibility of kibbutz family. Close to bus stop and main road. Holidays observed. HIV test compulsory before acceptance.
Kibbutz Movement: Takam.

(122) KIBBUTZ SHLUCHOT
M.P. Beit Shean Valley 10910; tel 06-6582111; fax 06-6582112.
Founded: 1948.
Members: 220+250 children. Volunteers: 5-20.
Work available: livestock, fish ponds, orchards, field crops, workshops for metal, carpentry, plumbing, garage, kitchen, dining room, laundry, children's house, clothing repair, carrot packing factory.
Volunteer organiser: David Sondhelm.
Free: small allowance for personal needs.
Accommodation: pre-cast and conventional rooms, 2 to a room.
Sports/Entertainments: weekly film, dances together with neighbouring kibbutzim. Sports facilities.
Facilities: libraries: English, Hebrew (secular and religious), swimming pool, synagogue.
Nearest town: Beit Shean.
Minimum stay: 1 month.
Other Information: ages 17-35. Religious kibbutz with Shabath and festivals religiously observed. Dietary laws followed. Regular religious study groups. Members originate from

Anglo-Saxon countries and Israel.
Kibbutz Movement: Hadati.

(41) KIBBUTZ SHOMRAT
D.N. Ashrat 25218; tel 04-9854611.
Founded: 1948.
Members: 320. Volunteers: 30.
Work available: furniture factory, textile factory, machine shop, avocados, cotton, gardens, services.
Working hours: 6-hour day; 6-day week.
Days off: 2 extra days free per month.
Accommodation: 2-3 in a room.
Sports/Entertainments: football, softball, basketball.
Facilities: swimming pool, two clubs, library.
Main Languages: Hebrew, English and Spanish.
Excursions: generally one day-trip per month. Longer excursions every 3-4 months.
Minimum stay: 1 month.
Other Information: The kibbutz is close to the main road. Ages 17¹/₂-35.
Kibbutz Movement: Ha'artzi.

(207) KIBBUTZ SHOVAL
D.N. Hanegev 85320; tel 07-916111/916220; fax 07-916569/916495.
Founded: 1946.
Members: 300. Volunteers: 20.
Work available: mainly poultry, cowshed, agriculture.
Working hours: 7-hour day, 6-day week.
Days off: 2 extra days monthly.
Free: aerogrammes and NIS220 monthly allowance.
Accommodation: 2-3 in new rooms with shower and WC. No kosher food.
Sports/Entertainments: 2 films weekly and discos, tennis and other sports.
Facilities: swimming pool, library, clubhouse, shop.
Main Languages: Hebrew, English.
Excursions: day-trip occasionally; 3-day trip every 6 months.
Nearest town: Beer'sheva 25km.
Minimum/maximum stay: 2 months

up to 6 months.
Other Information: ages 18-30. Groups, couples and individuals. Most holidays observed. Close to bus stop and main road. Possibility of kibbutz family.
Kibbutz Movement: Ha'artzi.

(6) KIBBUTZ SNIR
D.N. Upper Galilee 12250; tel 06-925511/06-925411; fax 06-951765.
Founded: 1968.
Members: 100. Volunteers: 20-50.
Work available: field crops, chickens, avocados, apples, kiwi fruit, cattle, gardens, garage, children's houses, kitchen, dining room, kiosk. Factory (including night shifts).
Working hours: 6-hour day; 6-day week.
Days off: 2 extra days free monthly.
Free: cigarettes, coffee, tea, soap, shampoo, newspapers.
Accommodation: 2-3 per room.
Sports/Entertainments: tennis, basketball, swimming pool, weight room, sauna soccer, weekly film, disco, rugby.
Facilities: library, clubhouse, shop.
Languages: Hebrew, English, French.
Excursions: day-trip per month, 3-day trip every 3 months.
Minimum stay: 1 month.
Other Information: ages 17-32. holidays observed. Possibility of kibbutz family. Accepts volunteers through Project '67.
Tourism: Banias, 5 minutes walk from kibbutz. Waterfalls and nature reserve. Kibbutz operates a kiosk at waterfall site.
Close to Mt Hermon, Tel Dan, Horshat and Metulla.
Kibbutz Movement: Ha'artzi.

(65) KIBBUTZ TEL KATZIR
D.N. Emek Hayarden 15165; tel: 06-6756921; fax 06-6756870.
Founded: 1949.
Members: 120. Volunteers: 20.
Work available: bananas, chickens, grapefruit, field crops, garage, kitchen,

dining room, garden, ostriches.
Volunteer organiser: Shiri Storm.
Accommodation: 1-3 per room.
Sports/Entertainments: volleyball, basketball, football, nearby sports centre, films, weekly disco.
Facilities: swimming pool, clubhouse.
Nearest town: Tiberias (25km).
Excursions: trips all year.
Languages: Hebrew, Spanish, English.
Minimum stay: 1 month.
Other Information: 1km from the Sea of Galilee.
Kibbutz movement: Takam.

(143) KIBBUTZ TEL YITZHAK
Doar Tel Yitzhak 45805; tel 09-694403; fax 09-696488/698358.
Founded: 1938.
Members: 150. Volunteers: 10.
Work: kitchen, dining room, gardens, factory, farm, swimming pool (summer only).
Working hours: 7-8 hours. 6-day week.
Days off: Saturday off, plus 2 days monthly.
Free: aerogrammes, phone tokens.
Accommodation: 3 to a room.
Sports/Entertainments: table tennis, TV room, pub (bar at weekends), discos.
Facilities: swimming pool, clubhouse, shop.
Languages: Hebrew, English, Spanish.
Excursions: trip every 6 weeks.
Minimum/maximum stay: 2 months up to 6 months.
Nearest town: Netanya (15 minutes), Tel Aviv (30 minutes).
Other Information: ages 18-32. Religious holidays and festivals observed. Centrally placed in Israel the Kibbutz has good connections to everywhere. Close to bus stop, railway station and main road. Possibility of adoption by kibbutz family.
Kibbutz Movement: Takam.

(102) KIBBUTZ TEL YOSEF
Tel Yosef 19132; tel 06-534793; fax 06-534095
Founded: 1921

Members: 350. Volunteers: 12 approx.
Work available: fishing, milking, orchard, printing house, field work.
Working hours: 6-hour day; 6-day week.
Days off: 2 days monthly.
Nearest towns: Afula, Bet Shean (15 minutes by bus).
Accommodation: 2 to a room. No kosher food.
Sports/Entertainments: tennis, horse riding (for experienced riders only), football, discos, films.
Facilities: swimming pool, library, shop.
Excursions: 5-days for groups who stay 3 months.
Minimum stay: 1 month up to 9 months.
Other Information: ages 18-30. Kibbutz Movement: Takam.

(130) KIBBUTZ TIRAT ZVI
D.N. Emek Bet Shean 10815; tel 06-6538011; fax 06-6534336.
Founded: 1937.
Members: 300. Volunteers: 5.
Work: agricultural, meat factory, services.
Free: aerogrammes.
Accommodation: 2-3 to a room. Food is kosher.
Facilities: swimming pool, sports field, workout room, library, shop, reading room.
Main Languages: Hebrew, English.
Excursions: occasional trips locally.
Nearest town: Beit Shean (15km).
Minimum/maximum stay: 2 months up to a year.
Other Information: groups with a Jewish religious background preferred. Ages 18 plus.
Kibbutz movement: Hadati.

(36C) KIBBUTZ TUVAL
D N Ma'ale Hagalil 25166; tel 04-9907907; fax 09-9907900.
Founded 1980.
Information: Tuval no longer accepts volunteers.

(222) KIBBUTZ TZE'ELIM
D.N. Halutza 85520; tel 07-9929211;
fax 07-9989222.
Founded: 1947.
Members: 165. Volunteers: 20-50.
Work available: field crops, poultry, dairy, mangos, tyre factory, kitchen, dining room, gardens, bed and breakfast.
Working hours: 8-hour day, 6-day week.
Volunteer leader: Sven Schmidt.
Days off: 3 extra days per month, 4 if you work in the factory.
Free: toiletries, coffee, tea, sugar, fruit, bus tickets (up to NIS 113 per month).
Accommodation: houses. 2-3 in a room. No kosher food.
Sports/Entertainments: basketball, football, tennis, weekly films, weekly disco and weekly pub.
Other Facilities: swimming pool, clubhouse with T.V., newspapers, magazines, table games, refreshments, shop selling confectionery.
Main Languages: Hebrew, French and English.
Excursions: 3-day trip after 3 months and one-day trips.
Minimum stay: 2 months.
Other Information: ages 18-30. Holidays observed. Possibility of kibbutz family. Individuals preferred.
Kibbutz Movement: Takam.

(173) KIBBUTZ TZORA'A
D.N. Shimshon 99803; tel: 07-9908222; fax 07-9908565.
Founded: 1948.
Members: 360. Volunteers 20-30.
Work available: agriculture, services
Working hours: 8-hour day; 5-day week.
Accommodation: 2 to a room. No kosher food.
Sports/Entertainments: basketball, tennis, self-organised dances.
Facilities: swimming pool, library, clubhouse, shop.
Main Languages: Hebrew, English.
Minimum stay: 2 months.
Other Information: ages 18-30. Indi-

viduals and groups. Kibbutz family provided. Close to bus stop and main road.
Kibbutz Movement: Takam.

(217) KIBBUTZ URIM
D.N. Negev 85530; tel 07-9920111;
fax 07-9920322.
Founded: 1946.
Members: 250.
Products: textile factory, jewellery box factory, cowsheds and field and orchard crops.
Facilities: swimming pool, library, clubhouse, shop.
Nearest towns: Ofakim (10km); Beer'-sheva (35km).
Main languages: Hebrew, English.
Other Information: no volunteers since 1997.
Kibbutz Movement: Takam.

(50) KIBBUTZ USHA
D.N. Kjar Hamaccabi 30031; tel 04-8458501.
Founded: 1937.
Members: 250.
Products: poultry, cows, garage, metal workshop, citrus groves, optical lens laboratory.
Facilities: swimming pool, library.
Other Information: no longer takes volunteers. All holidays observed. Close to bus stop and main road.
Kibbutz Movement: Takam.

(141) KIBBUTZ YAD HANNA
D.N. Lev Hasharon 42840; 09-8765490; 09-8765433.
Founded: 1950.
Members: 80. Volunteers: 10-14.
Work available: maintenance, turkeys, kitchen, dining room, dishes, chickens, avocados, citrus groves (seasonal).
Volunteer committee: Meirav Martin, Michael Hyde.
Working hours: 8-hour day; 6-day week.
Days off: 3 extra days monthly.
Accommodation: houses, 2 to a room. No kosher food.
Sports/Entertainments: basketball,

football, volleyball, pub, dancing.
Facilities: swimming pool (May to October), gym, library, shop.
Languages: Hebrew, English, German, Hungarian, Polish, Danish, Russian.
Minimum/maximum stay: 6 weeks up to 6 months.
Other Information: ages 18-35 Individuals preferred. Close to bus stop and main road. Kibbutzniks very receptive to new volunteers. Direct application by volunteers welcomed or through Project '67.
Kibbutz Movement: Independent.

(190) KIBBUTZ YAD MORDECHAI
D.N. Hof Ashkelon 79145; 07-6720500; fax 07-6720594.
Founded: 1943.
Members 400. Volunteers: 18.
Work available: orchards, field crops, poultry, cows, bee hives, laundry, children's house.
Working hours: 8 hours per day; 6-day week.
Days off: 3 extra days monthly.
Free: all work clothes and shoes, toiletries, tampax, aerogrammes.
Allowance: NIS 350 per month for the first 3 months, then NIS 650 per month.
Accommodation: blocks. 2-3 to a room. No kosher food.
Sports/Entertainments: soccer, volley ball, basketball, tennis, discos.
Facilities: swimming pool, library, clubhouse, well-stocked supermarket, gym.
Languages: Hebrew, English, German, Spanish, Yiddish.
Excursions: every 3 months, a weekend in the Negev or to the north in the Golan.
Minimum stay: 2 months.
Other Information: ages 18-30. Individuals preferred. Close to bus stop and main road. Tel Aviv 1 hour by direct bus or via Ashkelon, Jerusalem 1 hour, 15 minutes, Beer Sheva 45 minutes. Beach 10 minutes by car or 1 hour's walk through nature reserve.
Direct applications welcomed, but

must then go through a Kibbutz Office in Tel Aviv.
Kibbutz Movement: Ha'artzi.

(56) KIBBUTZ YAGUR
Yagur P.O. 30065; tel 04-9848665; fax 04-9848360.
Founded: 1922.
Members: 800.
Facilities: swimming pool, library, clubhouse, shop.
Nearest town: Haifa (12km), 30 minutes by bus.
Main Languages: Hebrew, English, Spanish, French.
Other Information: Ulpan only. Non-Jewish students wishing to take Ulpan courses have to have the permission of the Jewish Agency.
Kibbutz Movement: Takam.

(226) KIBBUTZ YAHEL
(Arava, North of Eilat)
D.N. Eilot 88850; tel 07-6357911; fax 07-6357051; e-mail yahel-office@yahel.ardom.co.il website www.aroom.co.il
Founded: 1976.
Members: 65. Volunteers: 15-20.
Work available: dairy, dates, flowers, gardening, kitchens, packing house, tourism.
Volunteer coordinator: Nadan Ghary.
Accommodation: comfortable houses with air-conditioning and heating. 2-3 to a room.
Free: nothing.
Sports/Entertainments: football, basketball, tennis, table tennis, pub (twice weekly), lectures, discussions etc.
Weekly films at the regional cultural centre (accessible by bus).
Facilities: extensive library, clubhouse, swimming pool.
Nearest town: Eilat (65km). Egged regional bus.
Main Languages: Hebrew, English.
Minimum/maximum stay: 1 month up to a year.
Other Information: the kibbutz runs organised tourist trips to the Arava and Negev deserts and seminars for Amer-

ican and Israeli youth groups on Reform Judaism, Zionism and Kibbutz life. Average age of members is 29. Mainly from Israel and North America. Religious celebration of Shabbat and holidays. A young energetic kibbutz deeply committed to Jewish life. Yahel has a small group of volunteers who come into close contact with kibbutz members and gain a good understanding of kibbutz life. Kibbut Movement: Takam.

(142) KIBBUTZ YAKUM
Yakum P.O. 60972; tel 09-9524650; fax 09-9524550.
Founded: 1947.
Members: 290. Volunteers: 10-15.
Work available: field, garden, dining room, kitchen, factory, plantation, swimming pool.
Volunteer coordinator: Gil Florsheim.
Working hours: 7-hour day, 6-day week.
Days off: 2 extra days monthly.
Accommodation: simple wooden houses. 1, 2, 3 or 4-person rooms. No kosher food.
Sports/Entertainments: football, horse riding, basketball, weekly films, barbecues, videos, discos etc.
Facilities: swimming pool, and nearby beach, clubhouse, shop.
Excursions: special trips in Israel.
Nearest towns: Netanya (20 minutes) and Tel Aviv (30 minutes).
Minimum/maximum stay: 2 months up to 6 months.
Other Information: ages 18-38. Groups and individuals. Applications direct to kibbutz considered. Close to bus stop and main road. Kibbutz Movement: Ha'artzi.

(45) KIBBUTZ YAS'UR
Asherat M.P. 20150; tel 04-9960111; 04-9960113.
Founded: 1949.
Members: 200. Volunteers: usually 15-18, but up to 27.
Work available: kitchen, dining room, toy factory, gardens, children's houses,

cows, chickens.
Volunteer Leader: Gerald Becker (e-mail gerald_b@mishkei.org.il).
Free: aerogrammes, work clothes.
Accommodation: 3-4 per room.
Sports/Entertainments: football, basketball, cable TV, pub, volunteers' clubhouse.
Facilities: swimming pool (summer), library, gym.
Excursions: trip about every 6 weeks.
Nearest towns: Akko (Acre) is 10 minutes by bus, Nahariya is 25 minutes by bus.
Other information: age from 18 years. German volunteers not accepted. Mandatory HIV test on arrival (no charge). Individuals and groups accepted. Must go through the kibbutz office (Kibbutz Program Center) in Tel-Aviv.
Kibbutz Movement: Ha'artzi.

(36) KIBBUTZ YEHIAM
D.N. Ma'ale Hagalil, 25125; tel 04-9856811; 04-9856064; fax 04-9856039;
Founded: 1946.
Members: 500. Volunteers: 20-25.
Work available: fields: organges, bananas, avocado, jojoba. Other: kitchen, meat factory, gardening, tourism.
Working hours: 8-hour day; 6-day week; overtime possible.
Days off: 3 extra days free monthly.
Allowance: volunteer allowance covers basic necessities.
Accommodation: 2-3 to a room in old houses with bath and WC in the room. No kosher food.
Sports/Entertainments: basketball, volleyball, football, tennis, table-tennis, video films, bar every night, weekly disco, TV in the volunteer club.
Facilities: swimming pool, library, shop.
Languages: Hungarian, Spanish, French.
Excursions: usually a monthly day-trip and a 3-day trip every 3 months.
Nearest town: Nahariya (30km).

Minimum stay: 3 months preferred.
Other Information: ages 18 plus. 6 km from main road. Five buses to kibbutz from town. Religious holidays and festivals observed. Stunning location overlooking Western Galilee and northern border. Crusader castle of Montfort nearby.
Kibbutz Movement: Ha'artzi.

(74) KIBBUTZ YIF'AT
Doar Yifaat 30069; tel 06-6548592.
Founded: 1952.
Members: 550.
Other information: has not taken volunteers since the Gulf War.
Kibbutz Movement: Takam.

(16) KIBBUTZ YIFTAH
D.N. Marom Hagalil 13840; tel 06-6952900; fax 06-6952698.
Founded: 1948.
Members: 220. Volunteers: 35-45 (summer); 20-25 (winter).
Work available: orchards, kitchen, dining hall, marble and plastic factories, building.
Volunteer leader: Hadas Israeli (e-mail hadasi@miskei.org.il).
Working hours: 8-hour day; 6-day week.
Free: tea and food etc. in the TV room, cleaning materials, toilet paper, newspaper, work clothes (but not boots).
Accommodation: good. 14 rooms, 2-3 to a room, all with toilet and shower, generally well-maintained, in own area.
Sports/Entertainments: indoor basketball/volleyball, pub 30 metres from volunteers' rooms, disco with pool table and bar, 2 videos daily, occasional visiting shows, singers etc (usually) in Hebrew, horse-riding occasionally possible.
Facilities: library (various languages), weight-training room (open 3 times weekly), swimming pool (May to October).
Languages: Hebrew, English, some Russian, German, Dutch.
Excursions: various walks in the area

(1-3 hours' duration). Regular volunteer trips.
Minimum/maximum stay: 1 month up to 6 months.
Other Information: picturesque, well-maintained kibbutz situated amongst hills. Good relations between volunteers and younger kibbutzniks. Many volunteers return two or three times, or more. Youngish population. Many triathletes among kibbutzniks. Mandatory, free HIV test on arrival. Passport required from each volunteer, returnable on departure. No Ulpan.
Kibbutz Movement: Takam.

(23) KIBBUTZ YIR'ON
D.N. Merom Hagalil 13855; tel 06-988311; fax 06-980888.
Founded: 1949.
Members: 180. Volunteers: 15-25.
Work available: dining room, kitchen, apples, nursery, garden, avocado, kiwis, zoo.
Free: toiletries, aerogrammes, coffee, biscuits, etc.
Accommodation: 3-4 to a room with show and kitchen. Rooms available for couples. No kosher food.
Sports/Entertainments: tennis etc.
Other facilities: swimming pool (summer), weight-room, gym, members' pub, library, shop.
Main Languages: Hebrew, English.
Excursions: no information.
Nearest towns: Safed (20km) bus 3 times a day from the kibbutz. Qiryat Shemona (27km).
Minimum/maximum stay: 2 months up to 6 months.
Other Information: ages 18-35. Groups and individuals. Bus stop on kibbutz to Haifa and Safed. Some way to main road. Some holidays observed. Stunning scenery and volunteers well looked after. Most volunteers come in a group. The kibbutz only accepts volunteers through the kibbutz office in Tel-Aviv. No Ulpan.
Kibbutz Movement: Takam.

(100) KIBBUTZ YIZREEL

D.N. Yizreel 19350; tel 06-6598259 (volunteer office); fax 06-6598239; e-mail yisrael@yizrael.org.il
Founded: 1948.
Members: 250. Volunteers: 12-15.
Work available: mainly dining room, kitchen and possibly gardening if there are enough volunteers.
Volunteer coordinator: Arnie Friedman.
Working hours: 8-hour day, 6-day week.
Free: toilet paper, light bulbs, detergent.
Accommodation: 4 to a caravan. Not strictly kosher.
Sports/Entertainments: basketball, tennis, volleyball, rugby, football, weekly films, occasional dances, disco-pub.
Facilities: swimming pool, library, shop.
Main Languages: Hebrew, English.
Excursions: every six weeks.
Minimum/maximum stay: 1 month up to six months (sometimes up to a year).
Other Information: owing to a shortage of volunteers, the kibbutz has been accepting applications direct and then informing the kibbutz office in Tel-Aviv. Direct applications must be made well in advance as the kibbutz also runs a small programme for Koreans (about five at a time): one month of English classes (2hrs a day, after a 6-hour work day). The classes are paid for by the Koreans. Ages 18-34. Holidays observed. Groups and individuals. Bus stop on kibbutz. Some way from main road. Possibility of kibbutz family.
Kibbutz Movement: Takam.

(229) KIBBUTZ YOTVATA (North of Eilat)

Doar Na Hevel Eilot 88820; tel 07-6357444; fax 07-6357400; website www.ardom.co.il/heilot/yotvata/yotvata.htm
Founded: 1957 (first kibbutz in the Arava Valley).

Members: 265. Volunteers: Up to 50.
Days off: 2 free days a month.
Work available: dairy plant, services, agricultural, tourist facilities, lifeguard.
Volunteer leader: Brigitte Berman.
Free: aerogrammes.
Sports/Entertainments: tennis, basketball, floodlit football, disco, cinema.
Facilities: swimming pool, weights room, large English library.
Excursions: possibility of hiking in interesting desert area.
Minimum/maximum stay: longer stayers preferred – up to six months, possibly longer.
Nearest town: Eilat 40km to the south.
Languages: Hebrew, English, French, Spanish.
Other Information: regional culture hall nearby, only half an hour from Eilat and water sports there. Possibility for non-Jewish people to do Ulpan.
Kibbutz Movement: Takam.

(187) KIBBUTZ ZIKIM

Hof Ashkelon M.P. 79140; tel 07-6746520; fax 07-6731420.
Founded: 1949.
Members: 170. Volunteers: about 30.
Work available: agriculture, dairy, kitchen, dining room, gardening, foam products factory.
Volunteer leader: Shai Weinstein.
Working hours: 8-hour day (6am to 3pm including mealtimes), 6-day week. Occasionally volunteers work Saturday and the hours added to their days off.
Days off: 3 days monthly, plus Saturdays.
Accommodation: new, permanent houses, 3 to a room.
Sports/Entertainments: basketball, football, tennis, weekly films, nightly videos, cultural activities and lectures.
Facilities: beach right next to kibbutz, library, swimming pool (summer), pub.
Nearest town: Ashkelon (20 minutes by car).
Excursions: 3-day trip every 3 months.

Minimum/maximum stay: 2 months; maximum 6 months.

Languages: Hebrew, English, French, Spanish.

Other Information: volunteers given 2 weeks probation and pay about NIS150 deposit (about $50) cash for room and pub kitty. Volunteer allowance is NIS 300 per month. Members' ages range 20-60 including second generation. Volunteers' ages 18-28. Written applications welcome. The kibbutz is 20 minutes walk from the sea.

Kibbutz Movement: Ha'artzi.

YOUNG KIBBUTZIM

Although there have been many new Israeli settlements created (and they are still at it in the West Bank, despite the Wye Peace Accord which called a halt to them), there have been no new kibbutzim founded since the 1980s. The ones below were some of the last to be created in the 1970s-80s. Consequently, they regard themselves as 'young kibbutzim.' Some have managed 'to make the desert bloom' while others have found the sparsely populated Upper Galilee region open to their grasp, and have strengthened the Jewish presence and economy of the area.

Kibbutzim which had the temerity to perch in the Golan, may find themselves dismantled, or moved back inside the recognised Israeli borders, under the anticipated terms of peace settlement with Syria.

The pioneering spirit is still an important factor to these younger kibbutzim and although conditions are not as harsh as those which wore down the early kibbutz pioneers, they still face the difficulties of establishing a new community. Though actively seeking new members, some will not yet have the facilities to take on volunteers but could do so in the future.

(157a) KIBBUTZ ALMOG
D.N. Bikaat Yeriko 90665; tel 02-9945200.
Founded: 1979.
Members: 45. Has had volunteers.
Agriculture: winter vegetables, dates, grapes.
Industry: factory producing electrical systems for cars.
Kibbutz Movement: Takam.

(225a)   KIBBUTZ/MOSHAV ASHALIM
D.N. Halutza 85512; tel 07-6557485.
Founded: 1976.
Members: 50.
Agriculture: field crops, orchards, poultry.
Tourism: Roadside restaurant.
Kibbutz Movement: Takam.

(229a) KIBBUTZ ELIFAZ
D.N. Hevel Eilot 88812; tel 07-6356200; fax 07-6356217.
Founded: 1982 (Kibbutz 1983).
Members: 35.
Agriculture: dates, vegetables, green-houses, jojoba.
Other Information: originally founded as a Moshav. Situation in the southern Arava. No volunteers at present.
Kibbutz Movement: Ha'artzi.

(54a) KIBBUTZ GESHUR
M.P. Ramat Hagolan 12942; tel 06-6764111; fax 06-6764008.
Founded: 1975.
Members: 95+.
Agriculture: grapes, apples, avocados, mangoes, cotton, arable farming, poultry, cattle.
Kibbutz Movement; Ha'artzi.

KIBBUTZ KADARIM
D.N. Hevel Korazim 12390; tel 06-6986222.
Founded: 1980.
Members: 25.
Agriculture: citrus, mango and avocado groves, hothouse for roses, onions, cattle, subtropical seedlings.
Industry: factory producing oil retainers.
Kibbutz Movement: Takam.

(175a) KIBBUTZ KALYA (QALYA)
D.N. Bikat Yericho 90665; tel 02-936222.
Founded: 1974.
Members: 80. Volunteers: 15-30.
Work available: dates, mangos, pomelos, dairy, turkeys, tourist shop and restaurant in Qumran Caves, water park near the Dead Sea, gardens, services.
Sports/Entertainments: tennis, basketball, gym, weekly discos.
Facilities: swimming pool (April-October), library, shop.
Nearest towns: Jerusalem and En Gedi (1 hour).
Other Information: reasonable transport. Pleasant weather in winter and hot, dry summer. Accommodation is air-conditioned. Written applications to kibbutz welcomed but not on-the-spot volunteers.
Kibbutz Movement: Takam

KIBBUTZ KERAMIN
M.P. Hanegev 84963; tel 07-6597111.
Founded: 1981.
Members: 50.
Agriculture: wheat, barley, potatoes, cotton, maize, vegetables, vineyards, sheep.
Other Information: situated west of the Hebron Hills. No volunteers yet.
Kibbutz Movement: Ha'artzi.

(42a) KIBBUTZ LOTEM
D.N. Carmiel 24900; tel 06-787222.
Founded: 1978.
Members: 100. Has had volunteers.
Agriculture: avocados, mangos, poultry.
Industry; factory producing irrigation equipment and piping.
Kibbutz Movement: Takam.

KIBBUTZ METZAR
D.N. Ramat Hagolan 12413; 06-763280.
Founded: 1981.
Members: 40. No volunteers.
Agricultural: orchards, avocados, hothouse vegetables, poultry.

Tourism: tourist facilities at the Hamat Gader hot springs and alligator park.
Kibbutz Movement: Takam.

(42b) KIBBUTZ MORAN
D.N. Bikaat Bet Hakerem 20195; tel 06-988911.
Founded: 1978.
Members: 130. Has had volunteers.
Agriculture: avocados, mangos, flowers for export, poultry and beef cattle.
Industry: factory producing technical plastic products.
Kibbutz Movement: Takam.

(54b) KIBBUTZ NATUR
M.P. Ramat Hagolan 12915; tel 06-763696; fax 06-763786.
Founded: 1980.
Members: 40.
Agriculture: avocados, apples, sunflowers, vetch, cotton, merino sheep.
Other Information: close to kibbutz Geshur in the southern Golan Heights, overlooking the Sea of Galilee.
Kibbutz Movement: Ha'artzi.

(19a) KIBBUTZ ORTAL
D.N. Ramat Hagolan 12910; tel 06-960711.
Founded: 1978.
Members: 100.
Agriculture: cows, apples, chickens, field crops.
Industry: factory producing lining for shoes.
Kibbutz Movement: Takam.

(36b) KIBBUTZ PELECH
M.P. Ma'ale Hagalil 25128; tel 04-986601; fax 06-886043.
Founded: 1980.
Members: 40.
Agriculture: poultry, goats, flowers.
Kibbutz Movement: Ha'artzi.

(52a) KIBBUTZ RAVID
Doar Tiberias 14100; tel 06-782562.
Founded: 1982.
Members: Members 30. Majority North American.
Agriculture: poultry, avocado and

mango orchards, hothouse vegetables.
Industry: 2 factories producing tie-dye,
cinder blocks.
Kibbutz Movement: Takam.

(223a) KIBBUTZ RETAMIM
D.N. Halutza 85550; tel 07-2711557.
Founded: 1983.
No longer exists independently as a
kibbutz – is part of Kibbutz Revivim.
Instead of the kibbutz there is a commercial guest house that belongs to
Revivim. Kibbutz Revivim takes volunteers – see main kibbutz section or
contact Gaby Cave (fax +972 7
6562240) for details. Situated about
50kms south of Beersheva and close to
Revivim. Some way from the main
road. Bus stop on site.

(229b) KIBBUTZ SAMAR
**M.P. Hevel Eilot 88815; tel 07-
6356711; 07-6356758.**
Population: 180 (including 80 children).
Volunteers: 6-10 maximum at any one
time; sometimes none.

Agriculture: dates (organic), animal
fodder, dairy herd, tropical fish, desert
tourism.
Other Information: located in the
southern Arava; very hot in summer.
Less than 40km from Eilat.
Kibbutz Movement: Ha'artzi.

(225b) KIBBUTZ TLALIM
D.N. Halutza 85545.
Founded: 1978.
Members: 40.
Agriculture: orchards, field crops,
dairy barn.
Industry: ready-mix concrete plant.
Kibbutz Movement: Takam.

(36c) KIBBUTZ TUVAL
Derech Doar Bet Haemek.
Founded: 1980.
Members: 75.
Agriculture: flowers, poultry, forestry.
Industry: factory producing film cases
and attachée cases.
Other information: ceased taking vol-
unteers.Kibbutz Movement: Takam.

For full details on application see pages 90 to 97.

Kibbutz Cross Reference

1	Misgav Am	44	Ein Hamifratz
2	Kfar Gil'adi	45	Yas'ur
3	Ma'ayan Baruch	46	Kfar Masaryk
4	Dafna	47	Hokuk
5	Dan	48	Ginossar
6	Snir	49	Afek
7	Hagoshrim	50	Usha
8	Menara	50a	Kfar Hamacccabi
8a	Lehavot Habashar	51	Ramat Yohonan
9	Kfar Szold	52	Lavi
10	Sde Nehemia	53	Ein Gev
11	Kfar Blum	53a	Kfar Charuv
12	Amir	54	Afik
13	Shamir	55	Hasolelim
14	Na'ot Mordechai	56	Yagur
15	Merom Golan	57	Mevo Yama
15a	El-Rom	58	Bet Oren
16	Yiftah	58a	Ha Hoterim
17	Gonen	59	Sha'ar Ha'amakim
18	Malkia	60	Ha'on
19	Ein Zivan	61	Alonim
20	Rosh Hanikra	62	Bet Keshet
21	Hanita	63	Kinneret
22	Adamit	64	Ma'agan
23	Yiron	65	Tel Katzir
24	Eilon	66	Degania 'A'
25	Matsuva	67	Alumot
26	Sasa	67a	Massada
27	Bar Am	68	Kfar Hachoresh
28	Hulata	68b	Hannaton
29	Gesher Haziv	69	Degania 'B'
30	Sa'ar	70	Bet-Zera
31	Kabri	71	Neve Yam
32	Ayelet Hashachar	72	Ein Carmel
33	Gadot	73	Ramat David
34	Ga'aton	74	Yif'at
35	Evron	75	Gvat
36	Yehiam	76	Afikim
37	Machanayim	77	Sha'ar Hagolan
38	Lohame Hageta'ot	78	Ginegar
39	Bet Ha'emek	79	Saird
40	Kfar Hanasi	80	Ein Dor
41	Shomrat	81	Kfar Harov
42	Parod	82	Mizra
43	Amiad	83	Dovrat

Young Kibbutzim

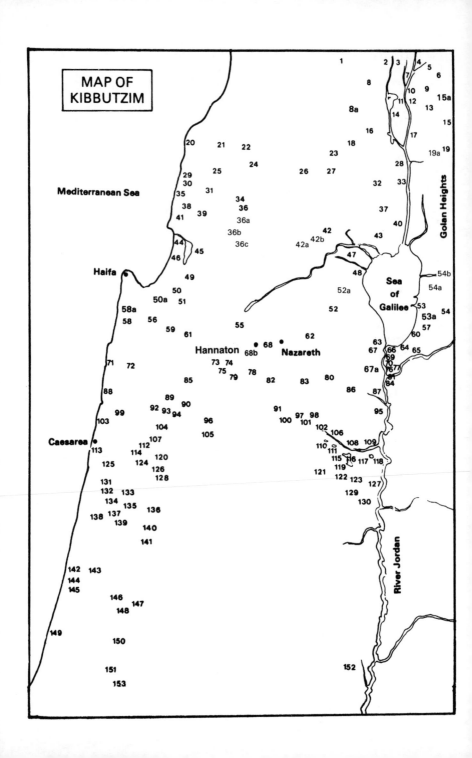

MAP OF
KIBBUTZIM

Mediterranean Sea

Golan Heights

Haifa

Sea
of
Galilee

Hannaton

Nazareth

Caesarea

River Jordan

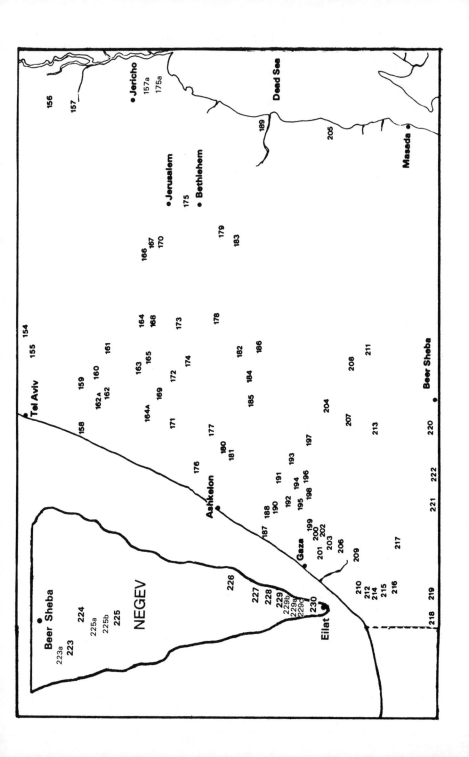

Vacation Work publish:

	Paperback	Hardback
The Directory of Summer Jobs Abroad	£9.99	£14.95
The Directory of Summer Jobs in Britain	£9.99	£14.95
Supplement to Summer Jobs in Britain and Abroad *published in May*	£6.00	–
Work Your Way Around the World	£12.95	–
The Good Cook's Guide to Working Worldwide	£11.95	–
Taking a Gap Year	£11.95	–
Working in Tourism – The UK, Europe & Beyond	£11.95	–
Kibbutz Volunteer	£10.99	–
Working on Cruise Ships	£9.99	–
Teaching English Abroad	£11.95	–
The Au Pair & Nanny's Guide to Working Abroad	£10.99	–
Working in Ski Resorts – Europe & North America	£10.99	–
Working with Animals – The UK, Europe & Worldwide	£11.95	–
Accounting Jobs Worldwide	£11.95	–
Working with the Environment	£11.95	–
Health Professionals Abroad	£11.95	–
The Directory of Jobs & Careers Abroad	£11.95	£16.95
The International Directory of Voluntary Work	£10.99	£15.95
The Directory of Work & Study in Developing Countries	£9.99	£14.99
Live & Work in Saudi & the Gulf	£10.99	–
Live & Work in Japan	£10.99	–
Live & Work in Russia & Eastern Europe	£10.99	–
Live & Work in France	£10.99	–
Live & Work in Australia & New Zealand	£10.99	–
Live & Work in the USA & Canada	£10.99	–
Live & Work in Germany	£10.99	–
Live & Work in Belgium, The Netherlands & Luxembourg	£10.99	–
Live & Work in Spain & Portugal	£10.99	–
Live & Work in Italy	£10.99	–
Live & Work in Scandinavia	£10.99	–
Panamericana: On the Road through Mexico and Central America	£12.95	–
Travellers Survival Kit: Mauritius, Seychelles & Réunion	£10.99	–
Travellers Survival Kit: Madagascar, Mayotte & Comoros	£10.99	–
Travellers Survival Kit: Sri Lanka	£10.99	–
Travellers Survival Kit: Mozambique	£10.99	–
Travellers Survival Kit: Cuba	£10.99	–
Travellers Survival Kit: Lebanon	£10.99	–
Travellers Survival Kit: South Africa	£10.99	–
Travellers Survival Kit: India	£10.99	–
Travellers Survival Kit: Russia & the Republics	£9.95	–
Travellers Survival Kit: Western Europe	£8.95	–
Travellers Survival Kit: Eastern Europe	£9.95	–
Travellers Survival Kit: South America	£15.95	–
Travellers Survival Kit: USA & Canada	£10.99	–
Travellers Survival Kit: Australia & New Zealand	£11.95	–

Distributors of:

Summer Jobs USA	£12.95	–
Internships (On-the-Job Training Opportunities in the USA)	£16.95	–
Sports Scholarships in the USA	£16.95	–
Scholarships for Study in the USA & Canada	£14.95	–
Colleges & Universities in the USA	£15.95	–
Green Volunteers	£10.99	–

Vacation Work Publications, 9 Park End Street, Oxford OX1 1HJ
Tel 01865–241978   Fax 01865–790885

**Visit us online for more information on our unrivalled range of titles for work,
travel and adventure, readers' feedback and regular updates:
Web site http://www.vacationwork.co.uk**